D0844173

Saturday Night Lives!

Kain and Augustyn, 1977
The Chinese, 1980
Telling Tales, 1986
Private View, 1988

For Paddye

Saturday Night Lives!

SELECTED DIARIES

[signature]

John Fraser

All the best

M&S

Canadian Cataloguing in Publication Data
Fraser, John, 1944-
Saturday night lives: selected diaries
ISBN 0-7710-3131-9

I. Title.

PS8561.R3S3 1994   081   C94-931545-1
PR9199.3.F73S3 1994

The publishers acknowledge the support of the Canada
Council and the Ontario Arts Council for their
publishing program.

Typesetting by M&S
Printed and bound in Canada
The paper used in this book is acid-free.

McClelland & Stewart Inc.
The Canadian Publishers
481 University Avenue
Toronto, Ontario
M5G 2E9

1 2 3 4 5   98 97 96 95 94

For my sister

Contents

Acknowledgements

~

I have a large debt that will forever remain outstanding to my gang at *Saturday Night*. Everyone there knows how much I love them and how much I'll miss them. This is especially true of the editorial staff over the past seven years: Dianne de Fenoyl, Dianna Symonds, Anne Collins, Charlotte Gray, Carmen Dunjko, Elizabeth Schaal, Sheilagh McEvenue, Meg Jeronimus, Ann Anderson, Teresa Tiano, Bruce Headlam, Ernest Hillen, George Galt, Scott Gibbs, Kaspar de Line, Bruce Ramsay, Chris Walters, and David Macfarlane.

My predecessor, Robert Fulford, and my successor, Kenneth Whyte, have been true allies and great friends. They helped, in different ways, to sustain me during difficult days and were wonderful to be around during good times.

I am grateful for the support and advice of my agent, Bruce Westwood; my former agents and friends, Stan and Nancy Colbert; and my new colleagues at McClelland & Stewart: Avie Bennett, Doug Gibson, and Dinah Forbes.

My stepmother, Mary Fraser, provided invaluable help with

the galley proofs. I thank her for this and for many other kindnesses.

These columns were initially edited by Barbara Moon, my closest and most trusted confidante at *Saturday Night*, both as senior editor and editor-at-large. All writers should be so fortunate as to have such an editor. All editors should be so lucky as to have an assistant like Anna Luengo, who tried to bring order to my chaotic ways. She never seemed to despair of this Sisyphean task, while her innate sense of loyalty to the magazine and its editor always left me awestruck.

Finally my wife, Elizabeth MacCallum, and my three daughters – Jessie, Kate, and Clara – gave me the kind of love and support that are the main reason for living. At the same time, they also kept my feet firmly planted on the ground which was useful, given the normal propensities of editors.

Working for Conrad

~

Richmond Street West, in the heart of Toronto's downtown business district, is a fairly depressing one-way thoroughfare. Its defining architectural features are backs of hotels and department stores and exits from multi-storey carparks where automobiles are disgorged onto an instant inner-urban raceway. It is a street people use to get somewhere else, fast. Paradoxically, during "rush" hour, gridlock takes over for three angry blocks and no one goes anywhere.

There is only one building of note on the strip between Bay Street and University Avenue, and that was where we were all gathered early in 1991 to honour a former editor of *Saturday Night*, Bernard Keble Sandwell, who had ruled "Canada's Magazine" from 1932 to 1951. It wasn't a monthly magazine at all in those days, but a three-section weekly broadsheet printed on a fancy rotogravure press with glossy paper. Although its circulation ranged between only thirty and forty thousand, the publication was holy writ for English-speaking Canada's social, business, and artistic elite. *Saturday Night* spoke to and for this affluent and influential constituency with the weight of a successful fifty-year publishing record and all the patrician confidence of the liberal ascendancy that largely defined Canada before the Second World War.

Sandwell operated out of a building worthy of *Saturday Night's* pretensions, positioned smartly on a *two-way* Richmond Street of elegant offices and smart shops. It is still called the Graphic Arts Building because the name is chiselled across its fourth and top floor on a long granite face stone, above handsome neo-classical columns that now look incongruous amidst the surrounding brutalism. The little one-block street that runs up the building's west side, also columnated, is named after the buccaneer-founder of *Saturday Night*, Edmund Sheppard, and the cast-iron railing that takes you up the first short interior flight of marble stairs still features an old *Saturday Night* logo. But that's as far as nostalgia will get you before the whiff of charbroiled meat takes over, because this chief remaining physical manifestation of the old magazine's glory days has dwindled into Hy's Steak House.

The handful of us who had gathered there to witness the unveiling of a plaque to B. K. Sandwell, commissioned by the Canadian Historical Sites and Monuments Board, were a rum little crew: a nephew of B. K., a few former employees, a few current ones, a few bureaucrats, and at least one street person, whose sleeping perch on a sidewalk grating near the new plaque had been temporarily usurped. I did not enjoy the ceremony one bit. In the weeks leading up to the official unveiling, I had been sourly contemplating the demise of *Saturday Night* after more than a century of plucky, if uncertain, life. Such thoughts, as Dr. Johnson famously pointed out, tend to concentrate the mind. It had not been a compensating comfort that, at the same time, Canada itself seemed to be going down the drain, harangued to death in unending constitutional wrangling: the magazine and the country seemed to me to be racing in tandem towards oblivion.

The warmly recalled anecdotes which surfaced that day did nothing to improve the mood. Someone remembered, for example, that when Jack Kent Cooke bought the magazine in 1951 at the end of Sandwell's reign, he made his first appearance on the premises when B. K.'s daily afternoon tea trolly was partially blocking the hallway outside the editor's office. After a less than happy encounter between the new proprietor and the old editor, Cooke left the office with typical impatience and kicked the tea trolly down the hallway, scattering uneaten sandwiches, tea cups, and a silver "slops" bowl.

Inauspicious as this reported meeting was, it nevertheless could be seen as emblematic of *Saturday Night's* plight for the next half century. The tea cups always seemed to be flying, and the exasperated grunts of subsequent proprietors regularly affronted the earnest efforts of a succession of editors. The saga entails one failed initiative after another. Once, in the mid-1950s, the old Social Credit Party of Canada got its hands on the magazine. A decade later, the redoubtable Arnold Edinborough gambled his own house on the magazine – and lost both. A decade after that, in 1975, Robert Fulford, whose achievements and duration (nineteen years!) as editor paralleled Sandwell's own, actually presided over *Saturday Night's* demise – obituaries and all. Fulford was and is a fighter, however, and before a year was out, he had secured new financing for the magazine and, along with the heartening support of *Saturday Night's* faithful subscribers, the old girl was revived.

That was then. On the day B. K.'s plaque was unveiled, Fulford had been gone for three years. A few days after Conrad Moffat Black had bought *Saturday Night* in 1987, the new proprietor, instead of kicking the editor's tea trolly down the hallway, had invited Fulford to lunch at his Hollinger Inc. headquarters on Toronto Street. Fulford had emerged convinced that he and the new boss were on different trajectories. His resignation came soon afterwards, amidst some confusion between Black and the former proprietor (Norman Webster) over who exactly was supposed to be paying whom for the magazine itself. The resignation caused considerable dismay because of Fulford's stature and accomplishments. There was also, as I recall, much gnashing of teeth over the "secret rightwing agenda" Black would be imposing on *Saturday Night*. This was my entry point as the twelfth editor. In truth, I would have preferred a different one because I had never sought to supplant Robert Fulford. How could I have? Most of my professional life as a journalist I simply wanted to work with him. He was my hero. He still is.

Unfortunately, there was nothing in Fulford's rescue of the magazine in 1975 that spoke to the dilemma *Saturday Night* was facing in the early 1990s. We already had a wonderfully well-off proprietor. Conrad Black kept saying that the losses at the magazine were "a pinprick," but he and I knew that in reality the increasing losses were fast approaching a haemorrhage. I also wasn't a fool. I had a fair sense of how long even the most generous of proprietors was prepared to countenance continuous losses that kept getting worse.

Nothing seemed fair about *Saturday Night*'s plight. The magazine continued to publish the best journalism in the country, regularly recognized by many awards. It was a showcase for the most celebrated and avidly read Canadian authors and a goal for the brightest young writers. Our circulation of approximately 115,000 should have kept us safe. In the United States, which had a population ten times the size of Canada's (and no French-speaking readership), parallel magazines such as *Harper's* (circulation 190,000), *Atlantic Monthly* (450,000), *The New Yorker* (660,000), and *Vanity Fair* (900,000) had far less "penetration" of their so-called market readership, but somehow they all seemed to have found ways to thrive.

Eventually I discovered all these U.S. publications were in dismal economic shape as well, but at the time the general perception of their "success" was used as a goad by media commentators and advertising agencies to taunt us. In any event, talk of our successful "market penetration" only left me with the queasy feeling that, like everything else in the wretched magazine business, even the jargon was inflated. Besides, in Canada, our circulation was seen by advertisers only in absolute, not relative, terms, while the editorial content was too often dismissed – unread – as boring. Even a dramatic doubling of our newsstand circulation (to 12,000 issues a month) and an expanding response to subscription renewals failed to impress anyone but me. The advertisers continued to yawn, and the yawns were starting to deliver us back to the merciless gaze of accountants for whom we had long been known as *Saturday Nightmare*. If readers in sufficient numbers couldn't be found, and if advertisers continued to balk at our offerings even at the pathetically low rates on offer, then there was only one future in store for Canada's oldest magazine.

When B. K. Sandwell's plaque was unveiled that day in 1991, the pleasant little memorial looked to me ominously like a cemetery plinth. Later, on a hot early summer's day when I was still having trouble sorting out what on earth I could do to save the magazine, I went into the cool interior of St. James' Anglican Cathedral near our offices to find some peace of mind. A little girl was also touring the premises with her mother and came across a plaque dedicated to a surveyor-general of Upper Canada in 1857. "What's a scurvy-general, mommy," she asked, or something like that.

I could see her moving on to B. K.'s plaque on Richmond Street East next: "What's a *Saturday Fight*, mommy?"

How do you ever adequately describe a love affair? And one that's not with a person, but with a publication, and not just with any publication, but one that seemed to me a glorious, soaring ideal. I didn't just love *Saturday Night*, I imbibed it and wore it and savoured it and cherished it and despaired of it and dreamed of it and found it very difficult when people talked dispassionately about its problems because my sense of identification with it was so complete.

On one level, this was a seriously silly, romantic vanity. Even if *Saturday Night* was a wonderful place for a working journalist to end up in, its ups and downs were perfectly susceptible to rational analysis. As a national, general-interest magazine, its primary task was to hold up a mirror to its audience, which is an honourable and exciting endeavour. In addition, the editor's post guaranteed contact with the most interesting minds and stories in the country. Traditionally the job was a writing editorship and offered one of the best soap-boxes in Canada. On top of all that, my proprietor was an outsized elemental force of nature who could never be taken for granted, but who surprised me at regular intervals in ways both great and terrible. Here was a daily jamboree that few professional writers ever get the privilege to preside over. For all that, though, it was a job and after seven years, when it seemed time to go, I was left zig-zagging the territory between job description and wild infatuation with the very notion of *Saturday Night*.

"B" brought this all to the fore the other day when he said he wanted to "torch" the magazine's modest archives. *Torch the archives!* "B" is a young writer and editor of considerable talent and in my less agitated moments I suppose I am capable of understanding where he was coming from. He likes bucking up against the status quo and questioning every sacred precept. Those qualities were part of the reason he was hired. He was rebelling against the 107-year tradition and stature of the magazine, which was symbolized by a small collection of books by past editors assembled in a wooden cabinet just outside my office. I think he found the stature stifling, but hey! I was the guy who put the bloody archives together, such as they are, so I felt like searching his office for any incendiary materials. The magazine

itself has few other historical artifacts on its premises. Everything was dispersed long ago by "B's" philosophical predecessors. The only complete set of issues is housed in the New York
City Public Library (there are *almost* complete sets in the
National Archives in Ottawa and the Metro Toronto Reference
Library), which is a neat irony. Personally, I found it endlessly
comforting to be near books by Edmund Sheppard, Hector
Charlesworth, B. K., Arnold Edinborough, and Robert Fulford
because they reinforced not so much a sense of continuity as the
notion that others before me had gone through some of the same
trials, and both they and the magazine had survived. I'm sure I
haven't been the only editor during the past half century who
has agonized about going down in the book of milestones as the
last editor of *Saturday Night*.

So what was this strange love flaming out of a book cabinet,
scorching the editor and mildly irritating an undereditor, a love
encumbered by tales of triumph and failure in the past and uncertain predictions for the future? Often enough, it was life
itself. It was hoping against hope that a terrific story we had been
forced to hold on to for four months – thanks to the terrible
deadlines of a monthly magazine and the manic perfectionism
of the editors – wouldn't be overtaken by other media. It was
quiet moments with young writers, on the cusp of greatness, as I
watched them struggle with tough decisions on their stories. It
was lunching with the great stars of our small world and being
humbled by the evidence of how precarious were their own
notions of achievement and success. It was watching the unfolding work of a master-editor turning a dog of a manuscript
into a trenchant article. It was reading letters to the editor from
the enraged and enraptured of every province and territory. It
was the moment each month when the new issue came in and I
would toddle off to the smoking room, copy and coffee in hand,
to turn each fresh page slowly through a comforting haze of
cigarette smoke. It was when we didn't seem to have a single

worthwhile clue about what to put on an April cover and out of the blue the best story of the year arrived over the transom. It was . . . it was . . . it was just the ordinary everyday stuff of life at *Saturday Night*, but we knew our ordinary stuff was better than anyone else's best stuff and even when we screwed up – which we did from time to time – everything mattered intensely because . . . well, we were *Saturday Night*. And, on top of all this, I had my regular encounters with Conrad Black, which were never ordinary.

I've listened again to a tape an English friend sent me that was taken from the popular weekly British radio program called "Desert Island Discs." It offers BBC listeners a charming conceit: distinguished guests are invited to discuss what music they would take with them if they were condemned to spend the rest of their lives on a desert island. The choices are themselves revealing of personality, but between playing snippets from the selections, the waspish host also grills the guests on their lives – sometimes in terms intimate to the point of embarrassment.

It was with some glee that I discovered that this particular episode of the program featured none other than the boss of bosses himself, that estimable friend of my school days at Upper Canada College in Toronto before we both got turfed out under separate dark clouds (I failed exams, he stole them). Conrad Black was not being interviewed by the BBC because of *Saturday Night*, obviously, but because by 1994 he had become a mighty press baron, owner of hundreds of newspapers and magazines around the world, including *The Daily Telegraph* of London, one of the most successful newspapers in the English-speaking world.

I was not in any way surprised by Conrad's musical choices: Beethoven's "Emperor" piano concerto, Paul Robeson singing "O Danny Boy," the Mormon Tabernacle Choir with "The Battle Hymn of the Republic," Cesar Franck's *Panis Angelicus* sung by Luciano Pavarotti, Tchaikovsky's *1812 Overture*, and so on. Conrad has never made any great claims to musical refinement, but he knows what he likes. I was far more amused that he managed to force onto the British airwaves a recording of General Douglas MacArthur's 1953 farewell address to the United States Congress, a speech bristling with hortatory warnings about the dangers of entering meekly into international conflicts. If Bill Clinton or John Major ever tried to rescue Conrad from his desert island, I suspect he'd take his chances on the next boat.

What I found transfixing, however, was the confirmation that the proprietor came across as someone manifestly caught up with the world as it is, brutally honest about that world and himself, colourful and original in his turn of phrase, disarmingly loyal to his causes and friends, and sober and pragmatic about ambition, power, and his own role in the scheme of things. This is exactly how I have always seen him, but I found it "transfixing" because there is no significant figure in Canada I have personally come across whose observable reality seems in such contrast to his public image.

I'm not sure exactly when it happened, but some time ago Conrad ceased to be an object of ordinary scrutiny in Canada. For many, undoubtedly, he became a capitalist hero, but for others – some of whom I seemed to encounter every other week during my time at *Saturday Night* – he was a mythic figure, a kind of dark household god, inspiring equal measures of loathing and envy. To some extent, I suppose, he is himself to blame for this, and it is not unfair to say that he wears his enemies proudly, supplying the fuel for their venom with rich and sometimes flamboyant rhetorical provocations. He does not respond humbly or quietly to accusations or assaults.

One of his English editors once said that the proprietor's bark was worse than his bite. While this may be true, it does not give due credit to the bark, for it is great bark, easily the most effective in the land. Why bother biting when such a bark will do the job? Early on in our *Saturday Night* relationship, when Conrad was still primarily based in Toronto, it was my practice to let him have advance knowledge of anything that was going into an issue which I thought would be of particular interest to him – or a problem. A responsible editor never purposely looks to annoy an owner, but occasionally there are moments when it is judicious to anticipate conflict and prepare the way. This happened rarely in our relationship, but when an article featuring the New Democrat member of parliament, Svend Robinson, bloomed into a cover story, I felt that it would be wise to alert the boss. Robinson had only recently acknowledged his homosexuality in public. He was the first MP ever to do so, and it was a brave act considering that an election was expected soon, an election in which he was to be triumphantly returned to Ottawa. We were featuring a noble black and white image of Robinson on the cover beside a large-type banner line which read: CANADA'S GAY MP.

Conrad is not a homophobe, and the writer of the article was a school acquaintance of ours whom he not only liked but had asked me to consider as a contributor, so I was fairly sure I was safe. Robinson, however, was the first socialist to appear on the cover of *Saturday Night* since Hollinger's purchase of the magazine, and I was not clear how Conrad would react to this. It was also at a time when the NDP were getting set to have a leadership convention after Ed Broadbent stepped down.

"We're running a yarn by your chum in the next issue," I said matter-of-factly to Conrad over the telephone. I had dropped this item into the conversation after we had talked about a host of other things.

"Oh fine," said Conrad. "What's he writing on?"

"Oh, its a West Coast politician in the NDP you probably don't know," I said casually. I mumbled the acronym for the

New Democrats in a low voice, hoping it might sound like PC or Liberal or Social Credit or anything *but* NDP.

"I hope to God it isn't Svend Robinson," said the boss.

"Ha, ha," I said, "aren't you a one. Well, no, I mean that's exactly who it is. Very fine piece."

"Have you taken leave of your senses?"

"No, really," I argued, "it's a great story, a great sociological story. I mean it's a political story of our times. MP comes out of the closet . . . . Can he win in his constituency of hard hats and blue collars? . . . He does win . . . . Our story talks to him and the voters to discern what's going on . . . . Good stuff, gripping read, blah, blah, blah . . ."

Despite this high and worthy anthropological glaze, I did feel I was dancing as fast as I could. In the midst of it, Conrad quietly interrupted:

"Well, if you think it is a good story, I guess it's okay. How on earth are you going to bury it?"

"Actually," I said very slowly, "it's the cover story."

"*The cover!*" he barked.

"C'mon Conrad," I said. "You know you and your pals on the board of Hollinger are going to sleep easier at nights if it turns out that one of your publications has in any way helped Svend Robinson's chances to become the new leader of the NDP."

The pause that followed this cheeky line was extremely long. Finally I heard that familiar and welcoming deep growl of a laugh: "That's a great line. I may use it if I have to."

There have been a few variations on this theme over the years, but that essentially was the way it was between Conrad Black and me. He was always interested in what we were publishing, not always pleased with the results, but always judicious and fair in debate. I have had so many people pumping me for evidence of cruel and inhuman editorial interference that I have become bored with the incredulity that always follows an anecdote like this. My happy understanding of the role of a good proprietor of a large publication stems from my seven years working with him and I can formulate it for you in three categories:

Responsible fiscal stewardship. Anyone who has studied Conrad's business career knows that "the bottom line" is the territory he has always headed for instinctively. At *Saturday Night*, as I have indicated, the bottom line has largely been defined as the depressing gap between costs and breaking even. At a particularly bleak moment in the magazine's relationship with Hollinger, when I thought the axe was going to come down at any minute, Conrad sent in some of his most trusted and senior executives to help us on the fiscal end. A good part of the reason I was able to leave *Saturday Night* in such good economic shape was because our parent company did not disdain to help us, small as the magazine was in the Hollinger universe. It took on the challenge of studying our minutiae with an aim to improving our cost base when most other owners would have kicked the tea tray down the hall and screamed "Enough!"

Enlightened support. In 1990, after *Saturday Night* had sustained yet another year of ever-increasing losses, I presented to Conrad and Hollinger a fairly cocky plan to rethink the traditional premises of distributing the magazine. With a recession winking on the immediate horizon, I suggested that we had to increase our 110,000 readership dramatically – nearly fourfold as it turned out – if we were ever to break out of the pernicious cycle the magazine kept finding itself in. Since I was proposing to increase circulation in an unorthodox way, by selective newspaper insertion, it was not a plan many people in the industry thought had much chance of support. But we got it and to my dying day I will be grateful to the proprietor for taking the gamble, for supporting the historic purposes and integrity of *Saturday Night*, and for believing in us at the magazine when we said we could pull up our own socks.

Editorial loyalty and acumen. The only thing that approached a proprietorial dictum came in a conversation early on. "I've never begrudged the Left its voice," Conrad said, "I just get angry when the Right isn't allowed equal play." That was it and, although he kept close tabs on the magazine and made many suggestions, he was as good as his word, even when I published articles far more irritating to him than the profile of Svend Robinson.

None, I suspect, vexed him more than James Bacque's important but highly contentious piece on the U.S. prisoner-of-war camps set up in Europe in the immediate aftermath of the Second World War. Bacque's thesis, partly supported by thitherto unexamined records in the U.S. Army archives, was that upwards of a million German soldiers held in captivity by the Americans died as a result of malnutrition and exposure. The magazine was careful to explain that there were parts of Bacque's thesis that could not be proved definitively: the actual number of deaths, for example, or the pivotal role in the affair ascribed to General Dwight David Eisenhower. The article spawned controversies that still rage and, although he never told me so explicitly, I believe it deeply offended the boss, especially since we put General Eisenhower on the cover and left the impression, according to Conrad, that the American hero was "a war criminal on a par with Goering and Tojo."

So what did Conrad Black, the proprietor, do? Well, he didn't fire me for starters, though that was always his right. He asked me to take him through our factual premises. As I recall, it was a fairly rigorous cross-examination, but once he was satisfied that we had acted honourably, that professional historians had been thoroughly consulted, that we had assigned the piece to our most demanding editor, that we had double-checked all the available documentation, that the areas of speculation were within boundaries established by the recently obtainable record, then he gave me wonderful editorial advice. Treat the whole issue as a legitimate debate, he said, and make sure the magazine's columns stay open to all reasonable participants. "And also make sure we aren't seen pronouncing anything definitive," he added. "Our role can only be that of a referee." I was very defensive at first – on behalf of the magazine's intentions and process, and the writer's bona fides – so Conrad had to repeat his advice several times. Eventually I not only saw the wisdom of what he was saying, but *Saturday Night* was able to run extensive commentaries – pro and con – which made for terrific and involving reading. And he did all this, as I said, for a piece he hated, which in my books makes him a prince among proprietors.

Let me leave you with a small but telling anecdote about His Nibs. In the early 1980s, a few years before he appointed me editor, Conrad invited me to lunch at Winston's Restaurant on Adelaide Street West in Toronto. Winston's was then the leading noshery for the movers and shakers of Toronto's business community and was run by the alarming Johnny Arena, a man who gave unctuousness its inner meaning. Winston's main dining room was heavy with "mahogany" panelling, self-importance, Art Nouveau decor, sycophantic waiters, and immoderately priced entrées of varying quality.

I knew Conrad was in a spot of trouble at the time thanks to an official inquiry into some of his business dealings. The inquiry ultimately collapsed of its own fatuity and he was completely exonerated. Nevertheless, as I discovered later in his autobiography, *A Life In Progress*, it was also a time of intense personal stress, and when he walked into places like Winston's, it was clear in his mind that some of the assembled Pooh-Bahs were measuring him up for prison garb.

A particular government functionary – call him "R" – was pushing the inquiry at a high accusatory pitch and there had been some gleeful speculative analysis in the local media the very morning of the lunch. At our table, though, we hardly discussed his ordeal. Conrad was facing out to the other diners, and as he was talking, midway through the meal, I suddenly noticed a large cockroach emerging from the wood panelling behind his head.

"Nice place you brought me to," I said, directing his attention to the cockroach.

Conrad turned his head and then, in an instant without a pause, he started snapping his fingers and bellowed out a summons like General de Gaulle at a staff meeting:

"Arena!" he shouted at the hapless manager across the room. Everyone stopped talking. Johnny Arena lumbered across his dining room with two liveried *garçons* in tow.

"Yes Mr. Black. What is the problem?"

"Arena," barked Black, pointing to the cockroach and making sure everybody was hanging on to each word he said. "I told you if you ever let 'R' into this restaurant, I would never come back. Eliminate him!"

The friends – and enemies – of Conrad Black broke out into spontaneous laughter and applause. Johnny Arena directed his *garçons* to capture the cockroach with their linen napkins. "R" had been temporarily routed, along with whatever anxiety had afflicted Conrad that day. I had a great yarn to tell my gang back at *The Globe and Mail* where I then worked. At the end of the day, the thought once again occurred to me that it might be fun to work with such a man one day.

As it turned out, it was.

The joys of editing *Saturday Night* are easy to enumerate. Even the economic woes are not particularly painful to recount because a half dozen of my predecessors had encountered them before me and, besides, I had been given the chance to do something dramatic about them and so far the new plan has been working quite well. But as an editor who was often enough accused of exulting in controversy (not an unfair charge), I certainly had a big problem with conflict. *I hated it.* I hated it between myself and staff members, with writers, and especially with subjects (and their lawyers) of our stories. It's not that I couldn't deal with it: a large part of the job of an editor is trying to bring conflicts of various sorts to some sort of resolution. Still, the motherlode of angst, bitterness, and wounded feelings that attend upon the consequences of print is really worthy of serious psychological study.

Print lingers in the minds of victims and festers terribly. Anticipation of what might be printed can be even worse. At *Saturday Night*, I inherited an excellent system of checking all articles, including quotes and narrative lines, before we published. This system didn't always keep us out of legal trouble, but its premises were honourable and aimed at the maintenance of veracity. Unfortunately, checkers also let some subjects know they were about to get into trouble. Also, it is possible to get a story past all the various hurdles, only to blow it with heads and decks and cover lines with which an article is adorned. The potential for conflict exists at every stage of the operation.

Few authors of stature in Canada have been more faithful to *Saturday Night* than Margaret Atwood, no stranger to controversy herself. I sought her out early on and asked for contributions, which she kindly provided. She graced our cover more than once and also offered us story ideas, which I always appreciated. The relationship got started on an off-note. In one of my earliest issues, we ran a short books column which claimed that the world-wide sales of an obscure Canadian religion writer were bigger than Atwood's. Boy! did she get in touch fast.

Out of this little brouhaha, however, I got a fix into a mysterious, scrappy, and *generous* woman. I've put "generous" in italics because, thanks to her wide fame and, like my proprietor, she has collected a coterie of detractors and they would howl at this adjective. But they're wrong and I'm right. It wasn't just her generosity to *Saturday Night* and to me personally. I am now something of a connoisseur of tales that feature a little touch of Atwood in the night. Writers in financial distress, an aboriginal writing group bereft of support, a poet down on his luck, an artist sideswiped by public criticism, a young writer dismissed peremptorily by his publisher, an established writer in a bind with his novel: the list is quite long, actually, and to all she has offered some sort of assistance – moral or professional or financial. It has all been done without any fanfare and I esteem her for it.

Like all creative people, she has her sensitivities and no-go areas, as I discovered to my chagrin when she was on our October 1993 cover. We had taken an excerpt from her new novel, *The Robber Bride*. One of the central characters, Zenia, is an outsized monster for whom the word "bitch" – while, no doubt, sexist – seems only barely adequate. So we put this terrific "sell" line underneath the author's image: "MARGARET ATWOOD / A sneak preview at her bitchy new novel." *Aaargh.* I found myself in the dog house after that because, I guess, she felt the magazine had capriciously fed into the agenda of her detractors, and she had been our friend, and what the hell was going on anyway? I admire and like Atwood so much that I struggled to make amends as best as I could. I think she's forgiven me, in her fashion! Shortly before I stepped down as editor, I got a greeting card from her featuring a large, toad-like man with a dunce's cap on his head, sitting on a stool facing the corner. Inside, handwritten, was this note:

> *Dear John*
>
> *I have been saving this card for the proper person & occasion and I believe this is it. The meaning is enigmatic – is this you? or your revered proprietor? In any case, our back yard is always open to you.*
>
> *Happy retirement!*
>
> *Peggy A.*

I studied the fat little fellow with the dunce's cap on the face of the card for quite some time and ultimately decided it couldn't possibly be offensive, or at least no more offensive than our cover line seemed to be, in which case all conflict was over. Thank God.

At least the divine Atwood has never come stalking me at my office. A lady bodybuilder did once, shortly before we published a story that alluded to her use of steroids. The mention of steroids, which she got wind of through the magazine's checkers, brought on a series of phone conversations of escalating tension and conflict that did not get resolved until she arrived, unannounced, at the magazine's reception area. When I was finally told who was out there waiting for me, it seemed the entire office staff knew ahead of me. Doors everywhere in the editorial department were closed. The ad sales people seemed to be leaving extra early for lunch. Even the mail-room clerk fled through the back door. It's at moments like this that you question ambition and rank in life.

I had about two minutes to prepare a plan of action, and briefly remembered the sad story of Sir Richard Squires, the last prime minister of the Dominion of Newfoundland, who fled a howling mob at his legislature disguised as a cleaning woman. I had to rule this option out because cleaning women didn't leave their clothing on our premises. Stiffening the sinews and summoning up the blood, I realized the lady bodybuilder didn't know what I looked like, so I decided to take stock of the situation by sneaking out the back way and coolly walking through the reception area to see just how big she was.

I sauntered in casually while whistling John Bunyon's great hymn ("He who would valiant be, 'gainst all disaster..."), but to my immense chagrin and surprise I was not immediately confronted with a karate chop to the neck or groin. Instead, I saw massive back muscles leaning over the reception desk, heaving up and down in great sobs. Oh shit, I thought, she's in stress.

George Orwell once said you should never get to know the face of your enemy because you'll discover he is human and fallible, just like you. The body builder was inconsolable. I took her into the nearby boardroom so we could talk in privacy and was not amused to notice that my faithful staff had suddenly emerged from behind their closed doors and were surreptitiously checking out the scene through a glass partition that looked into the boardroom.

"My life will be over if you print that article," she said, between more sobs. I tried to pat her reassuringly on her back, but the rippling muscles beneath her tight shirt seemed so daunting that my hand stayed indecisively in midair.

"It's not such a bad piece," I said. This was the truth. Perhaps the article was gently mocking of professional bodybuilding in parts, but it was quite sweet about her ambitions in the male-dominated world of grunting, pec-strewn weightlifters. There was one reference to trouble she had already got into with her professional organization over steroids and which she didn't dispute. The problem was the suggestion that she was still on them and this was, admittedly, based on incomplete evidence. The writer was still trying to track down the proof and the checker hadn't found it. I couldn't bear to see her so miserable, so I told her to phone me in a couple of days after I had got reports from everyone involved in the story from the writer and editor to the checker and our libel lawyer. I didn't promise anything, but my tone must have been sufficiently soothing for her to compose herself and walk out with a head held high above inch-thick neck muscles.

In the end, the writer couldn't prove the second instance of steroid use, so the reference was dropped from the story. Had I wanted a personal body building trainer, I could have had her gratis on the day I called to tell her the heat was off.

The heat rarely lifted whenever I was so ill-advised to try satire with my monthly "Diary" column. Some people can't help themselves, and I'm one of them when it comes to making salient points by indirection. I don't know why this is so. Ever since high school, I have been attracted to the great satirists in English literature, especially Jonathan Swift. I love the moral force of effective satire because when it hits home, the arguments linger in the mind for a lifetime, all the more effectively so because they have crept up on you on the sly. One of Swift's greatest satires, for example, was A *Modest Proposal*, his famous essay about "the Irish problem," in which his savage indignation was directed against English political grandees of his day who pontificated and prescribed without any understanding of the issues or the Irish people themselves. In A *Modest Proposal*, Swift took all the sensible, commonplace arguments he heard, *ad nauseam*, in Parliament or read in the respectable journals of the day and redirected them to a uncompromising conclusion: He had it on good authority, he wrote, that tiny Irish babies made tolerably good roast meat, and that careful attendance upon pregnant Irish women would bring a lessening of domestic violence in Irish homes, a fair balance of trade between the two islands, and – ultimately – provide a sensible solution for the overall Irish problem.

When I was a graduate student in England during the late 1960s, I once visited the "signature" gallery of the British Museum, which featured selections of original manuscripts and correspondence. I was thrilled to discover a letter to Dean Swift from a Whig peer chastising the writer for "the extremities" of his arguments in A *Modest Proposal*, but nevertheless concluding with a genial "thank you" for at least tackling the problem seriously and trying to come up with a solution. Talk about hitting home!

In this selection of columns I wrote over seven years at *Saturday Night*, you will find a number of efforts at satire. One in particular got me into as much trouble as I've ever found myself in. I incorporated Swift's own title – "A Modest Proposal: The

solution to the problems of Atlantic Canada is to eliminate it" –
to give a broad hint about tone and intentions, but, considering
the reaction, this was a totally vain effort. A few weeks before
I wrote the column, I had been part of a panel discussion in
Toronto which dealt with, among other things, the economic
malaise in Atlantic Canada. Having spent four of the happiest
years of my life in Newfoundland, I had developed special sensitivities to detect condescending paternalism among central
Canadians whenever a discussion on the Maritime provinces or
Newfoundland came up for discussion. These kinds of discussions always feature scare statistics, large-scale solutions devoid
of humanity, and the sort of blind pomposity that drives me right
up the wall. It must be a fairly comprehensive personal viewpoint because when the "Newfoundlanding" of Ontario occurred during the Great Nineties Recession, I found a certain
perverse pleasure in the parallelism and ironic justice.

Readers can make what they want of my attempts at satire in
this essay. I know it worked, even if it blew up in my face,
because the mail started pouring into the magazine – most of it
from Atlantic Canada and thoroughly outraged. Satire is successful, according to the classical rules, if its thesis has to be
discovered by indirection and its particulars are taken seriously.
This little satire, which assumed that no rational human being
would go along with the wholesale eviction of decent people
from their ancestral homeland, nevertheless cited genuine statistics to overload the case even as it distorted the true significance of those statistics. I'd figured out how to fix the figures
at the panel discussion. In making my points with a certain
amount of glee, however, I deeply wounded a lot of Maritimers,
not the least being the newly elected Liberal premier of New
Brunswick, Frank McKenna. To both my dismay and delight, he
decided he had to come to Toronto and set the record straight.
In such ways are writers rewarded for their trouble.

I got a phone call from the president of the Toronto branch of the Canadian Club informing me that Premier McKenna was coming to town the following week to address its large membership and that he had especially asked me to be invited to the head table. Now, I'm not entirely stupid, and I know a set-up when I see one. On the other hand, this promised to be an interesting encounter, even if I wasn't going to be given a chance to respond. So off I went and the predictable happened. McKenna decided to try a Churchillian address to defend the honour of everyone down East. I think he may have had stout New Brunswickers fighting off Toronto fascists on the beaches of St. Andrew's-by-the-Sea. At the head table, I couldn't stop laughing, which I suppose didn't make a great impression. Still, I was transfixed by the irony. There were ex-Maritimers who were outraged that I had written such awful things, and they lined up to pat Premier Frank on the back. But listen up! There were also lots of people in the audience who agreed with the satirical surface arguments, and they all came up to me afterwards. I smiled thinly as I was congratulated on my bravery.

I loved the freedom the "Diary" column gave me and I tried not to abuse this with too many satires. You will find, I hope, a fair bit of celebration – of people and events – and also some anger. Nearly two decades ago, for example, I was posted to Peking by *The Globe and Mail* and that experience touched me for life. This obsession, too, is reflected in the book, as is the sense of wonder for my own country and the small pleasures of life around us. To have such a forum was a privilege and I hope readers do not feel I ever abused it.

Midway through my sixth year at *Saturday Night*, I decided that it was time for a new editor at the magazine. In some ways, this decision still surprises me, because there's a part of me that would have stayed on happily till the day I died. Another part was restless and also recognized the limits of energy all directed to one end. A friend at the CBC sent me a wonderful quotation from the late Austrian-American nuclear physicist, Leo Szilard, which fed right into this mood: "Devote six years to your work, but in the seventh go into solitude or among strangers so that your friends, by remembering what you were, do not prevent you from becoming what you have become."

Magazines stay lively – and alive – by constantly questioning their mandates and their offerings. The danger sign is when, as editor, you think everything is exactly as it should be and there is no need for change. I'm a lucky man. Arranging a happy exit for yourself is more complicated than any entrance, but the rest of life is out there beckoning and the perils of the unknown seem magical.

PART ONE

Who Is That Writer Under the Editor's Desk?

Jean Chrétien

~

I n the spring of 1982, the justice minister of Canada, Jean Chrétien, made the last of several special trips to London, England, to acquaint Queen Elizabeth with the efforts of her Canadian administration to write a new constitution. This time, in contrast to all the other occasions, he had a "finished" document with him, a document that had gained the approval of the House of Commons, the Senate, and all but one of the ten provinces. The hold-out, of course, was Quebec, his own home and native land, but if Chrétien was brooding over the irony that it had formally fallen to a Quebecker to tell his sovereign of this imperfect conclusion, he wasn't showing a hint of it on the flight to London.

He had a number of officials in tow, along with a Canadian Press photographer and a couple of journalists, one of whom was me. Chrétien was pleased that the arduous process had finally reached a denouement, however messy, and he was charming and forthcoming with the journalists. When he arrived in London, he gave himself an hour or so to freshen up after the transatlantic flight and then dashed off to Buckingham

Palace. After the usual palaver with court officials and a traipse through the antechambers, he was duly announced and ushered into the royal presence. The queen looked at the *"p'tit gars"* from Shawinigan, eighteenth child of a unilingual machinist, with amused familiarity – and an amused echo of her greeting on a previous trip:

"You again!"

Him again. More than a decade later, Canadians woke up the morning after the federal election to ponder the triumphant return to power of "yesterday's man." In another country, or perhaps merely in another era in our own country, Jean Chrétien's victory at the polls would already have become the stuff of legend, even Lincolnesque legend. Instead, since this is Canada in the 1990s, there was far more interest in the catastrophic defeat of the Tories and the consequent rise in Parliament of the Reform Party in the West and the separatist Bloc in Quebec. Chrétien's victory, which was national and comprehensive in scope, seemed almost peripheral to the seismic shifts in the landscape of the political opposition. Canada remains a country fascinated by its losers and might-have-beens. The winner, who seemed always to have been with us, was almost a footnote.

Dismissing or underestimating Jean Chrétien has been a pastime in English Canada almost from the day he succeeded to the leadership of the Liberal Party of Canada in 1990. Overnight, it seemed, his image went from "colourful and original character" to "tired old party hack." In the ensuing years, I caught glimpses of what it must have been like to live such a marginalized political life. At candidate nominating meetings and fund-raising events, or in media scrums (especially during the traumatic federal-provincial constitutional meetings presided over by Brian Mulroney), Chrétien seemed hardly able to garner even the barest institutional media coverage. Out of it all he became almost a non-person, written off by many and ignored by the rest. As late as last summer, when Kim Camp-bell's star appeared ascendant, a senior Liberal Party official in Toronto solemnly informed me that Chrétien was merely "a transitional figure."

In his own province, the problem has been somewhat differ-ent and far more troubling. In 1990 at a fund-raising dinner for *Le Devoir* held in Montreal's Hôtel Reine Elizabeth (presiding ironies seem never to vary), I had a long and illuminating talk with him, not because I was such a fascinating conversationalist but because there were embarrassingly few people at the event who wanted to be seen talking to him. Quebec's tribal drums were beating very loudly that night.

In that conversation, he was disarmingly frank about the dis-like he seemed to arouse among the province's cognoscenti, at least during this period of Mulroney's domination. I asked him if the cold-shoulder treatment ever unnerved him. He smiled that loopy smile of his and answered indirectly but cleverly: "I'm a lucky man. I know *exactly* who all my enemies are. They give little clues, like calling me a traitor." Beside us, a man deep in another conversation swivelled to look at us when Chrétien said "traitor." His expression was stone-cold. It seemed to me that the word "traitor" hovered menacingly in the air, trapped in a historical echo chamber:

"I am branded in Quebec as a traitor to the French and in Ontario as a traitor to the English," observed Sir Wilfrid Laurier in 1911. "In Quebec, I am branded as a jingo and in Ontario as a separatist. In Quebec I am attacked as an imperialist and in Ontario as an anti-imperialist." Laurier was speaking the truth, but he went on to speak a far more important truth: "I am nei-ther. I am a Canadian. Canada has been the inspiration of my life. I have had before me as a pillar of fire by night and a pillar of cloud by day a policy of true Canadianism, of moderation, of conciliation."

We seem to learn nothing from our past, but then how could it be otherwise? English Canada doesn't retain its history long enough to see whether there is something actually worthwhile in it; French Canada retains so much history, refracted through such a warped filter, that it distorts and demeans most positive achievements.

Jean Chrétien looks out today across a fractured, bickering nation of immense possibilities. So once did George-Étienne Cartier, John A. Macdonald's great partner during and after Confederation. So also did Laurier, Louis St. Laurent, Pierre Trudeau, and, in a more symbolic way as the first French-Canadian governor general, Georges Vanier. All of them were charged with the care of a country that afforded them no safe refuge wherein to heal the inevitable personal wounds of political conflict. However fractious their careers proved, English-Canadian leaders have all had home constituencies, some sort of wall to protect their backs.

Whether it was during the Riel rebellion, the Manitoba school crisis, wartime conscription debates, or periods of militant, sometimes violent, separatist activity, all the French-Canadian leaders of Canada have – at one time or another – been accused of tribal betrayal. Nor did this negativity inside their home province produce any long-term political credit in English Canada, where, as Laurier pointed out, Quebec roots are usually a source of volatile suspicions. The truth is that summoning up the courage to transcend such elemental calumny has defined the vision of every one of them, and it is why I think that their vision has invariably been more coherent, comprehensive, and appealing than any English-Canadian leader's, save that of Macdonald himself. For one thing, they have automatically been impelled to abandon the politics of exclusion, the traditional wellspring of regional assertiveness in this country. For another, they have seen in the ideal notion of a tolerant Canada not only their own franchise but the only possible antidote to regional rivalries. All of this, I believe, grows out of the habit of diplomacy and compromise they have had to practise on the journey from Quebec to national leadership.

For a moment, then, let's take two givens: (1) politics is the art of the possible, and (2) Canada is impossible to govern. It is worthwhile considering this: at the heart's core of this glorious contradiction, which has so far endured for 127 years, there has always been a French-speaking Quebecker who has reached out and attempted the thankless task of national reconciliation. When some people in Canada complained in the lead-up to the last federal election that our politics is always held hostage, in one way or another, to a "Quebec agenda," they do not understand that the opposite is the case: that a particular Quebec agenda has been averted only because visionary Quebeckers have seen great merit in the humdrum realities and limitations of an imperfect federalist state. When Quebec fails to produce such leaders, within either the government or opposition parties, then, too, will Canada fail.

So what of Jean Chrétien, the latest in the line? Born in obscurity at the lower end of the economic and social scale, he has prevailed thanks to an adroit combination of benign parental influence, practical ambition, genial personality, some good luck and clever connections, a strong wife, and great powers of patience – all hitched to an evolving conviction that he and his country have a mutual destiny. Nevertheless, the cynic lodged in all of us knows that the political wheel of fortune keeps turning. There are setbacks, failures, and tragedies all waiting for this new government and this particular leader. These things are inevitable; the way they are dealt with is the only area of uncertainty.

Still, I think it's true to say that so little has been expected of Chrétien that he has some room to manoeuvre and even surprise us. Ever since Pierre Trudeau entered 24 Sussex Drive, we have – initially, at least – embraced unknown leaders in the wild hope that they would be an improvement on the known. This time we did something different: we have, at a dangerous time for Canada, chosen the only-too-well-known in an act somewhere between exhaustion and desperation.

Thanks to his equanimity of spirit and lack of vindictiveness, his courage and calm in adversity, and his natural instinct to reach out, there is more than a whiff of Laurier about Jean Chrétien, and we could do with another Laurier these days. It is enough, then, just to wish him well – and keep our fingers crossed.

February 1994

Strapped for Time

~

The week begins early and badly. Overslept. The two older kids have to be ferried to junior choir rehearsal before the 9:15 a.m. service, and I find myself cruising up Oriole Parkway (maximum speed forty km/h) at sixty-five km/h. This is foolish. For nearly five decades, the northern end of Oriole Parkway has been a notorious speed trap. Surely Metro Toronto's finest are resting on the Lord's Day? Even if they aren't, surely they wouldn't stop a bona fide Sunday-school teacher.

I am wrong.

At precisely the same spot where my twelve-year-old self spent many amused moments watching busy, irritated motorists wait with impatience for speeding tickets to be filled out, I find myself babbling inanities to a humourless, pint-sized cop. I am hoping the sight of blameless children and the judicious mention of good works will get me off the hook. It doesn't. I don't lose points, but the fine is $41.25. Less than it could have

43

been perhaps, but more than a conscientious Sunday-school teacher merits.

The thing that hath been, it is that which shall be; and that which is done is that which shall be done: and there is no new thing under the sun.

In humour as heavy as Job's, I take my seat in the pew and contemplate thin spiritual gruel. Why *do* bad things happen to good people? The traditional answer is bleak: because undeserved affliction ennobles the soul. This is not really an Anglican concept. We have values more rooted in reality, like: "Visible good works get you a seat in the front pew." Stuff like that.

Valpy arrives, with child, in the midst of this sour contemplation. All in a fluster, he hisses at me from the pew behind: "I got caught in a radar trap."

I ask Valpy what happened. "Apparently I was going seventy. I lost two points and the fine was $112. I told him I was on my way to church, but I had the feeling he'd heard the line before. Nasty little creep."

Two points! A $112 fine! For a difference of only five km/h! It must have been the Sunday-school business that softened him. Valpy has not yet volunteered to teach Sunday school and so, in effect, asked for the extra punishment.

I will sing unto the Lord a new song, for he hath not forsaken his servant.

Monday

Gruesome day. The full horror of how late we are with the February issue is revealed at the wretched production meeting. One senior editor is sick. The executive editor, usually our faithful scourge, is just back from two weeks' holiday, *en français*, and is still floating around the premises about six feet off the ground. She has not yet focused on our crisis, but we'll bring her back to earth before sundown. The production editor is threatening guerrilla reprisals or a walkout. The art director is talking enigmatically about far-off places. Over a hundred unsolicited manuscripts still await a verdict. Their writers barrage the office with plaintive or peremptory calls, and the pile of pink telephone slips on my desk is four inches high. It will all have to wait.

Read in the newspaper that Hollinger Inc., our principal owner, has set aside $10 million for redundancy payments and early retirement over the next fiscal year. Is this a message? Should I queue up early while the kitty is still ample?

Tuesday
My "Diary" is now three weeks overdue and what do you think is the major task of the day? A bra. I have been asked by my wife to purchase a bra. "Warner's Size xx-x." I have never before been asked to purchase a bra. Other things, yes, but never a bra. I think I don't want to do this thing; but there are compelling reasons domestically and, after all, I am a *Canadian* husband so I want to be seen to be caring and helpful. But a bra?

In the end, anthropological curiosity gets the better of me. I canvass female staff members in the editorial, advertising, and circulation departments. "Would you ever ask your husband or boyfriend to purchase a bra for you?" The answer is, without exception, no. The art director bursts into malicious laughter. "I don't think I'd have had the nerve to ask, but I really admire your wife for creating such an interesting challenge."

I ask the male employees two questions: (1) Have you ever been asked to purchase a bra? (2) If asked, would you do so? Double no. Without exception.

"I might ask George to do it," said the Ottawa editor, "if I thought he was having too wonderful a time at the office and was leaving me high and dry with the three kids. Because, you know, it's my experience that requests like this never get made without a subtext. It's interesting really. Do you often get asked to do this sort of thing?"

The Ottawa editor is paid to be suspicious, but I don't fancy the line of questioning. It is not possible to go through the working day brooding about bloody subtexts when the texts themselves are hard enough to read. The Ottawa editor, though, is relentless. She is also a great researcher, with far-flung nameless sources. "I have an acquaintance who worked in a lingerie department and she once told me men often buy such things – for themselves. I wouldn't go if I were you. I'm sure the salespeople will just assume you're a transvestite."

Nice. I end the day contemplating a potential item in *Frank* magazine: "Why, we wonder, would a national magazine editor and Sunday-school teacher be hanging around the ladies' lingerie department at The Bay? No doubt his wife asked him to make a purchase. No doubt he also likes to dress up for special occasions. No doubt . . ."

Wednesday
Editorial conference day. No "Diary." No time to respond to the unsolicited manuscripts. No time to buy the bra. I did find time, however, to check *Cruden's Complete Concordance to the Old and New Testaments* in hurried search of guidance, but found myself constantly cross-referenced to St. Paul and his advice to women. St. Paul doesn't seem to have foreseen this particular dilemma.

Thursday
Taking courage from the fact that even the prime minister is today wearing a white ribbon in his lapel to show solidarity with Canadian women, I set out to The Bay after a disputatious management committee meeting. The lingerie department, on the fourth floor of the store, can be approached obliquely. I take up a

surreptitious position two pillars away from a sea of very scary red-lace items. This is not simply to summon up nerve. I am also trying to get the lie of the land and scout out a motherly-looking salesperson who is at the same time efficient and *quick*.

At precisely 11:37 a.m., I stride briskly from behind the pillar to the cash desk at ladies' lingerie. I have rehearsed a line, but at the appropriate moment it evaporates. "This," I blurt out, as I shove her a piece of paper bearing the written specifications. "My wife can't come . . . very ill . . . trying to help. . . ."

She looks at the paper. She looks at me. She looks at the paper again. "Nothing easier," she says with a smile. "What colour does she want?"

"Colour?" I haven't foreseen this. Nothing has been mentioned about colour. I stammer. "I don't think it matters. I'm colour-blind anyway." *Why did I say that?*

"Well, you're not the one going to wear it, are you?" she says. There is a chuckle. It isn't motherly.

"Ma'am! White, I guess. Can you just get it for me so I can get out of here?"

"I'll just be a minute. Why don't you take a look over here. We have some wonderful gift ideas. Look at these beautiful . . ."

Lord, now lettest thou thy servant depart in peace, according to thy word.

Friday
Grotesque. I thought I had booked a power breakfast at the King Edward with a prospective sponsor of the "Wildwood" literary section. To my horror, a totally unknown person is brought to the table and says, "Hi John." He sits down, orders poached eggs in phyllo pastry, and then thanks me for arranging this friendly rendezvous. *Who is he?* How did this happen? The dawning recognition that a writer of an unsolicited manuscript has made it past all the screening barriers so carefully erected at the magazine is unnerving. A simple, silly mix-up of telephone slips.

Queen Victoria couldn't have been more astonished at finding The Mudlark under her bed. The writer turns out to be a real human being with experience and ideas and a gift of the gab, all of which makes me late for the meeting to write cover lines for the February issue. Being late for the cover-lines meeting is the first sign that the day may not turn out so badly.

(*Later the same day*) The week is nearly over. Even now, letters of rejection are being written wholesale to accompany dozens of unsolicited manuscripts. It is a heartless business, and our little letters are particularly unctuous:

> *Thank you for giving us a chance to consider the enclosed material.*
> *We have read it and decided that it is not suitable for our magazine.*
> *This is not a reflection on the quality of your work; it means only*
> *that your material and our needs don't happen to come together.*
> *We hope that they will at some point in the future.*
> *With good wishes,*
> *The Editors*

But then I remember how many times I have received rejection slips in my day. It all works out in the end. The February issue is still in crisis, but the bra has been purchased and gratefully received. Hollinger Inc. has not yet started to dispense severances from its Doomsday fund. I've been practising driving at forty km/h on major city streets. It's slow, but then so is inspiration for the "Diary," which is now finished. Thank God.

Sufficient unto the day are the needs thereof. Amen.

February 1992

The Last Refuge

~

O n May 22, 1990, a twenty-two-year-old Chinese man named Yi Zhibing (the family name is Yi and the whole name is pronounced approximately "yeh jer-bing") was brought before a two-person panel of the Immigration and Refugee Board in Toronto to determine whether he had a valid claim to refugee status in this country, or should be returned to the People's Republic of China from which he had fled in the wake of the 1989 Tienanmen massacre. Mr. Yi told the board that he came from Guangzhou (Canton of old), where he had operated a handbag and clothing stall in the downtown market area. A known supporter of and financial contributor to the students' cause, he had helped videotape footage of the massacre broadcast on Hong Kong TV, which he then circulated to family members, friends, and work associates. He had also participated in a small post-massacre demonstration in front of the Guangzhou provincial office which was closely monitored by the Public Security Bureau (PSB). After six of his fellow stall-holders with similar sympathies were picked up for questioning and not heard from again, he himself was issued a police summons to report to his local PSB office. Instead, he hid out for several days and, finally, was able to reach Canada surreptitiously via Hong Kong and Thailand. Not surprisingly, Mr. Yi didn't want to go home and asked the panel to decide in his favour to spare him the rigours of persecution from a very nasty Communist regime.

Mr. Yi's experience in China was harrowing, but not much more so than his later experience in Canada, for here he was brought before a newly created Canadian judicial entity during its first year of operation. In 1989 the federal government empowered the Immigration and Refugee Board of Canada to create special panels across the country to hear nothing but refugee claims. Each panel consisted of two members, along with a bureaucratic minder called a "refugee hearing officer," and its job was to determine whether outsiders who had made it unofficially into the country – by hook or by crook – were eligible for refugee status based on a realistic fear of persecution back home. These panels were given the sole right to accept or reject such claims. Their decisions can be appealed to the courts, but the judge in any such appeal can't just settle the case in favour of the claimant: he can only send him back for a new hearing before another panel. A rejection means the claimant will be dispatched back to his or her country of origin, or sometimes to some third country that has assisted the refugee in gaining admission into Canada.

The panels were the direct result of a choking backlog of refugee claimant cases, but they were a product also of a broad concern in government and (to judge from opinion polls at the end of the 1980s) among a considerable segment of the population over the ease with which refugee status in Canada could be obtained. Beyond this, they were the product of a general unease about multiracial immigration to Canada, an unease which kept drifting in and out of unthinking hysteria. This was amply reflected in media coverage of "queue-jumping" Sikhs landing illegally in Nova Scotia, "monster houses" sprouting in Vancouver, and gang wars in Toronto's Chinatown. It was fed by incidents like the Mashat affair, which seemed to prove that anyone – even a discredited Iraqi official – with a useful local connection could gain easy admittance here; by shocking accounts of illegal passport transactions involving a gilt-edged Canadian legal firm; and by heaven knows what else. All of it buttressed the notion that the world's rabble was on the move and heading our way. Refugee policy and immigration policy, which are two separate entities, had got hopelessly muddled together.

Spurred by this mood and confusion, the Mulroney administration threw in the refugee boards as a quick solution to the overall congestion and, at the same time, as a strong signal that Canada's famous leniency was at an end. At the theory stage, the boards must have seemed just dandy. Their hearings would be quick, their decisions would be public, and their mandate to weed out the noxious opportunists would inevitably receive public approbation. That was the theory, and no one should fault the government for trying to come to terms with immigration in a volatile and rapidly changing world. Now, however, we find ourselves having acquiesced in the creation of a judicial nightmare with these stupid and arbitrary refugee boards.

Let's pass over the well-documented horror stories of insensitive, ignorant, and well-paid (about $80,000 a year) panel members who, seemingly overdosed on stories of persecution and torture, make jokes about the wretched refugee claimants who are brought before them – although the cheap humour is a symptom. If anyone had supposed that this new arrangement was primarily intended to bring about a fairer evaluation of refugee status in Canada, the two annual reports the refugee determination board has issued should settle the matter. Where once the bulk of refugee cases were reviewed and determined on their individual merits, we now have a quasi-judicial apparatus that boasts a higher agenda. "The key to the success of the refugee determination system," the 1990 report states, "is sending clear signals to the international community that Canada will not tolerate abuses to the system." In other words, the "signals" take precedence over everything else. The same point is made in the 1991 report with a special pat on the back to the minister of immigration's "recent commitment to strengthen the enforcement and deportation activities of Immigration Canada."

Preceding these statements in the annual reports are the percentages for successful and unsuccessful refugee claimants. Since 1989, the board proudly points out, its little panels have been able steadily to increase the number of cases they hear (30,055 in 1991 compared to 21,469 in 1990), which is indeed evidence of a certain efficiency. Along with speedier decisions, however, the board also boasts a dramatically declining rate of successful applications. Eighty-eight per cent of refugee claims in 1989 were successful, seventy-seven per cent in 1990, and sixty-nine per cent in 1991. Any reasonable person can be forgiven the suspicion that an unofficial quota system is operating here, with an accompanying graph curve line. Who wants to bet 1992 won't be sixty or fifty-nine per cent? And who believes, given such publicly proclaimed objectives, that these panels aren't listening to the cases of refugee claimants with special suspicion?

In rejecting Mr. Yi's claims to refugee status, the panel cited "implausibilities" in his testimony which were "inconsistent" with its own documentary evidence of the situation and conditions in China. "First," continued the panel decision, "we note the claimant was not in any way a leader at any of the demonstrations. . . . It seems highly improbable that he would be sought by authorities." The panel observed that as "a business-man" he was unlikely to be detained because the authorities were after students. Even more unlikely, the panel said, was the notion that "a posse of representatives" (from the police, the Industry and Commercial Bureau, and Mr. Yi's neighbourhood committee) would "descend" upon his home to deliver a summons when he was not actually there. Why did this "posse" not stake out Mr. Yi's house and await his return? Finally, the panel observed, "It may well be the claimant was sought by the police for questioning. The documentary evidence makes it clear that many citizens were apprehended, questioned and released after three hours. Had the claimant chosen not to go into hiding, we have no reason to suspect that he would have been treated differently. . . . The claimant may indeed fear a penalty since he failed to comply with the summons. The panel is of the opinion that the claimant's fear in this regard is a fear of prosecution not persecution."

The panels are supposed to be assisted by researchers who prepare newspaper clippings and fact sheets on the countries the claimants come from and guide them in their deliberations. These data are sometimes cited by the panels in their decisions, to give authority to their findings. Although I have not been able to get my hands on any of these "country profiles," their substance can often be inferred from the decisions. In Mr. Yi's case, I infer that the country profile of China was criminally superficial. Consider just these points:

• The panel had before it no documentary evidence whatsoever – it doesn't exist – to support the notion that all Mr. Yi needed to fear was a routine three-hour quizzing. We are talking about the second most vindictive and unassailable police force in Asia. (This is a connoisseur's game, like comparing the Gestapo with the KGB, but Vietnam's is marginally worse.)

• The "posse" referred to by the panel consisted of officials from the three groups – his work unit, the local police, and the neighbourhood committee, who are the official snoops of private life in China – who controlled most aspects of Mr. Yi's life. The police put seals on his business, and the work unit revoked his licence, making him an instant pariah; the neighbourhood committee had total control over his residence permit and, without written approval from this ubiquitous organization, he could obtain neither travel documents nor food vouchers.

• Describing a twenty-two-year-old Chinese stall vendor as a "businessman" is to employ the kind of misnomer darkly hilarious to anyone who has been on even a two-week tourist trip to the People's Republic. Far more disheartening, the panel and its documentation team should have realized that this was a young man who had shown remarkable individual initiative in trying to create a better life for himself and his family by starting a small operation in one of the most precarious of all entrepreneurial settings. He is the kind of young man who could make a wonderful, contributing Canadian citizen. Hey! In the middle of a recession, that might not have been a bad signal to send out to the international community.

• There is plenty of documentary evidence from inside China, all of it well reported in the West, that, while many students were detained in the wake of Tienanmen and their leaders harshly dealt with, the "broad masses" of students received relatively lenient treatment. The real victims of vicious persecution were the workers, low-level officials, and "Western-tainted" small fry who took up the students' cause and tried to expand the protest. People precisely like Mr. Yi.

• None of the information available to the panel kept it from making the worst of all possible assumptions, summed up in its speciously epigrammatic argument that Mr. Yi might well have grounds to fear "prosecution" but not "persecution." *Carve this in stone*: in China today, no one is prosecuted unless his or her guilt and the sentence to be imposed are already determined and scripted. No arguments, no evidence, no personal testimony are ever allowed to displace the arranged theatrics of formal prosecution.

I wish Mr. Yi's case were isolated, but it is not. From examples that got caught up in the appeal process, a half-dozen randomly selected cases of Chinese nationals seeking refugee status in Canada in the three years following the Tienanmen massacre sketch a pattern of such consistent cultural incomprehension and smug ignorance that anyone with a tendency towards paranoia might think there was a special animus against Chinese refugee claimants. (It's an oddity, for example, that a "style guide" for specific use in turning down Chinese refugees was issued to the panels last year. The fact that the success rate of Chinese claimants has fallen precipitously from sixty-one per cent in 1989 to twenty-one per cent in 1991 also seems a trifle odd.)

According to the appeal records, different panels at different times in different parts of the country were able to cite as "implausibilities" everything from the notion that a Chinese citizen might be persecuted simply for belonging to a pre-revolutionary capitalist family to the idea that taking part in a pro-student demonstration was, in itself, grounds for fearing subsequent trouble with the authorities. One claimant was even refused refugee status because she waited three days after an initial PSB inquiry into her pro-student activities before going into hiding. The panel figured that she couldn't be all that afraid of persecution. *Carve this in stone, too*: they don't have to arrest you in China until they want to. I knew a brave young man who helped me and two other Western journalists find the site of a Chinese airplane crash in the outskirts of Beijing in 1979 (with the same crowd running the government and the police that are still entrenched today). For giving us street directions, he was ratted on by a close acquaintance and "inquiries" were begun at his place of work and in his neighbourhood. After ten days of rising innuendo, and with nowhere to hide out, he tried to turn himself in to his local PSB station simply to terminate the unbearable tension and to spare his family even worse trouble than it was already in. *He was turned away.* The authorities told him that they were not ready for him yet. An arrest came two days later, after which his trial, conviction, and sentence (three years of labour reform) were all tidily attended to in less than half an hour the next morning. This young man helped me and my colleagues on what turned out to be a ten-inch, page-twelve newspaper story and for that, as long as that rotten system endures, his life will be a comprehensive misery.

Mr. Yi's story has a good news/bad news denouement. The panel's decision was brought before the Federal Court of Appeal, also held in Toronto. Last June, after reviewing the evidence and Mr. Yi's testimony, Mr. Justice Mark MacGuigan ruled that the decision must be struck down. Although he was a minister of external affairs in the Trudeau era, this judge has never claimed to be an expert in the internal affairs of the Chinese Communist regime. Still, he managed to bring two humble ingredients into the process: common sense and common decency. In summing up, Mr. Justice MacGuigan noted that the panel's crucial disbelief in the claimant's story boiled down to its basic assumption that the authorities who came to deliver the summons would have waited around to make sure they got their man. "We may well wonder," the judge wrote in his decision, "whether this judgment does not involve the imposition of Western concepts on a subtle oriental totalitarianism, and whether it is correct to interpret Chinese law enforcement in the light of the more linear Western model, when the social control exercised by the Chinese State is omnipresent, through the co-opting of the vigilance of its citizens generally."

That's the good news. The bad news is that all Mr. Justice MacGuigan was able to do was call for a new hearing from another, differently constituted, panel. So it's off to the Immigration and Refugee Board for Mr. Yi once again.

October 1992

P.S. Within a year, Yi Zhibing got his second hearing with the Immigration and Refugee Board. This time, thanks to a good lawyer – and, no doubt, some press attention – the board thought better of its earlier decision and reclassified Yi as "a conventional refugee." He got his landed immigration status shortly afterwards. His lawyer, incidentally, later ended up being appointed to the board by the new Liberal government, which I guess represents some sort of progress.

Douglas Coupland

⌇

The day Douglas Coupland hid out under my desk was not the best day for me either. For one thing, the comptroller had snitched to the publisher that my editorial costs were up for the second month in a row. And, as usual, the undereditors were trying to make sure I ruled nothing around this place except my CD player (and *that* only if I kept the volume low). So this isn't just a cute column opener: it really was a bad day, right up to the moment Doug turned up, singed and distraught from an abrasive CBC interview.

He just barged right in, a bit before four in the afternoon – past the receptionist, past one of the undereditors, past my assistant, past all the people who are supposed to protect me. In my nearly seven years as editor at *Saturday Night*, there has never been a more serious breach of security, with the one exception of the lady body builder who came after me because we mentioned in an article that she once dabbled in steroids.

Mercifully, Doug has never been into steroids, just bric-a-brac. On this occasion, for example, he was carrying a plastic shopping bag with lots of stuff in it (scarf, notebook, one

running shoe, Sony Walkman™, a book, and various magazines). Now that I think about it, I guess the bag wasn't plastic.
Maybe heavy cotton. Definitely a breathing fabric. Dianne
noticed it when she came into my office. How could she not
notice, since she nearly tripped over it. She saw the bag even
before she realized its owner – our Douglas – was mere *inches*
away under my desk eating the last two Nice biscuits from the
lunchroom's Peek Freans™ Family Assortment (Commercial).

But I get ahead of myself.

What I remember clearly was that Doug's bag was
b-u-l-g-i-n-g. Like a street person's luggage. (I'd have said "bag
lady's" in the old days, but Doug has trained me never to be
gender specific unless I can see a safe exit.) I also recall the state
he was in. You could tell how upset he was because his voice was
high-pitched and he was letting out little moans as he dropped
the bag, crawled under the desk, and hugged himself in the fetal
position. I said, "Doug?" and he said, "Don't talk to me for a minute." So I went to our lunchroom to fetch the aforementioned
Nice biscuits because I thought he probably needed sustenance.
Doug's quite thin.

I put the cookies on a Melmac™ plate and gently laid it beside him on the floor. I was still feeling maternal towards him in
those days, thirteen months ago. Since then, I have met his real
mum in Vancouver and quickly realized I had to write myself
into a less redundant role. We communicate *ecrivano a ecrivano*
now, with joyous flashes of mysticism and religion. . . .

Eventually, the crystals on the Nice biscuits – a Prozac™
derivative, I'm sure – did their work, and Doug emerged from
under my desk, at peace with himself and the universe. Just in
time, too. He's young and can get away with this sort of thing.
I'm developing arthritic joints and sitting swami-like on the
floor to accommodate the sensitivities of a brilliant young
writer who is also an Olympic-class control freak is not my idea
of how to reach nirvana.

When we were both standing upright, we pretended that what had happened hadn't happened, so we shook hands and said "Hi" and "Great to see you" and "How's everything going?" and "Isn't that terrific news about the new book?" You can only do this with very special friends: mutual awareness, no explanations necessary. Doug and I always got along well, right from the first time we met at H's house. H, it is true, later killed himself. Although the suicide had nothing whatever to do with Doug or me, the stark fact of it nevertheless became a motif of our relationship, at least in my own mind. Clichés, mostly: *nothing lasts, don't waste the day, fame is fickle, wealth doesn't bring happiness, brief life is here our portion.*

Beyond the clichés, the simple truth of the matter is that I'm very proud of young Douglas these days. Very proud.

I was trying to explain to Barb precisely what a big deal Doug had become. Being difficult and judgemental, of course, Barb chooses to keep him "in perspective." This means that, so far as she is concerned, Doug is still in the "Michael Arlen mode" (bright young thing, spirit of his age, etc., but still not ready for the high jump). I reject this line entirely. I know Barb only too well, and if Doug ever went for her definition of "the high jump," she'd just raise the bar a few notches. I'd rather beat the drum for Doug just as he is today. I've seen his new book of short stories and I was smitten from the beginning. One at a time they came winging their way into *Saturday Night*'s offices, and my favourite can be found on page 46 of this issue.

Ever since he wrote *Generation X* three years ago and followed it up with *Shampoo Planet*, Doug has been a major literary and sociological event, especially in North America. In the States, he's cruising around in guru stratosphere: the Jack Kerouac of his generation (the post-boomer generation of disaffected techno-punks who don't know the words to either

"God Save the Queen" or "O Canada"), a new-minted McLuhan, Homer to the microserfs. He's been on the cover of *Wired*. The op-ed page of *The New York Times* uses him when it tries to appear mod and rad. He is equally important, but for different reasons, to *People* magazine and *The New Republic*. Even the Dalai Lama wanted to meet him during a recent visit to Los Angeles. Doug agreed and managed to fit His Holiness into a busy schedule, but he wasn't as impressed with the Lion of Lhasa as he wanted to be. His Holiness may be enjoying the glitterati too much, Doug seemed to indicate. I don't agree. I like the Dalai Lama and I like Doug Coupland, so I feel that if I had been in Los Angeles, it would have made a difference:

"Your Holiness," I would have said, "this is Douglas. He has his finger on the pulse of our age, and you need to know him if you want to understand young people today and the blockade they feel trapped within. He's a nice guy, too: he knows all the slick and clever things that make you laugh, but you can still push right past all that and get quickly to a core that is honest and decent and full of wonder for the world around him."

"And Doug," I would *also* have said, "for heaven's sake, this is His Holiness, the fourteenth Dalai Lama, who is a lovely, lovely god-man. Forget his relationship with Richard Gere, Doug. Think of the potential of his relationship with y-o-u. He is someone who would enjoy walking with you through the miraculous forest in Capilano Canyon as much as I did on that day I was feeling so low and you cheered me up. Think of the path His Holiness could lead you along, out and away from the blockade and into the sunlit uplands of life. He's shy and brave – very brave – and as full of the wonder of life as you are."

They should have got on famously, and I regret the missed opportunity to bring together two such good friends in a little cosmos of mutuality. A lost occasion is like a junked cassette tape: difficult to play again.

Doug and I have known each other for the better part of a decade. When I first met him he was a junior employee at filthy-rich *Vista* magazine, Frank Stronach's state-of-the-art, late-1980s, greed-and-exceed publication (which was not destined to survive the rigours of the recession). *Vista* was also where Doug developed and refined a lot of his theories for *Generation X*. The perspective was riveting from his own office cubicle, or "veal-fattening pen" as he called the pre-eminent work space of our time, isolating its sinister interior meaning.

I had just started as editor at *Saturday Night*, so when we first met he was on the make and I was on the take. That's the way it often is at the beginning of editor-writer relationships. If you're lucky, an opportunity arises for mutual respect to grow and entwine a relationship, like stubborn ivy. Well . . . ivy or a mass of neurotic nerve endings. Writers are such *creatures* at times, with equal measures of bravado and egotism masking hideous insecurity. Yet good editors are always on the prowl for new blood. Also, they always esteem and worry about their best writers in ways that sometimes not even lovers would understand. Before my very own eyes, Douglas grew from the nervy kid at *Vista* to the self-wrought oracle of our age, and he did it with a distinctive style and up-market hustle that still leaves me breathless. Not once, so far as I can tell, did he do a sleazy thing to get where he is. He trudged all the way on his talent alone. Owen Glendower could only "call spirits from the vasty deep"; Douglas Coupland dredges them up everywhere – from microchips to the refuse bags of plastic surgeons in southern California.

I have a prized cache of Couplandiana in my office: a collage on my wall, innumerable faxes in my files, a box of bribes he once sent me from southern California before he wrote *Generation X* and still had to hustle story ideas. It was a wonderful idea too, the best story idea I've not been able to get into print. Doug was going to go undercover at a McDonald's™ restaurant. He would stay there until he was either fired or named employee-of-the-month – whichever came first. Genius that he is, instead of doing it he identified "McJobs" as the highest sort of employment many members of his turned-off, cynical generation would be able to attain, and astutely left the grunt work of serving the fries to others.

Under my desk, I'm thinking of placing a brass plaque. This is what it would say:

On February 5, 1993, Douglas Coupland hid out here briefly to ponder his life thus far. Upon emerging, he headed directly to the next plateau. This space is now reserved for writers who, having achieved much, need a moment's rest before going on to do even greater things.

March 1994

Political Domination 101

~

T hanks to a new prime minister and an imminent general election, the question of leadership is before us again. I used to think this was a straightforward matter. Is there a coherent vision? Can the aspiring or established leader communicate this vision effectively? Is the leader astute and confident enough to surround himself or herself with intelligent colleagues, imbued with common sense, who will be a sturdy check on the inevitable drift into vanity, arrogance, and error?

I don't think this any more, or at least I don't see the leadership profile as quite so neatly summarized. In fact, with something of a tingle of self-revelation, I realized recently that for over twenty-five years I had been keeping a sequence of bizarre little mental notes on various qualities and characteristics that mark actual leaders. They certainly leaven the theories and embellish the Identikit.

Autumn 1965. Breezing out of the barbershop at the old Newfoundland Hotel in St. John's, I nearly crashed into John and

Olive Diefenbaker, who had just arrived to begin campaigning for the general election. He put his hand out immediately, which I missed at first because I was so transfixed by the baby-bottom texture of his facial skin. Eventually we did the squeeze-it-tight-and-look-him-in-the-face thing, *mano a mano*:

"What's your name then, young man?" asked John George Diefenbaker.

"John Fraser, sir."

"And your middle name. What's your middle name?"

"Anderson, sir. I'm John Anderson Fraser."

"John A.! Olive! Olive! Come and say hello to a John A. Now Olive, that's a very good omen."

True leaders assume that Destiny takes a personal interest.

Late summer 1977. Outside her house in upper-class New Delhi, over a hundred petitioners were waiting to make their cases to Indira Gandhi, even though she had been booted out of office, even though a judicial inquiry was even then unfolding in the Indian courts into illegalities her government had allegedly presided over. Inside, in her living room, she was cool and abrupt. Then, as now, it took me a long and circuitous time to work up to a really difficult question in a formal interview. With Mrs. Gandhi, there were two to be asked: Why had she condoned the perversion by Indian scientists of the Canadian-supplied Candu reactors towards nuclear-weapons research? How did she feel about the prospect of a prison term if the commission of inquiry found her guilty of breaking the law?

With a wave of her hand, she dismissed the first question – on the misuse of the Candu reactors – by briskly instructing me that "we simply had to let our scientists have a go at it." Leading up to the second, I blew it. I was trying to pull off a convoluted compliment underscoring her family's history of serving time in British prisons in the cause of independence. Instead of being explicit, my opening gambit was to say that she and her family were no strangers to the notion of hurling people into jail. Not unreasonably, she took this to be a reference to all the poor folk she and her arrogant son Sanjay had incarcerated during her years of power.

"That's an outrageous parallel," she said, glaring at me with dagger eyes. She got up from her seat and went over to the mantel, perhaps to summon up a more magisterial pose with which to put me in my place. "The difference is that when we put people in jail it was for political reasons only. But this government wants to put us in jail for criminal reasons. It's monstrous."

Righteousness is the royal jelly of leadership.

September 1978. The presidential palace in Hanoi, which once housed the governor of French Indochina, is a wonderful mixture of pomposity and domestic banality, almost anticipating the nasty crowd of thieving Communists who eventually moved in. I still have a vivid memory of sitting there in a minor audience chamber holding hands with Pham Van Dong, the Vietnamese premier, on one chair and me on another. This was not so much an interview as a little tea party. I had already submitted ten questions (out of an initial sixteen, six of which were deemed unsuitable for answer by the premier). The written answers, I was told, would be made available to me when the tea party ended. Our audience was to be informal, but I was free to ask questions.

"*Parlez-vous français?*" asked Pham Van Dong.

"*Comme une vache chinoise,*" I said, eliciting a stately chuckle from the premier. That's when he took my hand in his; he held onto it for the next twenty-seven minutes. My long-suffering wife was with me and volunteered to translate in order to avoid a Vietnamese interpreter. So we talked about this and that, about the weather and the banana crop, about state production figures and female labour, about the "rehabilitation" of the conquered southern part of reunified Vietnam, about local music and . . . well, would *Monsieur le Premier* care to discuss, ahem, the possibility – or perhaps, although this is maybe the wrong word, the inevitability – that Vietnam was about to, well, howdoyousayit? *invade* Cambodia?

Pham Van Dong squeezed my hand extra hard at this point. I could feel his veins throbbing and, although I can't swear to this, I believe there were tears of sincerity welling in his eyes.

"I promise you no Vietnamese soldier will ever set foot any-where outside Vietnamese territory."

I thought that this was decent of him to say. It seemed forth-right and unequivocal. Keeping hold of my hand, the premier tugged me to my feet, and together with my translating wife we went for a short stroll in the presidential gardens.

Later, when we were walking alone, I said to my wife that I thought the interview had gone well and the world's wire ser-vices would eat up Pham Van Dong's ringing assurances that no invasion would take place. As we talked, the rumble of tanks and troop carriers could be heard as they lumbered through the streets of Hanoi, heading who knew where.

"You forgot to ask him the follow-up question," my wife said.

"What follow-up question?" I asked kindly. I always try to be patient with someone not familiar with the higher levels of journalism.

"The one where you ask him to spell out exactly what he understands to be Vietnamese territory."

Vietnam invaded Cambodia four days later.

Lying and double-speak are justified means to policy ends. They are abetted when journalists fail to ask follow-up questions.

Early summer 1986. If you have any liking for history, and es-pecially for English history, a walk through the front door of 10 Downing Street and up the main staircase to the prime minister's office is a definite high. "How nice you could come," She said solicitously, as if it were the journalist who was doing the favour.

She was not contemptuous or impatient during the opening pleasantries, as I had been led to believe She would be. She was courteous and charming, as was her ubiquitous press assistant, Bernard Ingham, who hovered at hand. No one could have believed, as She patiently answered boring questions about Anglo-Canadian relations, that all She and Mr. Ingham were waiting for was a question on South Africa because this was the week the two of them had decided to kill the whole notion of sanctions as a moral imperative in the geopolitical scheme of things.

The fly didn't walk into the spider's trap for nearly twelve minutes, but when he did, a state harangue was unleashed that lasted more than eight minutes, during which time no interruptions were brooked. The journalist watched in awe as She shifted forward in her seat to make some particularly forceful point, and he marvelled as her voice went into a high nasal pitch not unlike that of a jet engine on takeoff. He thought to himself how clever She was, proved by the fact that by the end of the harangue She had established – to the perfect satisfaction of any debating judge – that those who were for trading sanctions against South Africa were duplicitous hypocrites and moral racists.

When She finished, She paused. The journalist did not realize until two days later that She would be deploying the same harangue on British journalists throughout the week, that he was simply the convenient tryout. So he did not understand fully why She then turned to nice Mr. Ingham who had been hugely enjoying the whole performance. "How'd I do?" She asked, like a little girl who had just finished her showpiece at a class concert. "It'll do very well," said nice Mr. Ingham. "A little long, perhaps, but you covered everything."

She was very pleased, though her opening and welcoming tone of voice was tinged with just a trace of impatience when *She* turned back to the journalist. "Now, is there anything else?"

Conviction is a matter of practice. It is not ever to be confused with what George Bush calls "the vision thing."

So there you have it. These nostrums being subscribed to, I see no reason why we can't expect the coming of a political messiah any old day.

March 1994

Citizens, Arise!

~

O ver the past several centuries, July has become the designated month for honouring revisionism. Revisionism is described in *The Collins English Dictionary* (*Saturday Night*'s bible) as "the advocacy of revision of some political theory, religious doctrine, historical or critical interpretation, etc." Don't be fooled by dictionary definitions. Revisionism means rewriting history to suit your current mood and purposes, and July, with its notorious round of political anniversaries, could well be christened Rewrite Month.

The round begins, of course, with the nationwide celebrations of Canada Day to commemorate Confederation. Many of the details of those far-off events in 1867 have necessarily become shrouded, so we are grateful to contemporary historians – revisionists all – for letting us know, each year, the newest authorized version. For example, where once as schoolchildren we had a serene sense of the Fathers of Confederation as united in one vision of the nation, we now have to accept that Maritime Canada in general was dragged howling into the strange

union, and that Sir Charles Tupper in particular was merely
looking after Number One:

"Premier Charles Tupper," observes P. B. Waite in the new
(second) edition of *The Canadian Encyclopedia,* "ambitious,
aggressive and confident, went ahead with Confederation,
convinced that in the long run it would be best for Nova Scotia,
and perhaps also for himself. Fortunately for Confederation,
Tupper did not test his electorate . . . sixty-five per cent of Nova
Scotians opposed Confederation."

But revisionism is more than a domestic phenomenon. On
July 4 our neighbours to the south persist in celebrating the
American "Revolution" (quotation marks around theme words
are the hallmark of the revisionist) despite the conclusive demonstration by Marxist historians, many decades ago, that the
disturbances of 1776 accomplished only a change in the board
of directors. For a revolution, the Marxists insist, the violence
has to bring about a transfer of power from one class to another.

It's clear that no such transfer occurred. Instead, every four
years, Americans simply elect King George III to the White
House. King George Bush, for example, can designate for his
cabinet anyone he cares to, without regard to the messy elec-
toral process – just like George III. He can start a little war
without recourse to his legislature – just like George III. He can
carry on in high office despite having both the legislative houses
opposed to and resentful of his authority – just like George III.
And he doesn't have to mess around with a secondary power figure such as a prime minister – *unlike* George III. So much for the
revolutionary pretensions of the Americans.

On the other hand, the Battle of the Boyne, of 1690, has been
revised into a true class struggle. The battle pitted the Protestant William of Orange against the last Roman Catholic king
of England, James II. Although Canadians barely acknowledge
"King Billy Day" any more, even in the old Orangemen's

redoubt of Toronto, whole previous generations grew up knowing that July 12 commemorated the most glorious/treacherous
day in history. The split was sectarian. But the revisionists have
decisively rejected any notion that religion – the despised
opiate – added anything other than local colour to the long
struggle by the bourgeoisie to shake off the shackles of economic
feudalism and prepare the way for the eventual triumph of the
working classes. In this light, William III and Mary II can be
seen as part of the advance team for the international proletariat, having made the first "gains" when they ascended the
throne in 1689.

The French Revolution, of course, has been a revisionist's
dream for years and the bicentennial this year represents something of a climax in the cult of reinterpretation. Still, people
tend to forget that it *is* a game. The author of a recent article in
The New York Review of Books was actually dismayed to find that
two new studies (*Citizens* by Simon Schama and *The French Revolution* by George Rudé) seemed to be at odds with each other:
"When it comes to the basic question of what the Revolution
achieved and why it evolved in the way it did, the two men flatly
contradict each other. For Rudé, despite all its blemishes and
frustrations, the Revolution left behind a glorious message of
social progress that was to inspire future generations. . . .
Schama sees the Revolution as a total disaster, in which the violence and chauvinism of a reactionary mob put an end to an
ancien régime that was already liberal in essence and fully committed to technological progress.

"With the best will in the world," the reviewer added plain-
tively, "it is difficult to see how they can both be right."

Why is it so difficult? Revisionism requires no more than a
strong opinion and a selective ferreting for supportive historical
data. Take the storming of the Bastille. In the strong opinion of
one sort of republican historian, July 14, 1789, marked the
liberation by the triumphant masses of Paris of the legions of

"oppressed peasants, workers, and intellectuals" who were languishing in the Bastille. The hideous prison itself had for years
stood as the symbol of the cruelty and arbitrary essence of privileged autocracy – an example of which was Marie-Antoinette
saying you-know-what. But another sort of historian, with
other fish to fry, not only turns up a much earlier reference to
"Qu'ils mangent de la brioche" as a popular catch phrase but dis-
covers that on the momentous day the Bastille contained precisely two madmen, four convicted forgers, and an aristocrat
jailed at his father's request for debauchery.

Like a film by Francis Ford Coppola, history offers a choice of
scripts. That being so, why should we not seize the opportunity
to present Confederation as the epochal event it surely was.
There is new research. Old research cries out for re-evaluation.
A strong argument shapes itself. Even by Marxian definitions it
will stand the proof.

July 1, then, marks the one true revolution since the Boyne.
The long class struggle of the bureaucrats against the peasantry
and stubborn entrepreneurial rabble of pre-revolutionary Canada ended in the bureaucrats' triumphant *coup d'état* – bloodless
admittedly, but not without fireworks. Only the bureaucrat class
would have had the wit to choose the ledger-sensible first day of
a month on which to seize power and set up the machinery of
government. Typically, its first acts were the requisitioning of fil-
ing cabinets and forms in quadruplicate on which to fire off
aides-mémoire – in both official languages. In short order, it then
forged three royal commissions, sixteen strategy papers, and
twenty-two drafts of specific legislation – including an act to forbid the grazing of horses or cows on Parliament Hill.

The new regime had already prepared its ground by making
alliances with the mercantile, banking, and legal fraternities,
and now moved swiftly to enlist the accountants. Under the
resulting onslaught of licensing requirements, credit checks,
property registrations, grant applications, customs and excise

reports, quotas, tax returns, and fine print, the breakdown of the old society was swift. While the voyageurs skulked off into the landscape, the farmers docilely set up marketing boards. Paperwork and red tape had vanquished adventurism.

There were problems, of course, not the least being the state of health of the bureaucrats' chief information officer, John A. Macdonald, whose chronically inflamed toenail caused him such excruciating pain that it slurred his speech, even at midday. Nonetheless Macdonald, and his fellow press officers (Cartier, Galt, *et alii*) were crucial in reconciling the nation to the surrender of initiative to middle-level management. Who will ever forget the words of the redoubtable James Mandiville Black (later Sir James), the first undersecretary of state for forests and waterworks, as he tried to give form to the embryonic, often inchoate longings of the raw young nation?

"We have not yet begun to enumerate fully the consequences of an unevaluated ecosystem," said Black on June 30, 1867, the eve of the historic march on Fortress Langevin. "Where one man might say, 'We have given you the tools, get on with the job,' it is our duty to point out that an improperly defined job is worse than a vacuum and all tools have to be correctly requisitioned and accounted for (departmental forms B-480/Y and B-480/MN2, with Annex-E copies to the minister of state's office). Let not our successors say we shirked our responsibilities, but instead let us pledge ourselves to establishing such a system that if the Canadian civil service and its mandarins last a thousand years people will say that this was their finest prioritization."

And they say our history is boring?

July 1989

Save the Last Dance

⁓

Mikhail Baryshnikov came back to dance in Toronto just a month before Rudolf Nureyev died in Paris on January 6. Baryshnikov was at the O'Keefe Centre, the theatre where he orchestrated his dramatic leap to the West in 1974 (and which he still lists as one of the worst performing houses in all of North America). Nureyev died in the city in which he made his own leap to a new life in the West in 1961. His memorial service was held in the ornate Paris Opera, a house he adored and where he often left dancers in tears, so outrageous were some of his harangues when he presided over the ballet company there in the 1980s.

Both men sported the news-wire sobriquet "Soviet defector," a special category of performing artist that will soon mean very little except as a historical footnote. Next to their obvious talent, however, it used to mean half of their mystique, half of *everything*: exoticism, artistic distinction, aloofness, unique star quality, being set apart from all Western-trained male dancers. Their overt sexuality on stage, differently expressed, was the other half. Critics were rarely explicit in discussing this, yet potency positively radiated from them during performances – from their costumes, mannerisms, athleticism, studied stage glances, even their curtain calls. Their artistry has formed the definition of male dancing for the last half of the twentieth century, but it was sex appeal that shot them both into the highest stratosphere of stardom.

Nureyev was gay and died of AIDS. Baryshnikov is straight and is still fathering children; he has had two with his companion, Lisa Rinehart. (An older child is the daughter of the film actress Jessica Lange.) Nureyev was promiscuous, almost to the end; Baryshnikov has settled down, though it was not so long ago that he led a merry chase through the ranks of ballerinas and movie stars where the risk of cross-sexual infection from the terrible disease is far more real than in, say, the middle-class enclaves of north Toronto. Many heterosexuals in North America still don't take the risk of AIDS very seriously. Not so in the world of the performing arts. Especially not so in the world of ballet. Safe sex is a contradiction in terms. Baryshnikov knows that; Nureyev laughed at it.

At the outset of his career in the West, Nureyev had two noble relationships with people older than himself that provided emotional and perhaps sexual stability. The first was with Dame Margot Fonteyn, the great English prima ballerina, and the other was with Erik Bruhn, the brilliant Danish dancer who loved him deeply. In each case, Nureyev gave generously of himself and extended his partner's performing career. In his fashion, he remained loyal to both, but his libido was restless and he was notorious for seeking out anonymous, dispensable lovers. This aroused endless pop-psychological speculation. Craig Dodd, the author and ballet critic who knew Nureyev in the 1960s, argued that this was his way of meeting people "on as nearly equal terms as anyone as famous as him is likely to do." Writing after Nureyev's death in London's *Sunday Telegraph*, Nicholas Farrell reported that some of the dancer's colleagues felt that "perhaps it could even have been a defiance of death – a sort of danse macabre."

What we do know is this: at the same age (their late thirties), Nureyev and Baryshnikov took dramatically different paths in their personal lives. Nureyev lingered on in dangerland and Baryshnikov headed straight for middle-class domesticity. And the impact of those personal decisions and directions has had a profound effect on their art.

When I was a dance critic at the dawn of time, nearly a quarter-century ago, I had my problems with Nureyev. I admired him enormously, of course. Only a fool wouldn't. He electrified every stage he danced on. Kid critics nevertheless had a responsibility for making sure the reading public didn't think we were overly awed by superstars like Nureyev, and I took my responsibilities as a *Canadian* kid critic very seriously in those days. After paying due attention to Nureyev's particular genius for three or four years, especially after he chose the National Ballet of Canada to be a handsome backdrop to his own expensive productions (his *Sleeping Beauty*, which reeked of dollars spent in the six figures, was notorious), I decided he wasn't sufficiently appreciative of the opportunities Canada had provided him. I detected unpleasant proof that the National Ballet was giving up too much of its mandate just for the thrill of having a soon-forgotten summer season at the Met in New York. I expatiated on all this, somewhat more pointedly than I am doing here, in the pages of the Sunday *New York Times*, where readers cared a lot more about Nureyev than about the future of Canadian ballet.

What a lot of fuss and bother ensued. By the time the dust and chicken feathers had settled, I'd managed to add to my list of blood enemies the legendary dancer/choreographer Martha Graham, the New York Times dance critic Clive Barnes, all the principal dancers of the National Ballet, and at least one American balletomane who took the trouble to mail me faecal material in a plastic bag. The article was published about the same time Baryshnikov defected in Toronto, so it was a wild time in my life. Curiously, the one person I didn't make an enemy of – in the long term anyway – was Nureyev himself. After he had whipped everyone up into a frenzy of loyalty oaths and assured himself the kid critic spoke for no one but himself, we collaborated on a book about the Canadian dancers Karen Kain and Frank Augustyn. (I did the legwork, he did the foreword.) During the course of this little collaboration, we agreed that we both listened to too much idle gossip. And then we gossiped idly and amiably through an affectionately remembered dinner and past all the damage we had tried to inflict on each other.

How I loved Nureyev after that, although I never really got close to him. Not close in the way I got to Baryshnikov, who walks on golden pathways as far as I'm concerned, and who understands human nature, and his own, in ways Nureyev could never have begun to plumb. You could see the proof of this in the dancing they both did after they had passed their prime. Nureyev clung to all the old forms. As he went on refusing to retreat from a field fit only for young men at their peak, he became for some a sad and desperate figure who allowed himself to be tricked out in his old costumes, half-dancing his former roles of glory. I caught one of these events in upstate New York. (He rarely took such efforts to main stages.) At first I was embarrassed for his sake and then I had a change of heart and thought the spectacle poignant and even beautiful in a weird way. For Nureyev, being on stage – any stage – was synonymous with being alive. I think it was as simple as that.

It's not at all that simple for Baryshnikov. He takes the

business of ageing very seriously. A far better technician than Nureyev, he always seemed to soar twice as high. The problem here, though, was that he lit twice as hard, and the damage to his legs over the years has been considerable. Unlike Nureyev, he has never had any interest in trying to perpetuate a former self. If he was middle-aged, dammit, he would dance middle-aged. His performances with Twyla Tharp in Toronto were a triumph: witty, sophisticated, but, most of all, wise. In Tharp, he has latched onto a choreographer/dancer who manages to confirm every dark, paranoid suspicion of the young Generation X feeling endlessly shafted by the hegemony of the baby boomers. Where once only youth was allowed to adorn the dance stage, Tharp and Baryshnikov announced that today's audiences don't really need the callow perspective of the under-thirty crowd. Here was a postmenopausal romp that embodied female independence, comfortable male self-acceptance, and a knowing deference to the realities and complications of relationships. Baryshnikov works around his game leg, makes a virtue of it, in fact, and once he and Tharp established the new rules and conventions of the game, they had us all cheering.

I suppose he can go on like this for a long time, and we may yet see him do a dance based on *The Old Man and the Sea*. He probably won't, though, because he is riddled through and through with common sense and a concept of decorum that is as natural to him as it was alien to Nureyev. This is not to detract from Nureyev. He was what he was and gave immense pleasure to millions of people. Anyone who saw him dance, particularly when he was in top form, is marked for life; to have known him, even fitfully, was an honour.

In private, he wasn't particularly nice about Baryshnikov – professional jealousy was as much a part of his personality as was generosity to young artists – but, like dominant predators who understand their mutual powers, they sniffed each other out early on and more or less kept to separate territories. And Baryshnikov, for his part, always understood Nureyev's appeal. "He had the charisma and simplicity of a man of the earth," Baryshnikov said after Nureyev's death, "and the untouchable arrogance of the gods." Those Russians! Those Soviet defectors!

March 1994

PART TWO

Sunday School Home
Truths

The Drag Scene

~

There is a smoking room on our premises. Actually, it is an official "separately ventilated smoking-designated area" in total conformity with draconian Toronto by-laws which, among other provisions, allow someone to telephone anonymously to City Hall and rat on fellow citizens for actual or alleged smoking offences. Although I haven't yet heard of anyone informing on his or her co-workers, I don't take any comfort from this. The mere existence of the provision (complete with serious fines of up to $5,000) along with the zealotry of nonsmokers and the darker motivations of human nature make for a combustible mixture. One waits for the knock on the door during the coffee break.

The nonsmokers at our place have been gentle. One of the few colleagues who have made noises about our "disgusting" habits is a glamorous hypocrite, having herself been known to indulge the vice during moments of high stress. We smokers know this type only too well, but we are a forgiving lot. Some of us have kicked the habit for periods of time in the past and fully understand both the missionary fervour that takes hold of some reformed smokers, and the righteousness that is the cheater's disguise.

In fact, thanks to our little room, we have come to know a lot about human nature. We have explored humility and encountered tact and mutual support. This is a very difficult subject to get across to nonsmokers, most of whom work from the premise that we are either lazy creatures of habit or pathetic victims of addiction – which may be true enough, but doesn't begin to explain the bond that now unites people who commit such socially unacceptable acts. Out in the sleet on the sidewalk, down the dark stairwells, in the designated cubbyholes, or wherever today's pariahs are forced to gather, there are no foes, only moments of egalitarian caring and merciful calm.

The most obvious manifestation of the bond, at least in our little smoking room, is the automatic breakdown of hierarchy. There we all are, randomly self-selected by our craving, from the editor to the receptionist, from the comptroller to a circulation rep, from the veteran editor-at-large who has seen *everything* to the newest kid freelancer desperately trying to get a foothold in a national publication. It is a true if unintentional collectivity, with exchanges of information that rarely happen elsewhere in professional life – interdepartmental grapevine stuff a lot of the time, but also pertinent news that can lead to story ideas. Sometimes, wonderfully, there are bursts of creativity that are shorn of agenda and objectives and challenges and all the other wretched encumbrances of formal meetings. Whether it's the theme for a new circulation campaign or a surprising twist to a complicated article, the smoking room is the only place in our small world that positively fosters a sustained and amiable dialogue among departments.

Our smoking room has been in existence for only two years, but already – at least in my mind – it has become the repository of ironic little grace notes in *Saturday Night* lore. Last year, for example, a writer came in after a heavy session with his editor. He slumped into a chair, lit up, and took such a deep drag that I thought he was going to implode on the spot.

"Trouble?" I asked solicitously. We had not yet been introduced, and I don't think he realized that I was the editor.

"X has just taken out my best paragraph. I can't believe she did it. It was so beautiful."

"Didn't she like it?" I asked. "What was the problem?"

"Oh, she agreed that it was beautiful. She said it was so good, it was threatening the balance of the whole article."

Smokers come in the usual variety. Some are fastidious, fully indoctrinated into being as inconspicuous as possible. They empty their ashtrays before leaving. The comptroller, on the other hand, is a pipe smoker and – occasionally – has his interminable computer print-outs spread over all possible working surfaces and his pipes and pipe ashes overflowing from all possible ashtrays. He is our Peck's Bad Boy and from time to time has to be gently admonished. Personally, though, I love the smell of his pipe, for it reminds me of my grandfather's pipes, especially the ones he kept in his library. The aroma, even when it is stale, is rich with nostalgia and serves me as the madeleine cakes did Proust in summoning up the remembrance of things past.

It is always amusing when nonsmokers make brief visits, twitching their noses at the smells when they first open the door. Even when they are coming to show that they acknowledge us as members of the human race, it is very hard for them to discuss anything but smoking. Smokers themselves rarely talk about smoking, but friendly nonsmokers can't seem to keep themselves from saying things like, "My boyfriend smokes, so I'm used to the smell," or "Not in the house but we have a nice veranda off the kitchen," or "Some of my best friends . . ."

They rarely stay longer than three or four minutes, and it has struck me more than once that they enter our premises in much the same way some people entered the hospital room of a friend who died of AIDS last year. They are trying their best to show support, but beyond the gesture it is best to move on quickly. Risk of infection, second-hand smoke, etc. etc.

Of course, of course, smoking is a terrible thing, and I am romanticizing our "separately ventilated smoking-designated area." I have children, you know, and am reminded daily – in ways various and cruel – that I live a troubled, depraved life. The children have all been prepped by their health teachers and have seen disgusting photographs of diseased lungs. To counteract this daily assault, I have my own private collection of smokers' support stories, which seem to amuse and comfort only me: for example, Pauline Vanier, of glorious memory, told me with glee on her ninetieth birthday that *they* had had to give up badgering her to stop smoking in case it shortened her life. One knows one is vile and weak, but still the day must be borne, and for some of us, a cigarette holds out more chance of relief than a cup of camomile tea.

I was principally responsible for the decoration – such as it is – of our smoking room. The furniture is ratty and used, like us smokers, but we like it. It does. There's an adding machine, a blue recycling box, and a hodgepodge of cast-off chairs. The only really controversial items are two framed photo portraits: one of the late René Lévesque looking slightly bemused, with a half-consumed cigarette clenched in his right hand; the other of Pierre Trudeau, looking superior and smokefree. The portraits once adorned covers of *Saturday Night*. Initially, I had them removed from our boardroom because they had a dated aura about them, and I put them up in the smoking room simply because they were at hand and the walls looked too bare.

Now they have taken on eerie, emblematic lives of their own. I once reviled Lévesque because he was trying to mess up my country and revered Trudeau because he was trying to hold it together. It's different now. René has become our friend and ally. "It's okay," he's saying, with a nice shrug and a wrinkled brow. "Life's a dog's breakfast. Have a puff. What the hell." In the smoking room, we are all separatists.

Not Pierre, though. His eyes are cold and censorious. Under that gaze, we smokers are variations on the theme of Margaret, and he's saying to us such things as, "You people had a choice and you chose to live in this cesspit. If you can't look after yourselves, maybe we'll have to do the job for you." Pierre is our warning never to forget what lies beyond the four walls. He's there to caution us of the doctors who don't want to look after us because smokers are vermin and an alleged drain on the health-care system. He's there to remind us that in every nonsmoker's mind there is a photo-identity picture of whoever lights up in which a red circle encases the head and a ban slash crosses the face.

Subconsciously, we know that out little smoking room cannot last forever. Now that we have been successfully isolated, I am at any moment expecting summary orders from City Hall or some ministry to place signs on the door. We know already what these signs will say: "DANGER! THIS ROOM KILLS" or "KEEP OUT! AUTHORIZED ADDICTS ONLY."

The director of consumer marketing, a longtime pal, told me the other day she was thinking of taking up t'ai chi, but the instructor said he wouldn't teach her unless she gave up smoking. Maybe she would try to kick the habit, she said. I've been blackmailed by my kids into promising to try the patch before the year is over (which doesn't end until 11:59 p.m. on December 31). If too much of this sort of thing comes to pass, our heretics' sanctuary will become even lonelier and then it will simply be proscribed. Something – a camaraderie, a rueful, generous culture – that I have come to value very much and that is incomprehensible to the unaddicted will be lost. The world will not be a better place and, after the last trace of second-hand smoke has vanished from the universe, our graves will still await us.

November 1993

Why Can't Quebec Listen?

~

I n Canada, the politics of language is invariably divisive. This is not because the difference between "yes" and "*oui*" is worth dying for but because the language debate has always been the outer dress of the twin solitudes that identify the Canadian soul. Now, a generation that thought it had bridged the essential linguistic and social contradictions of the nation has had to come to the realization that it simply met the necessities of its own era. We are still only a controversy or a court decision away from the familiar sense of self-destruction.

This is the main reason sensible politicians try to avoid the issue of language and would do almost anything – waffle, circumscribe, fudge, even hyperventilate – rather than tackle it. To embrace squarely anything that so risks inflaming French-English passions in this beloved aberration of a country is to flirt with the devil. There is always a price to be paid.

Journalists and academics are less sensible than most politicians. Ever since last December when Premier Robert Bourassa announced Quebec's intention to retain – despite a ruling by the Supreme Court of Canada – many of the particulars of its controversial Bill 101 affecting the use of French on public signs in the province, we've been for it in both official languages. A prominent and persuasive western journalist, for example, has argued that Quebec has played the separatist card once too often. "The whole prospect of Quebec's departure," wrote Ted Byfield, founder of the influential *Alberta Report*, "far from being an unthinkable disaster, has become in many minds a rather tantalizing possibility." Conrad Black, the proprietor of this magazine and a staunch defender of the French-Canadian reality, nevertheless wrote in his column in the *Financial Post* that Quebec has come very close to forfeiting its right to receive further transfer payments by treating the English-speaking minority so shabbily. In his nationally syndicated column, Allan Fotheringham – guru to the ungrateful and seer to the masses – journeyed to Regina, of all places, in order to heap scorn and disgust on Premier Bourassa for taking so long to denounce the torching of the Alliance Quebec offices in Montreal and for stating that the English-speaking minority in Quebec was privileged in comparison to French-speaking minorities in the rest of Canada.

The dateline of Fotheringham's column was the capital of the same province that nine months earlier had – like Quebec – declined to uphold its own national linguistic responsibilities. Hypocrisies abound whenever provincial politicians feel the need to march to local drummers. That Gary Filmon, a Conservative premier of Manitoba, should turn out to have had the biggest stick with which to beat Quebec is both fitting and ironic. The controversial "notwithstanding" clause invoked by Mr. Bourassa and denounced by Mr. Filmon was, of course, forced into the constitution – to safeguard parliamentary supremacy – by Filmon's predecessor as Tory premier of Manitoba, Sterling Lyon.

Perhaps a spirited debate on the language issue, or a larger one on the perpetual French-English divide, is just what we need. Somehow I doubt it. At *Saturday Night*, for example, we have been sending tart, remedial messages to French Canada for the past hundred years, all to no seeming avail. We have *nearly* got it into our heads that there is a society and a culture in Quebec that ignores the sensible editorial postures of English Canada. But judge for yourself. Here, for a start, is a genial little prescription from the magazine's founding editor, the redoubtable Edmund E. Sheppard, after he learned that the federal Parliament had voted in June 1891 to have a short recess in honour of St. John the Baptist, patron saint of Quebec:

"[English-Canadian politicians] are not [in Ottawa] to loaf around on saints' days; they are down there to attend to our business, and I imagine that if they quit this queer work and told some of the greasy haired Jean Baptistes to go and take a bath, there would be less of public money spent, both directly and indirectly, than now is being squandered on keeping some very unimportant people quiet."

Moving smartly on to the tolerant twentieth century, we find the fortunes of *Saturday Night* prospering and the first mention in the magazine (May 1909) of the bizarre notion of a bilingual Quebec:

"A bill has just been passed by the Quebec legislature which, if it stands the test of the high courts of the Empire, will force all common carriers, telegraph companies, etc., to have their waybills, contracts, tickets, in fact all documents with which the public come in contact . . . printed in French as well as in English. The business of the Province of Quebec so far as regards corporations is, of course, overwhelmingly English. The railways, the telegraph companies, the telephone companies, the shipping corporations, the manufacturing concerns and the large wholesale houses are, with very few exceptions, dominated by English Canadians. The French language is utilized when business necessities arise, but not otherwise. Now, however, a certain section of ultra French Canadians will have it a provision of law that the French language be placed on an equal footing with the English upon all documents issued by common carriers and corporations of like nature. Naturally the railways and business men are up in arms against it, and the chances are that the bill will find itself eventually in the cellar along with a lot of other fool legislation which is attempted in Quebec from time to time."

Three years later, in July 1912, *Saturday Night* told Quebec that it was an inevitable consequence of progress and demographic reality that "the use of French should gradually disappear from the Parliaments and Courts of Canada," adding, "There is hardly one man in a hundred of the citizens of Ontario and the West who gives a thought to Quebec except at election time."

The conscription crisis during the First World War, lest we forget, made the foregoing almost benign:

"This protest by French Canadians against French Canadians fighting the battles of Britain," editorialized *Saturday Night* in August 1915, "is the result of insular, bigoted upbringing, combined with dense ignorance. The French Canadian of the type who marches and riots as a protest against recruiting is perhaps more to be pitied than blamed. He is ignorant and he is narrow, and so he will remain just so long as his schools refuse him facilities for a liberal education. He knows nothing beyond his Province, and he cares less. All Jean Baptiste wants is to be left alone."

The following year, as English Canadian anger over Quebeckers' intransigence on conscription continued to gather momentum, some of the warning calls we still hear today began to emerge:

"The Province of Quebec must either go into the discard as a political factor or continue to be catered to and pampered by both parties as in the past. If catered to, conscription flies out of the window. The question is whether the present Government is big enough and strong enough, and sufficiently awake to the trend of public opinion in this country, to grasp the fact that Quebec is no longer essential to a successful political party."

By 1925, the magazine was striking a more positive – if pater-nalistic – note, undoubtedly induced by a few years of quietude. Readers were offered this cheery word sketch that could have captioned a painting by Krieghoff:

"It is pointed out that between 1911 and 1921 Northern Ontario's population of French origin grew from 45,000 to 63,000, out of a total population of 267,000. There is nothing surprising and nothing perilous as some would like us to believe in this migration of French Canadians to the 'back of the beyond.' The French Canadian is an ideal pioneer. Simple in tastes, industrious, ready and willing to put up with what we would consider considerable hardship, he is the man who fits naturally into our open spaces. He minds his business, does not join any Bolshevik clubs, behaves himself and brings up a large family, all good Canadians, who are in future generations likely to stick to the land, in place of decamping to the United States or gathering in our cities."

When the corrosive issue of conscription emerged once again during the Second World War to haunt the nation, a terse tone of minimal civility replaced the previous hysterics, but – as always – the underlying incomprehension and exasperation remained perfectly intact:

"We may as well be frank about these matters," wrote B. K. Sandwell in March 1942. Sandwell is still rightly regarded as one of the great editors of *Saturday Night* and is remembered particularly for his steely judiciousness in opposition to the internment of Japanese Canadians during the war. On the sub-ject of the perfidious French Canadian, however, Sandwell's judiciousness was tested to its limits:

"We may as well be frank about these matters. Active service against the enemies of Canada involves the risk of death. The unequal distribution of that risk among the different racial elements which make up Canada is the chief cause of the friction and bitterness that are developing over the question of conscription for service outside Canada. . . . There is among English-speaking Canadians a widespread feeling that the real motive of the French-Canadian attitude toward conscription is the desire to improve the numerical strength of that element in the Canadian population, by avoiding its full proportional share in the casualties."

In 1970, following the October Crisis, during which federalist Quebeckers were pitted against what was perceived as the ultimate separatist threat, another great editor, Robert Fulford, lamented the demise of a mythic peaceable kingdom where the various races had learned how to live together without violence. "Perhaps what we had before was based on illusion or stupidity," wrote Fulford, "but it was nevertheless important to us. It was our national dream – and what dream isn't based on illusion?"

The voices grow more tolerant in our pages, travelling from bigotry to elegy, yet they are united in being exclusively reactive. Quebec pushes, we deplore – or lament, wheedle, legislate, lecture, set up royal commissions, call out the troops.

And now, once again, dream and illusion in English Canada have collided with French-Canadian reality. Once again, Quebec appears to be changing the rules of the game. Once again, Quebec wants everything her own way. Once again, Quebec does not appreciate that English Canadians will take only so much. Once again, the solitudes have been reinforced. Once again, once again. . . . Like some long-married couple grown strange and crabby even as the partners cling to each other for warmth and protection, French and English Canada seem locked in a pattern of mutually irritating sufferance and unappreciated compromise.

Pierre Trudeau's creative new twist to our dilemma – that French Canadians should embrace federalism and break out of the traditional stockade of Quebec – has been so thoroughly assimilated that it's either taken for granted or enduringly resented. To some extent, in the reaction to the Supreme Court ruling on Quebec's Bill 101, and in the reaction to Quebec's response to that ruling, we are witnessing the long-delayed shakedown of the Trudeau era. Premier Bourassa's actions – which, despite the hue and cry in English Canada, have actually brought some bilingual relief from the earlier Parti Québécois sign-law legislation – simply return us to the rhetoric of the old impasse so familiar to *Saturday Night* centenarians.

If it is tedious, once again, for English Canada to have to react to an unacceptable action by Quebec, it is equally tedious to have to remind all Canadians that we have an obligation to come up with new solutions to maintain the central reality of our distinctiveness. Pro-free-traders in the West who resent the encroachments of bilingualism nevertheless are beholden to Quebec for making the difference in the free-trade vote. Anti-free-traders in Ontario who resent the spoiling factor inside Quebec nevertheless have to cling to the French fact of Canada as the most incontestable sign of our cultural originality. On and on it goes – the pluses are cancelled out by the minuses, and vice versa.

There is always the possibility of embracing a different logic, of creating an alternative script. It would be one that for English Canada begins with an understanding that not only is official bilingualism the glue that holds the philosophical and illusory notion of this nation together but that French-language rights have not been something we bestowed on an ungrateful Quebec; rather, they have been prised out of the English-speaking majority at some cost.

Then we might understand that Mr. Bourassa's "unacceptable" legislation is no more unacceptable than a dozen pieces of unacceptable federal and provincial legislation enacted to counter the passions of the day. Pierre Trudeau is no longer around as a public lightning rod to attract all the sullen anger against federal bilingualism; Robert Bourassa is. For those many other English-speaking Canadians who felt a program of comprehensive federal bilingualism should be sufficient to render Quebec "a province just like the others," the latest developments are equally repugnant. Quebec remains a special case, is undeniably different, and continues to seek protection for that difference.

Perhaps, in the 122nd year of Confederation, the vigour and consistency of the French-Canadian attempt to assert language rights could be acknowledged. Despite the engaged rhetoric, the essential defensiveness of Premier Bourassa's decision can be easily perceived. For much of the history of this land since the Conquest of 1759, French has survived in Quebec not because it has been the will of the majority of Canadians but because the speakers of French in Quebec have declined to relinquish their mother tongue. For some English Canadians, today as throughout our history, the whole notion of the French language surviving in North America is absurd. The assumption is that it will eventually die out and become a quaint relic just as it has in Louisiana. If you want to discover the engine that drives separatism in Quebec, that drove every reaction to federal or imperial incursions into the province in the past, it is here in the fear of the "ordinary common sense" in English Canada and the logic of the cultural trends in North America.

Let us find a different common sense. Let us, for example, concede that, during the past several decades of debate about the cost of Confederation, the territory of English-Canadian culture has been steadily expanding in quality and quantity. And who in English Canada has ever thought of rejoicing that our mother tongue is under no threat or that we can operate easily throughout most of the country in that language, even in those parts of it where bilingualism may always be a dirty word – like Calgary, or Quebec City, or Baie d'Espoir in Newfoundland? (That's Baie d'Espoir pronounced Bay Despair.)

Let us do it now, before we fall into the danger, once again, of turning the people of Quebec and their leaders into scapegoats – this time for all the festering, messily articulated misgivings so many of us in English-speaking Canada continue to have about the Meech Lake accord and whatever future it holds for the nation. Meanwhile, here at *Saturday Night*, we promise to sustain our century-old tradition of *evolving* towards civilized communication.

April 1989

Don't Have a Cow, Lord

~

S hopkeepers and secular humanists may have successfully manipulated Christmas into an amalgam of potent
sentiment and orchestrated debt, but for those still left
toiling in the vineyards of the Lord – Sunday-school teachers
like me, for example – it can be a gruesome time. We have been
especially afflicted over the past year or so with a new series of
gleeful books deploying archaeology, the historical method,
and modern theology towards a systematic demolition of the
biblical record, including most of the traditional trappings of
Christmas:

"The story of the baby being born in a stable at Bethlehem
because there was no room for him at the inn is one of the most
powerful myths ever given to the human race," writes A. N.
Wilson, the distinguished English author and journalist, in *Jesus*
(Sinclair-Stevenson, 1992). "A myth, however, is what it is.
Even if we insist on taking every word of the Bible as literally
true, we shall not be able to find there the myth of Jesus being
born in a stable. None of the Gospels state that he was born in a
stable, and nearly all the details of the nativity scenes which

have inspired great artists, and delighted generations of church-goers on Christmas Eve, stem neither from history nor from Scripture, but from folk-lore."

There's more of this stuff, more authoritatively documented in *The Unauthorized Version: Truth and Fiction in the Bible* (Viking, 1991; Penguin Books, 1992) by Robin Lane Fox, who at least does Christians the favour of first attempting to demolish nearly everything in the Hebrew scriptures before moving his wrecking operation from B.C. to the manger in Bethlehem: "There is a contradiction in Luke's story: if Quirinius was governor, the Roman census is credible but Herod is a mistake. There is also a contradiction with Matthew's story: if Quirinius or the Roman census is correct, Herod was not king and Matthew's stories of the Wise Men, the Massacre of the Innocents and the Flight into Egypt are all chronologically impossible."

Tackling all this and attempting to make it palatable to the remaining rationalists left in the church is John Shelby Spong's *Rescuing the Bible from Fundamentalism* (HarperCollins, 1992). Fox is a historian. Spong is the Episcopal bishop of Newark, New Jersey, and for some, serves Christianity much as Mikhail Gorbachev served Communism: like a way station on the road to oblivion. His concessions are tactical but sweeping: "Is any part of this [Christmas] tale believable to twentieth-century people? Do we believe in angels? Can they sing? In what language?" What's next? No doubt Kitty Kelley will soon be serving up exclusive details on the Virgin Mary's relationship with Quirinius during the census-taking.

Since faith transcends reason and is actually structured on the struggle with uncertainty, none of these cheerful jokers is too much of a problem for the battle-scarred Sunday-school teacher who knows better than most churchgoers – or agnostics, for that matter – the inconsistencies and literary extravagances of the Bible. The only truly irritating common denominator

in these books is the bald assumption that the beliefs everyone
is going to have to abandon are "Sunday-school beliefs."

Have they forgotten? Did they ever go to Sunday school? Do
they have even an inkling of what it is like to present yourself
before an inquisitorial court of kids from grades four or five or
six? Do they not know that these prepubescent sceptics have
their own exegetical texts? I quote from "Annoying questions to
ask your Sunday school teacher" published in *Bart Simpson's
Guide to Life* (HarperCollins, 1993):

"Wouldn't eternal bliss get boring after a while?"

"If someone's been decapitated, are they still headless in
heaven?"

"Why doesn't prayer bring dead goldfish back to life?"

"Can the spirits of your dead relatives watch you when you're
going to the bathroom?"

Such questions – all of which have been asked in one form or
another in my classes – are not unchallenging once you get into
them. (The film *Jurassic Park* opened up a whole new line of
inquiry, including an interesting side trip into the question of
whether dinosaurs had souls.) Curiously, though, unlike adults,
my pint-sized T-Rexes never seem to get hung up on mere
details or specific discrepancies in the Gospel accounts of Jesus
or, for that matter, in any of the heroic tales in the Jewish scriptures. God knows this is not because they lack inquisitiveness,
and I have struggled for some time now to understand what it is
in the grand sweep of the biblical saga that is so appealing to
children when it is not rammed down their throats.

For adults, part of the problem with the Gospel narratives,
which are missionary tracts written a century and more after
Christ's birth and based on several generations of oral (and
inevitably distorted) tradition, is that they are set up to seem
like historical – almost journalistic – records. Thus they invite
the methodology of historical scrutiny – and journalistic pok-
ing. A. N. Wilson's *Jesus,* for example, is a lively and often

fascinating roundup of modern scholarly inquiries into the New
Testament, but Wilson gets so enthusiastic in his investigation
that he ends up sounding like a *Washington Post* reporter on the
trail of Richard Nixon, a parallel the former president would
no doubt find apt. The search for the missing Jesus tapes and
the smoking gun (Judas Iscariot is "Deep Throat," by the way) is
great fun right up to the point where Wilson more or less ac-
knowledges that sufficient data don't actually exist for a proper
forensic profile of the suspect. Then the book veers off into the
familiar territory of re-creating "the historical Jesus" from the
slivers of objective evidence that *are* available. When Albert
Schweitzer tried the same trick almost a century ago in *The
Quest of the Historical Jesus,* the man from Galilee ended up
looking remarkably like a dedicated missionary doctor in Africa
who gave up everything to serve others.

Likewise with our chum Wilson. His Jesus, shorn of divinity
but embodying the ineffable spirit of humanity, ends up as a
man not without traces of arrogance but definitely a cut above
the proletariat (if he didn't go to Cambridge, he certainly could
have), and all in all one of the most decent men who ever
walked this earth. I daresay variations on this have been done
to "the historical Jesus" by most people who have inquired sympathetically into the available written record for the past two
thousand years. Back in Sunday school, though, things are different. You can't get away with wishful thinking, and you can't
get away with soft-headed rhetoric – or clever quips: kids always
see through bluster and can hurl back the quips effortlessly. And
then there are the other times when you get waylaid and utterly
humbled by both the reach and the wisdom of what you hear.

"How come everyone is always on a trip in the Bible?"
Rebecca asked me two years ago. *Huh?* "Well, no one seems to
stay home," she amplified. *Who's the teacher here?* We decided to
explore this thesis, and the more we explored it the more we
found out it was true. There's Adam and Eve, screwing up life in

Eden and off they go. There's Noah and his family, packing the ark. There's Joseph transported to Egypt. There's Moses on the return trip. There're Ruth and Naomi wiping the dust of Moab off their sandals and heading for Judah. There's Daniel diverted into a lion's den and Joshua stomping around the walls of Jericho. There are Mary and Joseph in the Christmas story going here, there, and everywhere. There's John the Baptist popping up all over the place. There is Jesus traipsing back and forth to Galilee, off on a mountain side, out on the water, in a desert, riding into Jerusalem, walking his cross. There's Paul criss-crossing the Roman Empire . . .

Where are they all headed? What are they all looking for? Sunday school is not Sunday school without some attempt at resolution, but to account for this restlessness – which resonates for my crowd with a lot of their favourite videos from *Robin Hood: Prince of Thieves* to *Star Wars* and *Hook* – is not all that easy. We agreed that everyone was on a quest of some sort, that the travellers weren't happy with things as they were. They listened politely to my own wrap-up which suggested that the Holy Grail was "the meaning of life," but I don't think they really bought it. Some of them wanted something more tangible, variations I suppose on the Golden Fleece. Others – like Rebecca – weren't so easily fobbed off:

"I don't think they know what they're looking for," she said, with that edge of retreating innocence that is the glory of a full-blown eleven-year-old. Again, *huh?* "Well, my dad said if you know what you're looking for you don't go running all over the place. You sit down and try to figure out where you left it. I think they are looking for something you can't find for sure."

I'll take the questions of Rebecca any day over the crushing certitudes of our own age. So have yourself a happy Hanukkah or a merry Christmas, and for heaven's sake watch out for A. N. Wilson. He looks remarkably like Darth Vader.

December 1993

Rushton vs. Rushdie

~

"All living mankind constitutes a single biological species (*Homo sapiens*) within a larger grouping or genus (*Homo*). Within the human species, *Homo sapiens*, a large number of populations may be differentiated genetically through readily observable characteristics (e.g., skin, hair, and face and body proportions) and through less obvious but more distinctive biological traits, such as blood type. These biological groupings within species are commonly called races, in man as well as in other living forms."

So begins the essay "Races: Subgroups Within a Species" in the fifteenth edition of the *Encyclopaedia Britannica* (1977). We are just a hop, skip, and a nervous jump away from the world of Professor J. Philippe Rushton, the University of Western Ontario psychologist whose ingenious correlation of race and intelligence (large-brained Orientals on top, blacks at the bottom, while whites get to play peanut butter in the middle) has provoked such agitation in the country.

Oddly, the Rushton affair, with its disquieting implications in a multiracial society, coincided with the international outrage over the fate of Salman Rushdie. The Indian-born British novelist had so inflamed a faction of the high Muftis of Iran in his latest book, *The Satanic Verses*, that their leader, Ayatollah Khomeini, took out a worldwide contract on the luckless author. With Rushdie, too, the Canadian implications turned out to be embarrassing – made so once again by the revelation of our presiding hypocrisies.

In the midst of all this, we were urged in *The Globe and Mail* not "to confuse these two very different cases," which was whistling into the wind because the two cases present fascinating parallels, as well as similarly awkward comments on the contemporary and still-evolving notion of Canada as a multiracial country. We keep trying to avoid the lessons Professor Rushton and Mr. Rushdie inadvertently teach us, but we avoid them at our peril.

On one level, the two controversies are opposite sides of the same coin: if, as the price of Western free expression, we are to insist that Islam is to bear the "slanders and profanities" of Rushdie's dream-representation of the prophet Mohammed, it seems that we are also going to have to accept Rushton's right to trumpet his insensitive conclusions on race. Along with this, apparently, we are going to have to accept a certain spasmodic institutional dither.

The federal government's response to the Rushdie affair, from the belated condemnation by External Affairs Minister Joe Clark to the temporary ban on importing the book by Revenue Canada, helps to define a nation forever awaiting signals from elsewhere on how to behave and act. Playing echo to the national penchant for indecision was the administration of the University of Western Ontario which, in handling the Rushton affair, managed simultaneously to defend its controversial professor while undermining its own credibility.

Both men must, of course, have known they were flirting with trouble. Rushdie is a lapsed Muslim and surely understood that the Koran is perhaps the most underinterpreted of sacred texts in world religion. Yet even the bedraggled, overinterpreted Bible can still arouse wild-eyed defenders – as the controversy over the filming of *The Last Temptation of Christ* proved. As for Rushton, he has subsequently shown some evidence of understanding that he was intruding on touchy ground. Both men test our affection for the principles we must uphold: Rushdie blasts away at Western sensitivities in *The Satanic Verses* (e.g., "British thought and British society have never been cleansed of the Augean filth of imperialism"), and Rushton – naively or otherwise – allies himself with unfortunate forces of reaction.

Perhaps, initially, both men felt protected by their immediate surroundings: Rushdie by the free flow of challenging ideas that forms the matrix of Western intellectual curiosity and typifies the literary milieu of contemporary London, England, where he lives; Rushton by the academic tradition of tenure as it is specifically honoured at the University of Western Ontario in London, Ontario. In the ensuing firestorm, however, both the milieu and the tradition have proved flimsy redoubts.

The cases are precisely similar on another level altogether. In the name of cherished principles – academic freedom, freedom of expression – both contrive to license the eruption of latent or active prejudice. Haunting all the accusations and recriminations in Canada has been a subliminal figure whose family name is consistently Race but whose given name is, variously, Relations or Prejudice.

Thanks to Rushdie, invoking the Ayatollah Khomeini permits an impenitent shudder at the thought of more Muslims getting into the country. Thanks to Rushton, it is amusing to be jocular in mixed company about genital size and moral habits. Cloaked in the semirespectable guise of deploring villainy, the complicated, spectral figure of Race keeps appearing.

What is clear is that we have not begun to come to terms with the challenges implicit in maintaining a coherent nation that is avowedly multiracial. Official multicultural and multiracial harmony in Canada is based on a simple naive declaration, mainly unencumbered by any of the complex accommodation such a declaration requires. In fact, Canadians think a lot about race, one way or another. We always did. In September 1906, for example, *Saturday Night* commented on the federal government's plan to bring in 5,000 Chinese to construct the mountain section of the Grand Trunk Pacific:

"We don't want Chinamen in Canada," the editorial declared. "This is a white man's country and white men will keep it so. The slant-eyed Asiatic with his yellow skin, his unmanly humility, his cheap wants, would destroy the whole equilibrium of industry. . . . We cannot assimilate them. They are an honest, industrious, but hopelessly inferior race."

Now, according to Rushton, they are an honest, industrious, and hopelessly superior race!

Understanding the saga of Chinese Canadians is instructive. As a community set apart, a community thought to be unassimilable, the Chinese were vulnerable both collectively and as individuals. Their solution was to keep a profile so low as to be almost indiscernible. Then, less than a decade ago, a blatantly racist national television documentary on medical schools (CTV's "W5" claimed "Asians" were taking over the classrooms) taught the Chinese community that lying low had become provocative and that it had a stake in claiming the full rights of Canadian citizenship (most of the "Asians" "W5" filmed were Canadian-born). The identification with the political structure since then has been astonishing – so astonishing, in fact, that some whites now offer the positive experience of Orientals to counter charges of racism against blacks.

Like Irish Fenians a century ago, some fundamentalist Muslims – and some Sikh nationalists – have trouble reconciling their divided loyalties. Many Canadians would prefer that those Muslims carrying signs calling for the death of Salman Rushdie had followed the Chinese path and embraced anonymity. They didn't, and in openly inciting people to murder they were quite possibly guilty of breaking the law. This was winked at to avoid further inflaming the situation. The winking was wrong, but it was apparently easier than dealing with the consequences. The authorities fudged the problem, just as the University of Western Ontario fudged a forthright approach to the Rushton challenge.

The essay that caused all the turmoil is entitled "Evolutionary Biology and Heritable Traits" and was prepared by Rushton for a symposium on evolution theory at the annual meeting of the American Association for the Advancement of Science held in San Francisco last January. To provide a handle on the work, here – in its entirety – is his study of "Social Organization" as a category of comparison among the races. In the overall presentation, it comes after a set of tables linking head size and intelligence, and genital size and promiscuity:

"Stable social organization depends on following rules. This can be indexed by marital functioning, mental durability, and by law abidingness. On all of these measures the rank ordering within the North American population is Oriental > White > Black. The 1.5 million individuals of Oriental descent are very rarely perceived as a 'social problem,' for they have significantly fewer divorces, out-of-wedlock births, or incidences of child abuse than Whites, and in fact they are very seldom studied. Black family structure, however, has been studied intensively. Since the 1965 Moynihan Report documented the high rates of marital dissolution, frequent heading of families by women, and numerous illegitimate births, the figures cited as evidence for the instability of the black family have doubled, almost tripled in some areas (Staples, 1985).

"A similar pattern of Oriental < White < Black is gained from figures on those confined to mental institutions or who are otherwise unstable.

"With respect to crime, in both North America and Western

Europe, race is one of the best predictors, and quite possibly, in other parts of the world too (Wilson & Herrnstein, 1985). The Chinese and Japanese, whether assessed in their home countries, North America, or the United Kingdom, have a lower incidence of crime than do Europeans. African descended people, while consisting of less than one-eighth of the population of the United States or of London, England, currently account for over fifty per cent of the crime in both places. Since about the same proportion of victims say their assailant was black, the arrest statistics cannot be blamed on police prejudice."

Even a failed Bachelor of Arts can see how explosive this research is, perfectly unadorned by even a hint of economic or social context. That it tends to confirm popular prejudice is part of its insidiousness, especially since it comes from a Guggenheim Fellow and a respected member of one of our best academic institutions. For all these reasons, Rushton's work should have set off alarm bells long before the paper was delivered in San Francisco. If the work is valid, the authorities at the University of Western Ontario should have had enough savvy to deploy a major defence. They didn't. They still haven't. All they have offered is the bald principle of academic freedom.

While a systematic, peer review of Rushton's work is still being awaited, with some impatience, amateurs can perhaps be forgiven for trying their hand on the text. Where, for example, in the discussion on "Social Organization" cited above is there any evidence that crucial parallel or comparative figures have been examined or even sought? We might want to know the figures for child abuse and civil crimes in large-brained Hong Kong, for example. We might want to have at least a footnote on how the low sexual appetites among the Chinese nevertheless result in an annual natural population increase more than twice as high as in the United States. Why is it that the same social disorders and malefactions attributed to race when found among small-brained blacks can be equally found among the mid-brained Anglo-Saxon underclass in the expansive slums of mid-eighteenth-century London? Why were native Canadians excluded from the study? Why are we never given contrasts in behaviour within the same racial group so we can make some sophisticated judgement of variations? And what on earth does it all mean?

The truth is that we have been left to our own resources in sorting out the possibly conflicting requirements of truth and tolerance, of freedom of expression and incitement to prejudice, of harmonious relations and cleaving to principle. Frightening as the prospect may be to our leaders in government and academia, there occasionally arise those moments when leadership is not only appropriate but actually needed. The Rushdie and Rushton controversies were such occasions. Instead, we had the curious spectacle of politicians and professors hurtling through the looking glass to attend to each other's business. While Ontario's premier, David Peterson, was telling the University of Western Ontario to fire its professor forthwith, numerous academics took to op-ed pages to instruct the government on its moral duty to defend Rushdie.

In the process, we were witness to government's inability to tell all Canadians that the law would be enforced, and we watched a university administration as good as admit that, when it came to incendiary research, peer review was a chimera.

The principles of free speech are grounded in the centuries-old struggle for parliamentary supremacy and are symbolized by the contradictory notion of "loyal opposition." If it is incumbent on new Canadians, whatever their conviction, to learn and abide by the responsibilities entailed in the word "loyal," it is equally incumbent on long-established Canadians, especially those running our governments and universities, to understand that opposition loses its truth-testing purpose if the original side abdicates the debate. A living democratic country breathes its

principles and statutes rather than setting them aside at inconvenient moments.

On the question of racial inheritance, at least, there is some
contradictory relief. One crucial part of the human anatomy
has escaped Professor Rushton's little tape measure: the heart.
As an organ of higher wisdom it appears impervious to most
kinds of "sociobiological" quantification. Nevertheless, as Pas-
cal taught us, it has its reasons. Among the various races, it is
only the heart's imaginative texture – its softness or hardness –
that limits the nature and usefulness of experiments in the
human condition.

June 1989

P.S. Professor Rushton is still at the University of Western
Ontario, clothed in the majesty of tenure. Salman Rushdie is
still under threat of death, although in the intervening time
since this column was written (June 1989) he has become more
adventurous with his public appearances.

The Middle of the Road

~

Ten years ago, during March and April of 1979, special agents of Beijing's notorious Public Security Bureau arrested the principal leaders – "troublemakers" was the phrase of the day – of China's short-lived democracy movement. In the swoop, a gentle man named Ren Wanding, founder of the Chinese Human Rights Alliance, was unceremoniously bundled through the exit that authorities in the world's most populous nation still reserve for ill-fitting cogs. It is an exit that leads to a prison or a labour-reform camp, which is to say to the land of nowhere, from which there is never an early return, if there is a return at all.

Ren Wanding announced the existence of his important-sounding organization during the great days of euphoria when Vice Premier Deng Xiaoping was making his bid for pre-eminent power. Throughout this period at the end of 1978, there were extraordinary manifestations of free speech directly encouraged by the vice premier in the streets of Beijing and numerous other major cities. In fact, he actively encouraged the manifestations right up to the moment when, his power fully consolidated, he had no further need of such expressions from the unpredictable masses. Then, very efficiently, the voices were stifled.

As the Beijing correspondent for *The Globe and Mail* during those remarkable democracy-movement days, I found life eventful and rewarding. The story was hot, it was out on the streets for the asking, and there was an international audience wondrously amazed at the things a hitherto silent proletariat had to say. I met Ren Wanding after tracking him down to the address he had supplied along with his name on a wallposter. In Chairman Mao's China, it would have been suicide for a member of the masses actually to identify himself. Even at this time, after the Great Helmsman's death, such an action was unheard-of, rash in the extreme.

Yet Ren thrived in the risky but spirited atmosphere. It was a time when the most incredible fictions about Maoist China were systematically being exposed. Young people today would scarcely believe the kind of idealistic rubbish that had routinely been pronounced about China's Maoist experiment by very distinguished scholars, pundits, and statesmen from the West. The country had become a blank canvas upon which any bizarre theory of human behaviour could be sketched, internally or externally. Common sense rarely intruded upon the process.

This was neatly symbolized by the film actress Shirley MacLaine who, during a carefully controlled tour of the People's Republic of China during the early 1970s, met a nuclear physicist on a farming commune who told her it was as important to learn how to grow tomatoes as it was to understand the mysteries of the atom. Such sweet egalitarian nonsense provided the genial glaze over a vicious epoch in which scientists were punished with field work and peasants lost valuable tracts of land to the greater good of cadre re-education. Among the lesser consequences of the Great Proletarian Cultural Revolution were historic setbacks for both agriculture and scientific research.

My friend Ren Wanding did not hate all these illusions as much as I came to – though he had had his ambitions to become an engineer cut short by the Cultural Revolution, and had been shipped off to the countryside to do manual labour. He was his own idealist and many of the more militant activists in the 1978 democracy movement tended to dismiss him as being far too naive. Nevertheless, he may have been the most difficult of the group for the authorities to handle since he was, absurdly, a socialist. I say absurdly because to cling to any faith in socialist theory in the quasi-fascist, egomaniacally run regime Mao bequeathed his successors suggests a state of mind that not even Holy Mother Church required of her faithful when promulgating the doctrine of the Virgin Mary's own immaculate conception.

But Ren believed that, run strictly on democratic lines, socialism was the key to a more prosperous and fairer future in China. To this end, the creation of the Chinese Human Rights Alliance was "to assist" the authorities in living up to the country's constitution as it struggled to bring in "genuine" socialism. The contempt held for this collaborative line of reasoning by other, and more ferocious, activists was considerable. Impatient and heroically reckless, they did not understand a genuine middle-of-the-roader, even though Ren Wanding was paradoxically under fewer illusions than they about how far the state would permit free expression. Poor man! He only wanted to provide a form of "loyal opposition" to a government in transition which should have grabbed the chance with gratitude. Instead, the authorities were too insecure and too stupid to recognize the great gift this obscure young citizen was offering them – the gift of a fairer face for the image of an oppressive state.

Perhaps, in the end, Ren was too implausible a figure for that state to treat seriously. He was poorer than a Maoist church mouse. He wore (thanks to a severe astigmatism) glasses with Coke-bottle lenses of which one was badly cracked. Whenever I met him, little pieces of paper always seemed to be falling out of his pockets and he was forever about the business of picking them up. As a strategist during a new era in China, his master-stroke was to keep all his activities above ground. He was, as I have said, the first to sign his real name to a wallposter. When he gave interviews to Western journalists, he did so not furtively, down back lanes or in foreigners' automobiles, but outside the very gates of Zhong Nan Hai, headquarters for both the government and the Chinese Communist Party. Seemingly alone among the billion Chinese, he treated the Chinese constitution – with its assurances of freedom of speech and association – as the truth.

The constitutional promises, however, turned out to be as much of a fiction as Miss MacLaine's enthusiastic scientist-farmer, as much of a fiction, indeed, as the Chinese Human Rights Alliance, of which Ren Wanding was "chairman." The organization was just a few individuals who put out a badly printed magazine and, when the time of testing came and the Public Security Bureau picked up poor Ren, even those associates deserted their leader and fled the scene. In China, the cock doesn't even get to crow once before betrayal. Ren Wanding was led off from the Xidan Democracy Wall on April 4, 1979, after trying to paste up a wallposter protesting the new wave of arrests of democracy activists. I have a picture of the arrest taken by a journalistic colleague who was at the scene. It is blurred and shot from behind, but what is going on is very clear. Three burly officers of the Public Security Bureau surround Ren. His head is being forced down and his right arm is being jerked up behind him. He is a man of sorrows.

It was the last sight any of us outsiders had of him. From this moment on, he simply disappeared into the great void. Despite strenuous efforts by Amnesty International, nothing could be learned about his fate. No show trial was reported in the media. Discreet inquiries through precarious Chinese contacts and sources served only to underline how completely someone can become a nonperson in the People's Republic even after the Maoist era.

And then, just a few weeks ago, another journalist – Andrew Higgins of *The Independent* in London – ran across him in Beijing. He was alive! Out of prison! And his spirit was unbroken. Ren, it emerged, had never been tried or even charged. Nevertheless, he was forced to spend nearly five years in prison and now pieces out a dreary existence as a factory worker regularly subjected to official harassment and administrative searches of his tiny apartment. "I don't know why they let me out," he told *The Independent*. "Perhaps they just got fed up with me."

They probably got fed up with him for much the same reasons as the other activists did. He does have his own views and they conform neither to those of a stereotypic dissident nor to a model citizen's. According to Higgins's report, Ren never stopped proselytizing inside prison, which infuriated his guards. "They kept ordering me to confess, to tell them who I had met, what we had discussed. I told them that everything I had done was open, so that there was no need to repeat it."

Typically, like Lear's fool, he has not abandoned his own truths – including his faith in socialism – and thereby mocks the hypocrisy of others. "The authorities always said I spent too much time thinking, that I let my fantasies run away with me. But we must have some ideals, something to work for. After all, every great change began as no more than a fantasy." No wonder he was kicked out of prison. He was probably undermining all the good work in re-education and thought control.

Other democracy activists, notably Wei Jingshen, Xu Wenli, and Liu Qing, still languish somewhere behind bars. Like Ren Wanding, their names are virtually unknown to Westerners. This is due, in part, to cultural myopia (the names themselves, with the surnames coming first and all those strange combinations of letters, are hard to register as adding up to real human beings) and also to lingering double standards (Chinese human-rights abuses have never aroused the same concern in the West as those of the Soviet Union or in Central and South America).

Thanks to his own merits and perseverance, then, Ren Wanding is out and, judging from the report in *The Independent*, it is hard to see what the regime can ever do to hurt him again, short of killing him. His life appears to have entered into a very clear, lucid territory that anyone who has attempted to understand the nature of persecution will know as the true land of the brave and home of the free. When asked if he dreaded being locked up again, Ren Wanding answered quietly: "I am no longer afraid. I've already died once in prison. Once you have been there, you are never really afraid of anything again."

March 1989

P.S. Ren Wanding was rearrested following the events in Tienanmen Square a few months after this column was published (see "The China Syndrome," p. 261). He remains in prison somewhere in China as of mid-1994. Amnesty International has taken up his cause for several years, to no perceivable effect.

PART THREE

Elegies from Rideau Hall

A Modest Proposal

~

When the last remaining residents of Prince Edward Island recently held a plebiscite to decide if they wanted a bridge or tunnel built to connect them to the mainland, there was intense interest throughout the country. Not that anyone west of Atlantic Canada was in any doubt about the outcome. The proposed link would cost between $500 million and $700 million, and this fact alone guaranteed that a majority of the Islanders would be for it. Fortuitously, the wildly impractical scheme was being touted at the very time the rest of the country was finally waking up to the harsh realities of the postmodern age.

We have the proposed free-trade deal with the United States to thank for this propitious development. No matter which side of the fence Canadians find themselves sitting on with free trade, they can all be grateful that the debate itself heralded an infusion of common sense and sound business logic into the national consciousness. In coming to terms with global economies and North American trade imperatives, people seem finally to have realized that the witless romanticism which has plagued Canada from the beginning has to be replaced by tough, bottom-line thinking.

The first step in this process is to examine the premise of whatever has been deemed the problem. Once this basic breakthrough in perception has been made, the problem itself may disappear. In Vancouver, for example, the city's orchestra was in a terrible pickle a few months ago. Falling revenues, a massive deficit, insufficient support from the various levels of government, an unimaginative board, lacklustre subscribers: all of these elements conspired to suggest a major disaster in the imminent offing. Instead, look what happened when the local community redefined its premises. Alternatives to live orchestral concerts were widely available, whether it was the plethora of records, tapes, and digital discs in neighbourhood stores, or CBC-FM's exciting range of snippets from the classics. In the past, the community has always thought of such things as peripheral. The breakthrough here came when Vancouver finally realized that *it was the orchestra that was peripheral.*

The jump into common sense requires imagination and decisiveness. Vancouver has risen to the requirement, and the citizens have their reward: there is no longer an orchestra problem because there is no longer an orchestra. In similar fashion, the federal government has solved the dilemma of escalating numbers of aliens being allowed into the country. Thanks to the adroit application of common sense to new immigration legislation, refugees will now be directed anywhere else but here. Not only does this remove the source of a specific problem, it brings subsidiary benefits such as eliminating the onerous burden on refugee support groups and relieving the security services of the need for unlawful surveillance.

These and other developments, occurring at the same time as the Prince Edward Island plebiscite, point the way to a creative solution for a problem that has been with Canada since Confederation. Justifying the link-up to the New Brunswick mainland – whether a bridge or a tunnel, or a combination of both – is not in itself the issue. Nor is the specific cost. Nor even is the fact that PEI can no longer grow an honest potato and must annually deploy a mountain of suspect fertilizer to supplement its fraudulent soil. Grotesque as all these things are, they are gossamer on a summer breeze compared to the historic blackmail the rest of Canada is obliged to pay to keep the whole of Atlantic Canada in the style to which it has become accustomed.

Consider even these isolated items:

• Every year since 1949, Canadians have had to cough up the outrageous tab for maintaining Newfoundland's wasteful coastal ferryboat service. Last year alone the cost to Transport Canada was $27.3 million. This "contract," enshrined in an appendix to the British North America Act, is valid in perpetuity and inevitably indexed to inflation. There seems to be no solution.

• Like the other three Atlantic provinces, Nova Scotia elects several Members of Parliament during federal elections. Occasionally, some of these MPs make it into the cabinet and feel obliged to look after their impoverished ridings. Senator Allan MacEachen, for example, was the Liberal MP for two ridings (Inverness-Richmond, and Cape Breton Highlands-Canso) for a quarter of a century, much of it during Liberal rule in Ottawa. Over that period, hundreds of millions of Canadian taxpayers' dollars were diverted to such dubious projects as the National Philatelic Centre in Antigonish, the Nova Scotia Nautical Institute in Fort Hawkesbury, and a heavy water plant in Point Tupper, not to mention the Cape Breton coal industry and the Sydney steel plant. Despite such provocation, Maritimers cannot simply be disfranchised, because our democratic institutions are too precious to jettison, so here too there seems to be no solution.

• As symbol of the abiding sinkhole in the east, New Brunswick last year received a grand total of $1.335 billion in federal transfers. This figure is just the tip of the iceberg. It doesn't include unemployment payments, family allowances, and the usual panoply of handouts to "nongovernmental" agencies, private "companies," councils, co-operatives, and Indian bands. Once again, the bitter word "insoluble" surfaces.

Atlantic Canada, as even so sympathetic a source as the University of Toronto's eminent professor of history, Michael Bliss, recently pointed out, is an idea whose time not only never came but has already run out. *There is no longer any point to it.* Academic judgement is arid without the follow-through, however. The old rationale – that the region was part of the price we all had to pay in a Confederation where each was supposed to receive according to his needs – simply collapses under the exigencies of such comprehensive and intractable need. The price is no longer right and everybody knows it. Confederation today is a much more practical and realistic proposition which must hold to the basic economic principle that each receives according to his merits – or, in simple layman's terms, God helps those who help themselves.

This principle is not unfamiliar even in Atlantic Canada. The brightest and best from the region, in hundreds of spontaneous acts of fiscal responsibility, have already moved westward and are leading moderately productive and useful lives. Unfortunately, the exodus has left an increasingly isolated and desperate population facing the inevitable risk of inbreeding. Already, one has heard terrifying tales of entire communities given over to TV-mart mania by night and regional expansion programs by day.

This is a situation to prick the consciences of everyone because the state of Atlantic Canada is a savage indictment of the way the rest of us have condoned drift and compromise. It is as much our fault as theirs, for they too – the least among us – remain our brothers and sisters. So far, desperate questions have been the only response: how much more will we have to pay? How long can this madness continue? Once again, creative scrutiny of premises suggests better answers: no more and no longer. It is time everyone in Atlantic Canada cleared out and moved on. Fortunately, the path of practical common sense leads to the realm of decency. The compassionate solution is a comprehensive relocation of the entire population.

Maritimers, to give them their due, have shown superhuman tenacity in unlikely and untoward settings. The hardiest could properly be sent to the new settlements in the high Arctic where Canada intends to make its presence felt on a permanent basis. This is in the national interest and should have the highest priority. Elsewhere, a sensible screening process should be able to place several thousand lost souls in the expanding service industry. In Toronto and Vancouver, and perhaps some day soon in Calgary and Edmonton once again, there is an urgent need for mothers' helps, messengers, window cleaners, copy boys, church vergers, ticket takers, cleaning ladies, laundresses, knife grinders, shoeshiners, and comptrollers.

As for the rest, they constitute a direct challenge to our better instincts. Most are not trained for work, yet must be somehow housed and fed – preferably in well-organized camp allotments where welfare and disability payments can be easily delivered and redeemed. Local customs should never be denigrated where they do not harm others, and precedent suggests we follow the Newfoundland example of the mid-1960s when hundreds of benighted outport residents, foolishly mired in modest self-sufficiency, were successfully moved to more appropriate welfare settlements. The populations of all four Atlantic provinces are conveniently located near the mouth of the St. Lawrence River and could be transported to several locations in just the sort of

commodious barges the former Liberal premier of Newfoundland, Joseph R. Smallwood, made available to his own people.

The vacated territory would, of course, remain part of every
Canadian's heritage. The boundaries of existing national parks
and wildlife sanctuaries could be extended until they actually
joined each other, thus ensuring federal protection for the entire
area while legally discouraging squatters and ending forever
pollution in the environmentally threatened areas of North
Sydney and Saint John. A cadre of armed wildlife security officers would cost scant pennies in comparison to the onerous *bil-
lions* doled out over the years to keep this unprofitable scrubland
populated.

Humane common sense, as it turns out, is also sound business
sense. In embracing the bottom line in Atlantic Canada, we will
be saving countless tax dollars as well as eliminating the most
vexing and enduring social problem in the country. There is
nothing modest about this proposal: it forms a natural corollary
to the national dream.

May 1988

Accidents of Birth

~

T
he day Pauline Vanier died in Compiègne earlier this year at the great age of ninety-one, Shen Zhong-hua slammed his dilapidated bicycle into a delivery van at the foot of a hill on Christie Street in Toronto. The two events are hitched in my mind because, seconds after I had hung up on the long-distance call from Madame Vanier's son Jean, in France, my sister called to say Mr. Shen was in hospital getting a broken leg put in a cast. He had been charged with reckless driving, she added, and the van owner was demanding exorbitant damages.

Grieve for the dead, worry about the living: life sometimes comes in bizarre clumps. Mammy, as Pauline Vanier was called by everyone who was close to her in her last two or three decades, lived a life as full as anyone's in the old Canada. Consort to the only truly great governor general Canada has ever had, Georges-Philéas Vanier, she had "retired" to a small village outside Compiègne to live out her last years at the mother house of the international L'Arche movement for mentally handicapped adults founded by Jean Vanier. The terminal illness, lasted less than a week and then her mighty spirit fled her body.

Mr. Shen is only thirty-eight and was born into a poor Chinese peasant family in Shanxi province, the fourth of six children and the only one in the entire history of his family to get a higher education. An agronomist, he was on an exchange visit to Canada at the time of the Tienanmen slaughter and virtually jumped into our arms when my sister made the mistake of expressing some concern over his plight. Since I once worked as a journalist in China, I bear the heavy burden of being the Chinese expert in the family, and before long Mr. Shen and either my sister or I were to be seen making the dogged rounds of immigration and manpower offices in Toronto.

Mammy died surrounded by people who loved her for herself and for all that her remarkable life represented. Her sons and daughter were nearby. A network of people associated with the L'Arche movement around the world held vigils in her honour and cradled her in their hearts on her final passage. In Toronto, Mr. Shen is for practical purposes all alone save for our family, which is small comfort in the night when he goes about his work at a twenty-four-hour gas station.

The job comes complete with illegally low wages and a boss who cheats him of a few dollars most weeks by alleging accounting inaccuracies. Since Mr. Shen never makes mistakes with money, this is more than a grievance: it strikes at his sense of honour and fairness. There's nothing he can do about it, though, and he always gives in because he knows – as his boss knows even better – that there are a dozen people ready to take his job at any given time.

In his spare moments, Mr. Shen holds down another (part-time) job, gives volunteer tai-chi-chuan instruction at a neighbourhood YMCA, and attends an ever-increasing variety of self-improvement courses. He lives in a closet of a room in a boarding house a few blocks from where he had his accident, buys six-month supplies of staple foods at emporiums I never knew existed, clothes himself at Goodwill, and never fails to listen to the "World At Six" on CBC Radio after he has awakened from the four to five hours' sleep he allows himself six days out of seven. On Sundays, he does his intensive studying and his laundry. He writes letters to his wife and two children back in China, sometimes visits us, and – wherever else he goes – makes a point of avoiding Chinatown (for reasons that seem obvious to defecting Chinese and overwrought to middle-class native Canadians).

The bicycle accident was a catastrophe, a far bigger one than most of us could even begin to comprehend. He was returning from the gas-station job. The half-hour ride got him home around 7:30 a.m., and the leisurely free-wheel down the final hill was one of the few enjoyable moments. Until, that is, this particular morning when he applied the brakes and discovered he didn't have brakes any more. He tried to slow the bike by skidding along the sidewalk curb and dragging a foot, but everything was happening too fast and the next thing he knew he had crashed into the parked van and was splayed on the sidewalk in agony, his right leg twisted at a queer angle.

The owner of the van never once helped him, but instead shouted obscenities along with what Mr. Shen described as "unfriendly" observations on the Chinese race. Within minutes, prompted by a telephone call from the van owner, two squad cars were on the scene. An officer in the first car talked to the van owner, then demanded some identification of Mr. Shen, and finally charged him with reckless driving. An officer in the second car helped him up and drove him to a hospital. The crumpled bicycle was abandoned and presumably ended up in the garbage; it was certainly not returned to Mr. Shen.

The nice cop said that the nasty cop's rap could probably be beaten, but at this point Mr. Shen wasn't taking too much in. He was wondering how he could hold on to his two jobs, how he could avoid disappointing the senior citizens at his tai-chi sessions, how he was going to get to his own classes. He thought of Chairman Mao's favourite fable, of the old man who moved a mountain, a parable from Cultural Revolution theology meant to spur the masses to impossible tasks, but then ruefully remembered that the old man had two working legs when he moved all the earth and stone.

A week after she died, Mammy's body was flown back to Canada for a state funeral in Quebec City. It may be a cliché to say that funerals are for the living, but clichés, too, are for the living. My wife and I needed an occasion fixed on some proximity to her to focus the awful sense of loss. Our friendship had been one of the few pure perquisites of a life in journalism. On the way to a posting in Beijing nearly fifteen years ago, I had badgered my way into her life on the excuse of an interview. She refused me twice but my wife and I just turned up at her door anyway. She let us step over the threshold. Not a year passed, after the China posting, that we didn't spend time with each other, either here or in France. The telephone bills have been ridiculous. She has held each of my daughters in her arms and the force of her crunching bear hugs is implanted deep in whatever understanding I have of what it means to be truly alive. *Nothing* was going to keep us away from Quebec City, so my sister volunteered to look after the children. And Mr. Shen.

The Queen sent a wreath. The governor general came. Soldiers of her beloved regiment, the Royal Twenty-Second, ushered people to their seats in the cathedral, bore her body through the nave, and carried it to the vault hollowed out of the rock of the Citadel, where she was placed beside General Vanier. At the service, Jean Vanier said that his mother at her end was no different than she had been throughout the lifetime he had known her. She was a little girl, he said, longing to be loved. That was true enough, but I also remembered when she was in St. John's, Newfoundland, in 1966 and let loose a flash of her Franco-Irish ire at a tree-planting ceremony in Bowring Park. It was less than a year before her husband was to die in office, and a civic official, self-important but no doubt well enough intentioned, roughly and noisily barred a stray ragamuffin from getting a closer look at the viceregal couple. Eyes flashing with anger, Mammy left her husband and barged past the official to get to the child. She jackknifed her large frame to bring herself to his level and, in the subsequent brief encounter – a gesture to be sure – she transformed the circle of onlookers into penitents in the cause of simple decency.

After the burial, the regimental band of the Van Doos played "O Canada" and the regiment marched past the crypt. It seemed that in burying Mammy Vanier we were also sealing up a notion of Canada in the cold stone high above the St Lawrence River. The notion is hard to express without sounding maudlin, but you could point to the old lady and say, "She was it."

Mr. Shen's court date was twice postponed. He turned up alone both times at the courthouse at the old city hall in Toronto and was sent away both times. The van owner and the police constables – the "witnesses" – never seemed to be there and inquiries by Mr. Shen simply led to a new date. The business left him confused but unbowed. It was while he was preparing for his third date that he finally told my sister what was going on. She phoned me and the two of us immediately called an emergency meeting with him.

We told Mr. Shen that he must have a lawyer. He wouldn't hear of it. He had already somehow insinuated himself into the library of Osgoode Hall Law School and read everything connected to reckless-driving charges. Lawyers, he announced, were too expensive. I had learned by this time not to proffer money, as either gift or loan. He was extremely proud of his independence and the few dollars he had been forced to accept from me when he first made his penniless decision to try to remain in Canada had been returned within three months – with interest (calculated at the prevailing rates, which he had checked out with two banks and a trust company).

He also confided to my sister and me that if he didn't have to go to prison he would be bringing out his wife and children under the Canada-China family-reunification program. We tried to disengage him from this wildly premature scheme. While Mr. Shen had shown ingenuity in holding on to both his jobs since the accident, despite crutches and with even less sleep, he was clearly not sufficiently well set up to cope with the considerable extra burden of the family. My sister and I know a lot about these sorts of things.

"I think it's all right," said Mr. Shen quietly. "I've saved fifteen . . ."

"For heaven's sake," we said to him, "do you have any idea what it will cost just to fly them here? Fifteen hundred dollars might bring one of them."

"Not fifteen hundred," he said, still quietly. "Fifteen thousand."

"*Fifteen thousand!*" we exclaimed. "That's one, five, and three zeroes."

"Yes," he said, and he smiled this time. "One-five-zero-zero-zero. I've saved it. I think it's enough to get started. My wife's English is not very good, so she will have to go to school for six months before she starts a job."

My sister and I stared at each other, our collective debts crashing against Mr. Shen's fiscal acuity. Together, without saying a word, we retreated from the role of advisers, though we had the grace to keep ourselves – at least for the moment – from soliciting financial advice.

The next day, Mr. Shen and I met outside the courthouse fifteen minutes before he had been told to turn up. He was clutching a file which contained various papers he was going to use in his defence. Everything had been copied by hand from the law books. He had gone over them with us the night before and it was all perfectly incomprehensible. My sister and I had quietly worked it out that, if things went badly, I would try to intervene and get another stay in the proceedings so we could hire a bloody lawyer. That was as close to a strategy as we could come up with.

Together Mr. Shen and I entered the courthouse and found our way, through a jungle of well-dressed lawyers and their nervous clients, to the designated courtroom. It was a woman who was presiding on the bench. We arrived just as she was pronouncing her verdict on some hapless youth and she was severe with him. She seemed in an irritable mood. Truly, the karma was not good. Mr. Shen had begun shaking quite visibly the moment we walked through the portals and, as he sat beside me, we might as well have been hooked up by electrodes so completely had he transmitted his terror.

Shortly after 3 p.m., a court official called for "Mr." – (long pause) – "Shungagungawhee" and told him to approach the bench. The judge looked down at me and asked Mr. Shen if I was his legal counsel. "No," I said, almost in a whisper. I was really upset. "I'm his friend. I guess I'm his sponsor."

She snorted. Or at least it sounded to me like a snort.

Mr. Shen was sworn in. He looked very small before the judge's bench. I had the impression of his slowly being engulfed by the whole setting.

"What's that you're holding?" Her Honour asked peremptorily, pointing to Mr. Shen's file of papers. "Let me see it."

The papers were taken by the court official and handed to the judge. After reading some documentation of her own, she spent an agonizing two minutes perusing Mr. Shen's file before handing it back.

"Well?" she said to the official. The tone was unmistakably brusque.

"Your Honour," he said. "The witnesses are not here."

"Of course they're not," she said. Her eyes were . . . angry. Very angry. "This man has already had his case postponed twice. What an introduction to our justice system." She rearranged her papers. "You're free to go, sir."

Mr. Shen was locked into his position. His head swivelled towards me, but his feet couldn't turn. The court official approached him. "You can go," he said.

I got up and went to the bar and motioned. "Come on," I hissed, "let's get out of here."

"I'm free?" Mr. Shen asked.

"You're free. It's all over."

I know I said that because when Mr. Shen later regaled my sister with what had happened he said that's what I said. All I can really remember is trying to fight back tears. In the judge's face, I had seen Mammy's eyes.

December 1991

P.S. Mr. Shen continues to amaze me. Since this column was written he has changed many jobs and taken other courses, but he now works with a small group of Chinese-Canadian business people who shun (the verb sounds the same as his family name) any linkage between trade and human rights. This has put me in my proper place, along with my opinions on this particular matter (see "The China Syndrome," p. 261).

Karen Kain

~

I n the performing arts, entrances are far easier to arrange
than exits. The wonderful German soprano Elisabeth
Schwarzkopf wisely concluded in 1975 that age had sufficiently diminished her vocal range to call a halt to paid performances, and she thus set off on a final, nostalgic tour of concert
stages throughout the world. So successful (and, no doubt,
lucrative) was this farewell circuit that she decided to post-
pone the day of reckoning a whole year to hold a second "final"
tour. A critic irritated her when he warned that she was in danger of becoming a case of "not gone, but forgotten."

Still, singers and actors have always had a rich and diverse
repertoire to plunder in order to carry them through most of the
seven ages Shakespeare's Jaques allotted mankind. An Olivier
may begin stage life as Romeo, but *Lear* is there to embrace him
at the end. Schwarzkopf could soar with Richard Strauss's *Four
Last Songs* in her prime, but Schubert's middle-range lieder
waited patiently to be adorned by a majestically receding voice
three decades later. In ballet, the cruellest of the performing
arts, the logic of the body is far swifter and more brutal. This

autumn marks the twentieth anniversary of Karen Kain's professional stage debut with the National Ballet of Canada. The
best Canadian ballerina to achieve a wide and significant international reputation, she is only thirty-seven and dancing beau-
tifully. Nevertheless, her dancing days are all but over and that
seems, for those thousands of us who have followed her shining
career with proprietary pride and fussiness, an awesome reality.
Her retirement from the stage may come next year, or the year
after, or even five years from now. But it is approaching ever
more swiftly, and so we come to watch her now with special
intensity, knowing how careful she is in choosing her roles –
wary of those (like Aurora in *The Sleeping Beauty*) where she no
longer feels fully in control and embracing others (like Alice
Liddell Hargreaves in Glen Tetley's highly regarded *Alice*) with
the luminous intensity of summation.

For many dancers, the prospect of retirement is too horrid
to contemplate. Such things are not a natural source of contemplation at the age of thirty-seven. This is a time when keen professionals are plotting their big push to the top: an occasion for
back-stabbing, not stepping back. Also, Kain has more opportunities for lingering on stage than most of her fellow dancers.
Margot Fonteyn of Great Britain, Carla Fracci of Italy, and
Irina Kolpakova of the Soviet Union are all examples of great
ballerinas who were able to dance on into their fifties, manipulating the aura of their stardom and the remnants of their technique for yet another rendezvous with the audiences they could
not bear to leave.

It was said of Fonteyn at the end of her career that her curtain calls alone were worth the price of admission. Up to a point
that was true. If you had never seen her in her prime, at least you
could say you had seen her. And those curtain calls *were* beautiful. The Queen never curtsies, but if she did she would have to
do as Fonteyn did or suffer the comparison. The greatest ballerina of the postwar era had a special aura, but still it would have

been better had she not gone on as she did. And on. And on again. Karen Kain won't make the same mistake. She says it to anyone who cares to listen, and anyone who knows her well understands that it is not idle talk. She will retire before too long because she has pride in her career, pride in herself, and ambitions for the rest of her life which a fantasy of her former self on the stage does not fit into.

The late Erik Bruhn, who loved her, used to say that Kain would never become one of the ballet world's reigning super-stars because she wasn't sufficiently bitchy to command the domain. He even said it to her face once, as a goad maybe, or perhaps to help her understand that she – like him – was des-tined to be remembered for artistry and stage stature rather than unsuppressed ego and unsubstantiated gossip. It wasn't so much a cruel shaft as a misdirected one. Bruhn didn't fully understand how determined and courageous a person Kain was or that sometimes the strength of fine human characteristics can sustain the same sort of dynamic stage presence as ruthless egos and selfishness. Last spring, for example, the press reported that she suffered a miscarriage several days after appearing on stage at Toronto's O'Keefe Centre as host of the first Erik Bruhn International Ballet Competition. What wasn't known was that the miscarriage had occurred the day before the perfor-mance and that she had stoically gone ahead without telling anyone, for the sake both of Bruhn's memory and of the less than stoical fund-raisers of the National Ballet of Canada. Here, as elsewhere, her response was part of a lifelong pattern that has established her as an artist of conviction. There has also been a Gretzky-like tolerance brought to bear on the circus elements of her life, while her guileless civility in the face of some of the reckless or brain-dead things written and said about her is awesome and affecting.

We cannot say for sure when it will be that she will announce the last dance. All that is known for certain is that

these are shimmering, golden days for Karen Kain. She is dancing at that still point where her last great burst of physical bra-
vura is joined to a lifetime's understanding of her art. It is one
of the magical times in a ballet career, paralleled only by the
formal debut in a leading role or a performance in a dancer's
absolute prime. Catch her when you can. Her equal may be a
while in emerging.

December 1988

Praise the Lord

~

I first began collecting old hymn books more than a quarter
of a century ago when I was still a university student. Some
might call this a strange leisure-time occupation, but aren't
all such private enthusiasms ultimately strange? Lord Thomson
collects Krieghoffs, Mikhail Baryshnikov collects Pushkin
memorabilia, and Conrad Black collects papal legates – each to
his own according to his means:

> The rich man in his castle,
> The poor man at his gate,
> God made them, high or lowly,
> And ordered their estate.

Soon, inevitably, the novice collector begins to specialize –
an innocent form of protoscholarship that proves his serious-
ness. Quite early on, then, I developed a special interest in
dreadful hymns, or at least hymns that strike more modern sen-
sibilities as dreadful. Over half a century ago, for example, "The
rich man in his castle . . ." was excised from most hymn books as

an embarrassment in the otherwise blameless and still popular "All Things Bright and Beautiful." Yet was there ever a more telltale comment on the class structure in nineteenth-century England?

The value of such masterpieces as "A Mighty Fortress" or "Now Thank We All Our God" is perennial and transcendent. The value of hymns (or stanzas of hymns) that drop a clanger is anthropological. Perhaps nothing else so clearly betrays the indefensible pieties of each succeeding age.

Christian hymns, deriving from the Jewish custom of psalm singing in the temple, date from the earliest days of the Church, and there is still in existence a fully preserved Greek text, *circa* A.D. 200, of "Go, Gladsome Light." The Protestant Reformation, though, is chiefly responsible for the spate of topical hymns that came to be bellowed out from choir stalls and back pews. Starting in the mid-eighteenth century with the evangelical revival under John and Charles Wesley, hymn writing became less an act of adoration than an opportunity for personal exhortation – inevitably couched in the sentiments currently prevailing. Sin, for example, would remain an ongoing concern, but the remedial benefits of sanguinary bathing appealed most specifically to the earlier writers:

> *There is a fountain filled with blood,*
> *Drawn from Emmanuel's veins,*
> *And sinners plunged beneath that flood,*
> *Lose all their guilty stains.*

That was actually from the pen of a rather good poet, William Cowper. More typical of the genre was the Reverend Mr. Lowry's "Nothing but the Blood of Jesus":

> *What can wash away my stain?*
> *Nothing but the blood of Jesus!*

What can make me whole again?
Nothing but the blood of Jesus!
Oh, precious is the flow,
That makes me white as snow!
No other fount I know,
Nothing but the blood of Jesus!

Hymn books of the high Victorian era are especially notable for the confidence they assume in the Christian mission to worldwide conversion and in the force of logic behind colonial expansion. These are hymns of empire, of Great Britain chasing the never-setting sun, of the United States making trade treaties in the wake of its gunboats, of the Church Militant bringing in the sheep in mystical, far-off places. You can sniff the trade winds in their stanzas while following the path of purposeful young curates, export/import grandees, and solemn viceroys and governors:

From Greenland's icy mountains,
From India's coral strand,
Where Afric's sunny fountains
Roll down their golden sand,
From many an ancient river,
From many a palmy plain,
They call us to deliver
Their land from error's chain.

"From Greenland's icy mountains" appeared in a hymn book called *The New Lute of Zion* in 1856. Eight years later, this gem was perpetrated:

I often think of heathen lands,
(Far away, far away!)
Where many a pagan temple stands,
(Far away, far away!)

And there each hapless child is led
To bow to idol gods its head,
Whilst many a mutter'd charm is said –
Far away, far away!

Four years after *that*, in the *New Standard Singer*, we get:

Go, *sound the trump on Afric's shore,*
And bid the negro weep no more!
(Negro, weep no more! Negro, weep no more!)
From cruel chains and gloomy grave,
The lowly Saviour comes to save.

Go, *sound the trump on Judah's shore,*
And say to Israel, weep no more!
(Israel, weep no more! Israel, weep no more!)
The Lord of glory, slain by you,
Will yet restore the guilty Jew.

Today, of course, we balk at the arrogant notion of "error's chain" or "heathen lands," and wince at the casual bigotry. Yet the missionary movement of the nineteenth century – in both its best and its worst guises – was, of all the causes to rally the idealism of youth in the West, the most widespread and durable. A century later, young people of the same sort, their idealism updated, were driving ambulances in the Spanish Civil War; their children flocked to the Peace Corps, and their grandchildren are fighting to save the rainforests of Brazil. *Far away, far away.*

The Victorians were also the first to conceive of children's hymns as a distinct subspecies. These had a direct connection with the missionary salvos in that some of the writers of children's hymns clearly regarded their little charges as having untutored and quite possibly heathen souls:

I'm thinking of my sins,
What wicked things I've done,
How very sinful I have been,
Although I am so young.

The cure for wicked little souls was discipline, outward recti-
tude, and constant reminders that the larger world of adults –
and the deity above – was keeping close tabs on vacant minds
and idle hands. Lord Baden-Powell had not yet invented Boy
Scouts when "Keep to the Right" was first published in *Fresh
Leaves for the use of Sabbath Schools* in 1868; but he was just
around the corner, no doubt taking notes:

March along together,
Ever firm and true,
Many eyes are watching,
Taking note of you:
Pleasant winds or foul ones,
Cloudy days or bright,
Keep to the right, boys,
Keep to the right!

Victorian hymns for children encompass, and reinforce, most
of the terrors little minds are capable of harbouring. They
also, inadvertently, provide a kind of check list of social and
physical conditions. It wasn't just sin and redemption the hymn
writers relentlessly harped on. Illness and death were ever-
present themes, inspiring numerous hymns overloaded with
Victorian morbidity and sentimentality. "Safely folded" is a
good example:

Gentle Shepherd, thou hast still'd
Now Thy little lamb's long weeping:
Ah! how peaceful, pale, and mild,
In its narrow bed tis sleeping!

And no sign of anguish sore
Heaves that little bosom more.

All dreadful hymns eventually and quietly disappear. First
they are left neglected in hymn books for a generation, and
then, either in new editions or total revisions, they are
dropped altogether. One of the old hymnals had a delightful category – "Hymns Suitable For Burial" – to which they could be
metaphorically consigned. But other hymns-of-the-times, of
course, replace them. As the missionary drive started its slow
recessional at the beginning of this century, for example, the
temperance movement took up the slack:

Mourn for the thousands slain,
The youthful and the strong;
Mourn for the wine-cup's fearful reign,
And the deluded throng.

The old Canadian *Methodist Hymn and Tune Book* has many
more in this vein, which seem amusing and quaint from today's
vantage point, until you try replacing the references to demon
booze with crack or heroin. Then they don't seem quite so
funny.

Canadian hymn books even track our own tortured sense of
national identity. *The Book of Common Praise*, compiled in 1908
for the Church of England (Anglican) in Canada, has an
alternative version of "O Canada" which rings of a country we
hardly know any more:

O Canada, our heritage, our love,
Thy worth we praise, all other lands above,
From sea to sea, throughout thy length,
From pole to borderland,
At Britain's side whate'er betide
Unflinchingly we'll stand.

Indeed, writers of dreadful hymns are an ever-industrious crew, toiling hopefully in the fruitful vineyards of contemporary relevance. They are toiling even now:

> *God of concrete, God of steel,*
> *God of piston and of wheel,*
> *God of pylon, God of steam,*
> *God of girder and of beam,*
> *God of atom, God of mine:*
> *all the world of power is thine.*

Or, if you prefer the activist ideo/theology of the late 1960s, try "Sing we a song of high revolt":

> *He calls us to revolt and fight*
> *with him for what is just and right,*
> *to sing and live Magnificat*
> *in crowded street and walkup flat.*

Most of the new hymns seem not really to have caught on, the "happy band of pilgrims" today preferring the tried and true classics which have endured for centuries. Somewhere, though, someone must be singing them before they lapse into oblivion. Maybe at the First Church of Christ, Sociologist. As a collector and a specialist, I always lament the passing of dreadful hymns. Like tail fins on cars or bell-bottom pants, they bespeak particular trends at particular times. If anyone wants to know what was relevant to some deep-thinking Christians in the post-Woodstock, pre-AIDS late 1970s, let him look no further than Hymn 202 of the joint Anglican-United Church hymnal:

> *Now thank we God for bodies strong,*
> *vitality and zest,*
> *for strength to meet the day's demands,*

the urge to give our best,
for all the body's appetites
which can fulfilment find,
and for the sacrament of sex
that recreates our kind.

December 1989

The Governor General's Man

~~

E smond Butler, who was private secretary to the last five governors general of Canada, died last December in Ottawa at the age of sixty-seven. It was a death more noted in the media of the United Kingdom than in his own country, thanks to the usual conspiracy of embarrassment with ignorance that afflicts Canadians when they have to deal with whatever doesn't fit neatly into the here and now. Yet this was a man who tried as much as anyone in our time to reconcile the complicated, fractious remnants of our colonial heritage with the desire for a singular nationhood. His death, although it came four years after he was discreetly but shamefully removed from office, draws a clear dividing line between the constitutional conception of Canada that many of us grew up with and the uncertain future that lies just ahead.

There are many Canadians today who will snort at the notion that a governor general – let alone his private secretary – has much to do with anything of significance on the national agenda. This is the result, in part, of a series of inept appointments of discarded or inconvenient politicians to Rideau Hall –

a practice that continues unabated and has now become its own tradition. It is also a result of the growing ambivalence many Canadians feel towards the notion of a constitutional monarchy. Yet if anyone tried harder than Esmond Butler to marry the old order of things to the mostly inchoate longings for egalitarian nationhood, his or her name does not spring immediately to mind.

For more than a quarter of a century, and particularly in the latter part of his time in office, this son of an Anglican clergyman from Manitoba provided most of the consistency and constancy in Rideau Hall, unobtrusively nudging untoward types into some semblance of viceregal dignity and significance. He did it with quiet humour, kindliness, a sang-froid that insecure folk occasionally and incorrectly took for haughtiness, and an uncomplicated but deep sense of service and loyalty.

It does not take very much to reduce the paraphernalia of monarchy and viceroyalty to the level of comic opera. When you have a natural in office, like the late General Georges Vanier (who raised Butler from a press attaché to the post of private secretary and considered him almost an adopted son), the role of the private secretary is relatively uncontroversial and straightforward – though not therefore undemanding. Vanier's biographer, Robert Speaight, observed that whoever had this unique job, which is in effect the deputy ministership to the head of state, must be "tactful, affable, intelligent, and discreet, acquainted with constitutional usage, moving at ease within the limits of protocol." Speaight formed the definition from the general expectations of private secretaries to the sovereign, but more directly from the practice of Esmond Butler himself.

On the other hand, when a buffoon – or, worse, a homegrown autocrat – becomes governor general, then the secretary needs all his wits about him to avert any number of catastrophes. If none of our recent governors general has soared to the true potential of an increasingly confused office, it is also true that none has actually shamed us and for this we have Esmond Butler to thank.

I first encountered "the secretary" in the outports of Newfoundland in 1967 discreetly shepherding Roland Michener through his first official tour as governor general, a tour that I was covering for the St. John's *Evening Telegram*. In my recollection, apart from a few memorable anecdotes, much of the business is now a hazy collage of boy scouts, ladies in white dresses from various Orange Lodges, fish-plant workers, faceless civic dignitaries, veterans, school children, sealers – and Esmond Butler, utterly responsive to local ways and totally in control of the task of transforming Mr. and Mrs. Michener into impressive but approachable personages.

This was not so easy a task as you might think. The Micheners were an appropriately dignified couple, but they were quite unprepared for the curious mixture of circus and circumstance, pomp and happen-chance, that crowd the official day of a viceregal office-holder. In Twillingate, the whole town had assembled to greet the governor general, who had arrived offshore in great state on a Canadian naval destroyer. A helicopter flew the official party from the ship to an open field about a mile out of town. Here was assembled a remarkable local cavalcade of "presentable" automobiles, led by a venerable and largely dilapidated Chevrolet convertible which was to ferry Mr. and Mrs. Michener to the town centre.

As Mrs. Michener looked on in some dismay at her rusty conveyance, Butler walked briskly over to the driver and spoke a few words which left the man beaming. Whatever it was that Butler said, I suspect the driver briefly joined those many Canadians who felt momentary confusion over who exactly was the governor general: the secretary or the actual incumbent. In any event, from inside his attaché case Butler removed a small viceregal flag standard attached to a metal mantle. He licked the suction cup at the bottom and slammed it down authoritatively on the hood of the Chevrolet. A piece of chrome trim on the side of the car immediately fell off from the impact.

"This is the coach, Your Excellency," he said to Mrs. Michener, who was still looking on aghast as local fishermen crowded to get a closer look at the swells from the Mainland. "And our driver assures me he knows how to keep out of all the potholes."

"All right, Esmond," said Mrs. Michener, "if you think it's safe."

Within a few minutes, the makeshift cavalcade had approached the town centre where everyone was assembled. A loud public-address system was delivering a jaunty air which Butler, with his impeccable ability to anticipate problems, immediately noticed and recognized as the middle bars of the "Marseillaise." "Hmmm," he said, quickly scanning the order for the greeting ceremony. It called for the playing of the first half of the royal anthem the moment the governor general alighted from his car. "This could prove interesting."

By the time the cavalcade had come to a full stop, the tune had shifted to "The Star-Spangled Banner," and it was clear that the PA system was hooked up to a recording of national anthems from around the world. The mayor of Twillingate approached the Chevrolet. Mr. Michener got out. There was a terrific introductory drum roll over the PA system. Everyone stood to attention waiting for the opening strains of "God Save the Queen" – everyone except Butler, that is, who had quietly moved up to right behind the governor general. When instead of "The Queen" the assembled throng was greeted with a particularly militaristic version of "Deutschland, Deutschland über Alles," Butler turned without a twitch to the mayor of Twillingate and said: "What a fine day you have provided Their Excellencies, Mayor Manuel. Why don't we go and inspect the school first? We can do the anthems later, if you like."

"Excellent idea, Esmond," said the governor general, turning to Mrs. Michener, who was still fingering her program in utter perplexity. "Come, my dear, we're going into the school." A loud scratch came from the loudspeakers and suddenly the dying strains of "O Canada" were to be heard.

Mayor Manuel smiled tightly in grim relief and prepared to move off with the viceregal party, but not before turning to a colleague and saying in a loud whisper: "We're going into the school. Why don't you go over to Harold and pull his thumbnails out for me?" Harold, it was subsequently learned, was the Twillingate town councillor who was manning the PA system.

In 1958, Esmond Butler went to work in Buckingham Palace as assistant press secretary to the queen. He arrived in the wake of an almighty royal brouhaha. Lord Altrincham had written what was then regarded as a sensational attack on palace officials, accusing them of shrouding the sovereign in secrecy and irrelevance. Butler was the first official appointed to the palace from outside a close-knit group who considered that, according to London's *Daily Telegraph*, "any journalist who did more than copy out the Court Circular should be languishing in the Tower."

During the next sixteen months, this judicious but affable Canadian brought some fresh breezes to the business of reporting on the monarchy. Journalists, long used to the genteel contempt of the palace, were amazed to get luncheon invitations from an official who was actually interested in their problems and was prepared to give straight answers. It seems small stuff now, but in its day – and in those circles – it was virtually a house revolution. Another thing happened too. As he got to see at close range how crucial, yet how fragile, was the whole notion of symbolic leadership, Butler made a private commitment to an ideal. He returned to Canada and Rideau Hall (he had been assistant to Governor General Vincent Massey's secretary before the Buckingham Palace stint) and brought with him a strong conviction that the institution he was prepared to serve for the rest of his professional life needed both a structure of stability and a capacity for change.

He then set about furnishing exactly that: providing stability by remaining in a job he could easily have used as a stepping stone to more powerful or lucrative positions, and encouraging change by endorsing sensible reforms. It was a balancing act and, if he erred on one side or the other from time to time, his larger goal – to preserve the office of governor general – was never once out of sight. In Canada, there was no one more astute than Esmond Butler about the niceties of practice and propriety in a still evolving constitutional monarchy. Each new appointment brought forth individuals who wanted to leave particular marks on the office. Ed Schreyer, for example, liked breezy informality, while Jeanne Sauvé felt more comfortable with an updated grandeur. Jules Léger had to deal with chronic illness, and Butler had to finesse a much larger role for Madame Léger. General Vanier had to be protected from exhausting himself and Roland Michener from exhausting everyone else.

More than merely accommodating the office to different styles, and vice versa, Butler had the primary responsibility not only of advising our governors general on sticky constitutional questions, particularly during minority governments, but wherever possible trying to head off problems before they turned into sticky questions. He never once disdained whomever a prime minister might name to the office, however inappropriate. It is also true, however, that he did not shirk from reminding a governor general of the boundaries of acceptable action in public or, occasionally, private life while he or she held the office. This did not always win him friends.

Two years before his retirement, Butler was unceremoniously removed from his post and dispatched, in the delicate prose of his obituary in The Daily Telegraph, "to the consolation of the ambassadorship to Morocco." That might seem a perfectly pleasant last hurrah to many people, but for Butler it was exile.

The tragedy here is quite clear. It wasn't that one of our most distinguished public servants was being robbed of a well-deserved grand exit so close to retirement. It was because his loyalty, sacrifice, and consummate skill were deemed to be of no value and were peremptorily discarded.

I knew something of the battles he was having with Madame Sauvé and her husband, Maurice, during the first year of the new governor general's office. Personality undoubtedly had much to do with the turmoil. So also did other matters that cannot yet be discussed in print but were a source of concern to some members of the high bureaucracy. One evening in London, England, just before he took up the post in Morocco, I tried every journalist's trick to get more of the story out of him. It was like trying to talk to the Sphinx, and for my efforts I was rewarded with an unsolicited, and not particularly enjoyable, lecture on the importance of defending the office he had served so faithfully.

He was a model civil servant, then, and went uncomplainingly. With much the same dignity, he bore the terrible wasting effects of Lou Gehrig's disease, which took his life. It is not entirely clear even now why this loyal, decent, and effective servant of his queen and country was handled in such a shabby manner. Certainly small and unappreciative minds were behind it, but so also was the presiding atmosphere of a country grown confused and almost querulous about the institutions that have served it well and could serve it better still if allowed a decent chance.

April 1990

A Leadership Guide for
a Crabby Nation

~

The topic of leadership is with us again. Ho hum. This
month, the New Democrats meet in solemn conclave
in Winnipeg to find a retread to succeed the estimable
Ed Broadbent. Next June, the Liberals will be ditching the
crypto-tragic John Turner for the tragicomic Jean Chrétien (no
bets allowed, foregone conclusion). And the Tories? No fear.
They are still hard at work trying to find a way to remodel Brian
Mulroney. Presto! Three new leaders. Welcome to the 1990s.

If this prospect is not sufficiently depressing, consider also
each party's national agenda. With the Tories, it stretches no
further than the latest opinion poll. The Grits are so far from
any coherent vision of the country that they are staging the
finale of their leadership convention the day after the deadline
for final ratification of the Meech Lake agreement, thereby
cravenly obviating the need to have any collective opinion on it
at all. As for the brave New Democrats, formerly conscience to
the nation, their vision has dwindled to persuading the voters
that good socialists make great business managers.

It is at a peculiar juncture that we find our federal parties preparing, lazily, to proffer leaders to carry us into the last decade of the twentieth century. In the circumstances – with all three overwhelmed and exhausted by the struggle to be all things to all people all of the time – the notion that Canada is actually poised at a historic and potentially extraordinary moment sounds like a bad joke. Yet that's precisely where the country is and it's only the dumb-show cast in Ottawa that isn't scrambling for a new script. God knows it's needed when you look at the current one.

In central Canada, where the logic of two official languages and North American economic interdependence is most compelling, the long Trudeau hangover continues: Ontario wrestles with fissures brought on by bilingualism and fear of free trade, while Quebec stares uncomprehendingly into the reality that it has already won all of the victories – and then some – sensibly available in a pluralistic society. Atlantic Canada persists in its miasma of inferiority and comfortable complaint under regimes collectively incapable of concocting any imaginative breakthrough in the historical cycle of poverty and dashed hopes. And the West bides its time menacingly, waiting for the energy and agricultural games to pick up momentum so it can once again thumb its nose at the rest of the country.

Our national talismans and symbols – from the monarchy to the Canadian Broadcasting Corporation – are lurching ominously towards the discard heap. The environment is in a mess and the palliatives being advanced are on the order of shipping PCBs to Wales. We have allowed a stupid panic over illegal immigration to lower our humanity and self-interest several significant notches. The land is strong, but the mentality is static. Who would want to be leader of such a crabby, increasingly desiccated political wasteland?

Ironically, having now travelled so far along the road to nowhere, Canadians find themselves at the crossroads to anywhere. It's a nice, bracing location in political and social cartography, full of omens and possibilities, challenges and dangers. Just wait and see. The leaders of the 1990s who manage to articulate the deep-rooted concerns and inchoate ambitions of Canadians won't know what hit them, so passionate will be their following. The residue of cynicism from the 1980s, when politics was all tactics, will be obliterated in a twinkling when a well-thought-out program of action based on the new realities is effectively presented.

The collective desire for a changed agenda is so palpable you can just about sniff it in the air. We need new thinking on the environment that is intelligently tied to resource management, something that will break the deadlock between the doom-sayers and the polluters. We need a new regional policy for Atlantic Canada, one that emboldens the four provinces to take their cue from the West European drive towards union and push the federal government – and the rest of the country – away from pork-barrel tokenism and towards hard-edged utilitarianism. We have no coherent employment and immigration policies based on reality from any of the parties. What they do have, based on fear of unemployment and of outsiders, has to be rejected because fear simply leads to reaction.

The process of re-education has to come from a strong leader with equally strong party backing. The need for a positive approach to newcomers, for example – especially from the Third World – is intimately tied to how we will be able to compete with American industries and firms under free trade. Our sense of what constitutes fit employment for Canadians, new or long-arrived, hasn't even begun to acknowledge the potential of the new age. Why are we not, for example, training the greatest cadre of resource managers the world has ever known? Do our political leaders really have no ideas for expanding the crucial service industry beyond being friendly to fast-food chains and ensuring plenty of McJobs for young people?

Foreign policy follows suit. Away with tremulous reaction long after events. Canada has for so long considered itself of no particular worth internationally that the wish might almost have become reality were not the rest of the world much wiser than we. Illegal immigrants do not flee to places of no worth, nor do foreign companies voluntarily buy into dead ends. A country that recognized the envy with which so many outsiders viewed it should not be seeking to build barriers around itself but exploiting – economically, socially, and intellectually – its unbounded fortune.

We pride ourselves too much on our sterling human-rights record. It is not so shining. If there is a common denominator in the history of the northern half of North America, it is the continuing inability to deal seriously with aboriginal rights. They are different from constitutional rights, and that gap in understanding constitutes the definitive and enduring Canadian tragedy – a tragedy perversely unifying our diverse geography, scattered population, linguistic incompatibility, and fractured drive towards some semblance of chartered order. The natives remain restless, and most of us continue unconcerned or irritated.

Perhaps most importantly we have to come up with plans, programs, and organizations that will harness the idealism of young Canadians who have been left to twiddle their thumbs for a generation or two. The battle to save the environment is probably the single most potent appeal to young people today. Why should we want to stop them improving the world? Where are the programs to deploy this rising desire to do something? Where are *any* exciting programs for young people? Even mundane projects from the past should be dusted off and re-examined for their potential, from interprovincial exchange visits to summer projects at home and abroad – especially within the Commonwealth. Most of all, the middle-aged baby-boom generation – which had it all and is still taking it – has to make room, physically and spiritually, for the challengers coming up.

This is not an idealistic agenda, but a list of positive responses a country like Canada could make to national malfunctions with which we live daily, or to events already afoot. Free trade is here. Immigration pressures abound. Repercussions from world developments – from the looming catastrophe in Hong Kong to the increasingly dynamic West European competition for traditional Canadian markets – will be affecting us directly. Young people are drifting in and out of drugs. People on the fringes, a gathering constituency of despair, are now being shafted as a matter of course. It makes far more sense to push our political parties to find the right sort of leaders to deal with these challenges than to let them go through the potentially vacuous process of a leadership convention unattended by public concern.

Even old leaders can be transformed. My favourite parlour game is taking Brian Mulroney seriously. Apart from upsetting friends on both the Right and the Left, this novel exercise fosters the idea that, under certain conditions, people can surmount their limitations. Look what Stephen Lewis did by wrapping himself in the United Nations. As for Mulroney, what other English-Canadian prime minister has risen so confidently out of the heartland of French Canada? Which other Canadian politicians have so efficiently – i.e., electorally – straddled east and west and made the centre buy it? Who, since Laurier, has had the courage to champion continental trade logic, and, unlike Laurier, pull it off?

Okay, okay, he sounds like a slow tape on all-night FM. He shillyshallies around policy like a freshly caught eel. He undermines his assets with overkill and underachievement. Neither the prime minister nor anyone else in his government has a clue about how to inspire and ignite the country after the free-trade victory. Et cetera.

No one's perfect. None of the leaders of our future will be perfect either. They'll still have this hodgepodge of a nation to hold together, however it is reconstituted. But if we are going to be optimistic about Canada at this potent juncture, why should we exclude The Man? We need to push him too. Start taking your neighbourhood pollsters seriously. Tell them unmistakably that we need a new rhetoric for a new era.

November 1989

The Wicked Witch of the East

~

The name of the last empress of China, Tz'u-hsi, looks unpronounceable (it isn't; just say "zoo-she") and means almost nothing nowadays to people in the West. But in her time – she lived from 1835 to 1908 – she was internationally notorious as a scheming monster who had usurped power from the child emperor and his lawful regents, and for nearly five decades wielded it with the murderous depravity of a Lucrezia Borgia.

Her lasciviousness and profligacy were bywords. At a time when her country's navy was sorely in need of new battleships, she was reputed to have built herself – at enormous expense to the public treasury – a boat-shaped marble pavilion to grace her sumptuous summer palace on the outskirts of Beijing. Her chief eunuch was said to be no eunuch but one of her many lovers. Like her lust, her appetite for intrigue was believed to be insatiable, and she was identified as the manipulator behind the Boxers, the rabidly xenophobic secret society that massacred missionaries as part of its uprising against the Foreign Devils in China at the turn of the century. It was perfectly understood that she had her heirs murdered, along with anyone else who threatened her position of power.

When the 2,000-year-old Chinese empire collapsed in the wake of her death, "the old whore of Peking" was held responsible, and her depravity and "cold-hearted cruelty" were soon cemented into all scholarly and popular histories of her country and her era. Indeed, nearly a century later, a current edition of the *Encyclopaedia Britannica* sums up her record as follows:

"Ruling through a clique of conservative, corrupt officials, [Tz'u-hsi] maintained an iron grip over the Manchu Imperial house, becoming one of the most powerful women in the history of China. But her power was maintained only through the suppression of badly needed governmental reforms, and the dynasty collapsed soon after her death."

Coyly, for such an august arbiter as the *Britannica*, the rest of the account is punctuated with phrases like "It was even rumoured . . ." or, when referring to the deaths of heirs, ". . . possibly from poison" and ". . . presumably from poison."

It's all lies.

The story of the systematic blackening of Tz'u-hsi's reputation is little short of astounding because just about every one of the "facts" – the profligate spending, the sexual licence, the hatred of foreigners, the poisoning of relatives, the criminal intriguing, the unbridled exercise of power – can be traced to one man: an English researcher, Sinologist, and pornographer named Edmund Trelawny Backhouse. He lived in Beijing during the last years of the dowager empress's life and, because he could speak fluent Mandarin Chinese when few other foreigners – especially the crucial resident correspondent for *The Times of London* – could say even *ni hao* (hello), his mischievous fabrications and fantasies were taken for gospel. He had no access whatever to the empress or her advisers and only marginal contact with the court, yet journalists and diplomats waited breathlessly during major events to be briefed by Backhouse.

He came to China first in 1899 as a young, meek, and hopelessly devious remittance man and attached himself to the *Times*'s man in Beijing. Britain's imperial power was at its zenith, *The Times* was the world's leading journal of record, and the convenient Backhouse, who offered himself as translator, interpreter, stringer, news source, and consultant, simply wrote the script on China and its rulers for the outside world. In the event, he was the actual author of the *Times*'s obit on the dowager empress – an important promulgation of his scurrilous portrait – and he went on to collaborate on two histories of Tz'u-hsi's reign that were accepted as definitive sources. His motives seem to have been sheer perversity along with a twisted malice towards his own mother, but he was aided in the enterprise, obviously, by journalistic laziness and – as all foreign correspondents and observers have encountered it throughout this century – by Chinese secrecy.

Sir Edmund Backhouse, as he later became, was hugely admired during his lifetime and his bequests to the Bodleian Library at Oxford of rare Chinese books – some copies or crude forgeries, the rest looted by him during periods of fighting in Beijing – earned him high honours. The truth did not even begin to emerge until 1976 when the English historian Hugh Trevor-Roper wrote *A Hidden Life: The Enigma of Sir Edmund Backhouse*. Trevor-Roper exposed Backhouse as a forger and con man who had supported himself in Beijing by creating and selling counterfeit Chinese documents including court papers and court diaries. But revelation of the extent of his fraud had to wait until last year when Sterling Seagrave's massive new biography of the dowager empress, *Dragon Lady*, was published.

In reality, Tz'u-hsi was a woman of sheltered upbringing and ordinary intellect pitchforked into power by the circumstance of being the first of the emperor's wives to produce a male child. She nevertheless struggled to do what was right for her country at a time when, having neither unity nor solid defences, it was prey to grotesque foreign interventions. Far from lavishing money on carnal pleasures, she had to live through the destruction and repeated looting of her ancestors' residences by foreign troops; the Boxer Rebellion was provoked not by her wicked plotting but by the hysteria and casual atrocities of Westerners; she had perilously few options in governing the world's most populous country, and even the few she might have had were curtailed not by "evil courtiers" but by the governments of Britain, Japan, Germany, and the United States. Synonymous with evil during her lifetime and for most of this century, she was in fact plucky, kindly, full of curiosity, and tragically torn by the plight of China.

Tz'u-hsi's fate in history is pertinent today for two reasons. One is specific to China, a place where Western observers continue to make large judgements based on scant information and too little common sense, and where ignorance is still abetted by state secrecy and a long tradition of demonizing state enemies. Just over a decade ago, for example, the myth was promoted that Chairman Mao Tse-Tung's widow, Chiang Ch'ing, embodied the worst evils of the Communist excesses during the Great Proletarian Cultural Revolution. Everyone seemed to buy the notion: the Communists to sustain their ideology, outsiders because it supported their prejudices, everything from academic Marxist philosophy and the "great man" theory of history to the proverbial "inscrutability" of the Chinese. But when the lady herself finally took the stand at her own trial in 1981, she told the stark truth – which no one has paid attention to, then or now. "I was Chairman Mao's dog," Chiang Ch'ing said at the time. "I bit whom he asked me to bite."

Poor Chiang Ch'ing. Poor Tz'u-hsi.

For people love their illusions: that is the second lesson from the fate of the last empress. Backhouse's genius was in understanding that truth is too strenuous to be attractive to many reporters, many observers, and much of the public at large.

They prefer the pat drama of demonology, hagiography, and all the other fairy tales.

Today, four years after the Tienanmen slaughter of 1989, the Tz'u-hsi process is at work again. Knowing the true face of the Communist regime, knowing its propensities to corruption and its hatred of democracy, many Westerners in business, politics, and journalism are nonetheless happy to fantasize a tranquil and lucrative future – which is about as likely as the pope turning Protestant.

June 1993

PART FOUR

The Dalai Lama Sends
His Regrets

On a Wing and a Prayer

~

My fascination with angels began when I was six years old, in 1950, the year my mother conceived, authored, and directed a Christmas pageant at our church. My sister got stuck with being a dumbstruck shepherd, but I was elevated to a select choir of cherubs. Although the cherubim occupy only a subordinate position – behind the seraphim – in one of the three great hierarchies of angelhood, a cherub is nevertheless so much higher than any earthbound shepherd that I actually felt pity for my sister. She may have been two years older, but in this universe of the Christmas pageant she was the merest speck of mortality. I, on the other hand, had wings of delicate tissue paper and a halo of pure cellophane. These gleamed like the galaxy on a clear night when caught by the single, flickering arc light of the production my mother had so lovingly put together.

If you brood about angels, hierarchy is very important. As a consideration, it comes well before any debate about how many can dance on the head of a pin and immediately after the definition of their primary function: to intercede between God and men and women. In a cursory study of Hebrew scriptures and early Christian texts, you could be forgiven for thinking – as St. Paul did – that there were only five different ranks; in addition to being confused about women, St. Paul was sloppy in his enumeration of angels and other holy entities. It wasn't until the pioneering census of Dionysius the Pseudo-Areopagite (*circa* A.D. 500) that we learned there were nine choirs arranged into three orders: seraphim, cherubim, and thrones; dominations, virtues, and powers; principalities, archangels, and angels. This was once considered very useful information because these strictly graded extraterrestrials governed all relations between God and the world. Not surprisingly, the three orders paralleled the early Christian church's three-tiered hierarchy of bishops, priests, and deacons. As in the church, function is less important than status, but it is true that the Bible specifically builds up archangels as major players.

Our group leader in the church pageant was the archangel Gabriel, played by a tall teenager named Penny. Although my memory of the pageant comes filtered through a nostalgic haze of childhood mysticism and pride (my mother's script was considered good enough for national emulation and was published in *Chatelaine*), I do remember vividly the special aura of stern sanctity surrounding Penny/Gabriel. She wore a shimmering gown of white gauze surmounted by a silver-mesh bodice which shone five rankings stronger than the wings of the cherubim. She was also the means of my first discovery of how actors become their roles. During rehearsals, and sometimes even in the midst of performances, the cherubs occasionally became restive and crabby, but one look from Penny/Gabriel could send us rocking back into celestial obedience. This archangel did not brook unruly minions.

Gabriel is one of only three archangels actually given name and form in the Bible. The other two are Michael and Raphael.

This trio bestride both the Old and the New Testament as heralds and interpreters of God's will and word. Michael, for example, appears twice in the Book of Daniel as a kind of career counsellor to the Israelites as they come to grips with the burden of being "the chosen people," but he also pops up in the Book of Revelation as a soldier on the side of Christian metaphysics doing battle with a dragon. Michael, Gabriel, and Raphael hovered around the books I read when I first discovered how horrible had been the history between Jews and Christians for most of the past two thousand years. They grieved at this tragic heritage, and – it still seems to me – they also offered solace simply by being a bridge between the two religions.

More solace, certainly, than my sister – the Darth Vader of all shepherdesses – was prepared to provide when Jane-the-cherub smashed my left wing immediately before my first stage entrance on opening night. The cherubim had been assembled in a side chapel and were being herded towards the manger scene at centre stage when I bent down to get something irritating out of my toe. (Cherubs went barefoot in this pageant.) Jane-the-cherub fell on top of me, crushed the tissue wing, and nearly started a collective pile-up. There was nothing to do but keep moving after this disaster but, as the cherubim picked their way through the assembled mob of shepherds, wise men, and farm animals, I heard the voice of my sister hiss at me and my crumpled wing: "Mummy's going to kill you."

After the sixteenth century, when Copernicus exploded the biblical conception of the cosmos, and along with it the landscape formerly occupied by the celestial hierarchy, angels came in for a rough time. If heaven wasn't above, hell below, and earth in the middle, where oh where did the angels abide? Sexless and amorphous, they were banished by rational minds along with pixies, sprites, and all denominations of hobgoblins. They resided in this nether world of decreed superstition until their rescue in the late nineteenth and early twentieth centuries by psychoanalysis. Someone with a more ordered and scholarly mind than mine could make a very good case that the spirit of an age can be discerned from its attitudes towards angels and their dark cousins, the devil's court of demons (also hierarchically ranked). The revival of the heavenly and hellish hosts in this contemporary and utilitarian guise even incorporates the traditional pre-Copernican division of the universe, as an essay on the subject in the *Encyclopaedia Britannica* makes clear:

"The tripartite cosmos was re-mythologized into a tripartite structure of the personality – the superego (the restrictive social regulations that enable man to live as a social being), the ego (the conscious aspects of man), and the id, or libido (a 'seething, boiling cauldron of desire that seeks to erupt from beneath the threshold of consciousness')."

For me at this time of year, there has been a wonderful conjunction of memory and reality as, usually sitting in a pew beside my mother and sister, I have watched my own daughters walk through their roles in various Christmas pageants. I look at my sister on such occasions and wonder how it came to pass that the crowing little shepherdess became one of those rare people who light up other people's souls, and what it is that leads her on through life with such resilience. A few years ago, for example, she got caught in a freak accident trying to rescue an old woman from the residual spray of a chemical paint-remover. It's a somewhat complicated tale, but the net effect was that in rescuing the woman she got a faceful of the chemical herself. For several days it wasn't at all clear whether she would ever regain her sight, yet apart from cursing the fact that her blindness had left her with a haze of her least favourite colour – beige – she simply kept herself busy consulting the Canadian National Institute for the Blind and figuring out how she could best carry on as if nothing had happened. Her sight eventually returned, but not before everyone who crossed her path understood that she had no complaints to offer fate.

Eventually I discovered that I had been on a journey with my sister through the triple cosmos first formulated by Dionysius the Pseudo-Areopagite. The Church, which has always had an obsession with anything that comes in threes (from the Holy Trinity to the pope's triple tiara), reasoned that the journey to true understanding took three stages. First came the "purgative," when you got rid of evil or destructive thoughts. Then you moved on to the "illuminative," in which special insight replaced guesswork or superstition. At the end of the process came the "unitive," where a sense of oneness with all things took over your life. And that's exactly the way it was with my sister and me. In the process, I think I finally got angels straight.

Each stage was punctuated with an insight:

Purgative. Shortly after she held me, when I was eight, in a powerful hammerlock in the basement of Eaton's, she told me the facts of life. I thought angels brought babies, so I have been grateful ever since for the update. Over the years, she has performed the same admirable service on subjects ranging from child-rearing to the unsuitability of writing about family for public consumption. *Illuminative*. For me it was not a "born again" flash point. Instead, by the time I was twenty, I simply understood not only that she had evolved into my best friend but also that her capacious heart expanded proportionately to the demands placed upon it by anyone or any group who came into her orbit. I cannot think of a downtrodden cause or a forlorn victim she would not embrace if the root of the case was elemental justice. *Unitive*. Despite the fact that my sister is generally dismissive on the question of religious beliefs, my mother and I long ago came to the conclusion that Gabriel, Raphael, and Michael have not yet abandoned this world for retirement in the realms of glory. Even in the midst of so much cruelty and selfishness, we have seen evidence of their specific, careful work. Sometimes, as in the case of my sister and much to her irritation, they can team up to inhabit a single mortal frame.

December 1992

The Mark of Zero

~

April 1, 1994

Office of the Commissioner
Harassment & Discrimination
Ministry of Education and Training
Queen's Park, Toronto

To All "H & D" Officers:

Unfortunately, since the release last year of the ministry's *Framework Regarding Prevention of Harassment and Discrimination in Ontario Universities*, some reactionary academic and media circles have generated negative commentary about our policy of "zero tolerance for harassment and discrimination at Ontario universities." For example, a rump group at Trent University in Peterborough managed to get coverage by demanding "the right to be offensive," and no doubt there will be other silly outbursts from time to time. We do not want to exaggerate the impact of this criticism. Most university administrations in the province have complied with the principles of the *Framework* by the March 1994 deadline.

At the same time, there also appears to have been some confusion over interpretation of key concepts in the *Framework*. The Council of Ontario Universities, for example, has implied that our definition of "harassment" is somehow hazy and ill-conceived. This is nonsense. Harassment is not only clearly defined as "one or a series of vexatious comments or conduct related to one or more of the prohibited grounds that is known or might reasonably be known to be unwelcome/unwanted, offensive, intimidating, hostile, or inappropriate," but examples are specified to include "gestures, remarks, jokes, taunting, innuendo, display of offensive materials, offensive graffiti, threats, verbal or physical assault, imposition of academic penalties, hazing, stalking, shunning, or exclusion related to the prohibited grounds."

Nevertheless, to forestall any further misunderstandings and at the same time to equip H & D officers to deal with practical, real-life situations, the Office of the Commissioner has designed a short question-and-answer information sheet.

As a veteran white male professor of economics who lectures on Third World development to mixed classes of over 300 students, none of whom is known to me personally, I confess I am worried about inadvertently making "one or a series of vexatious comments . . . that is known or might reasonably be known to be unwelcome/unwanted." Should I be?

Not at all. You will *always* be given formal notice following a complaint or accusation and your university should already have established a tribunal at which you can try to defend yourself.

I am a female graduate student with an alternative life-style. Our history department has invited an international scholar named Simon

Schama to lecture here next month. The title of his talk is "Dykes and Discord: the role of land reclamation in seventeenth-century Dutch domestic policy." Posters have been plastered all over our campus, causing snickering, and I have been made to feel uneasy. Does the Framework *have any remedy?*

You bet it does! There is "zero tolerance" for anything that makes you feel a loss of self-esteem, and the *Framework* clearly states that "visitors to campus should be subject to complaints if they engage in prohibited conduct." Depending on how your academic administration chooses to police the *Framework's* guidelines, you have a range of options – from demanding prior access to the visitor's lecture to cancellation of the lecture itself and having the speaker barred from campus. As for the posters, they clearly come under the grounds of "poisoning the work or study environment," and the *Framework* is very specific about this: "A complainant," it says, "does not [even] have to be a direct target to be adversely affected by a negative environment. It includes conduct or comment that creates and maintains an offensive, hostile, or intimidating climate for study or work."

I am a young contracted instructor who has strict views on hard work and excellence. Will I be in trouble if I fail a student who consistently declines to turn up for lectures, refuses to hand in term papers, and writes rap lyrics on a final examination paper?

You are *already* in trouble on at least three counts: (1) the imposition on students of academic penalties is clearly included as an example of harassment; (2) depending on the race and gender of the student, a failing grade could also be determined a discriminatory act; and (3) the negative implications with which you invest "rap lyrics" indicates the potential on your part to create a negative study environment. It is also possible that your attitudes generate unconscious, systemic harassment/ discrimination, which the *Framework* defines as "policies, practices, procedures, actions or inactions, that appear neutral, but have an adverse impact associated with one of the prohibited grounds." This problem, however, would require a fairly extensive investigation, which I am required to inform you we have already begun.

I am a second-year student with strong Judaeo-Christian/humanist leanings who is dating a woman torn between choosing an academic career or a life as a Carmelite nun. My university insists on holding its year-end examinations during Lent when I am entirely focused on sexual abstinence, materialistic denial, fasting, and gender/race remorse. I feel that to write examinations during this period undermines my efforts to adhere to my faith, but my professors and administration are unsympathetic. Who is right?

You are 100 per cent right. You should immediately bring an action against the administration and any specific professors who have made you feel uneasy about the practice of your religion. The *Framework* specifically cites the setting of examination time periods that conflict with "important religious events" as an instance of systemic harassment/discrimination.

As a male English literature lecturer whose specialty is seventeenth-century social drama (excluding Shakespeare), I have felt insecure in the department ever since the appointment of a new head, whose specialty is contemporary feminist poetry. Will this new Framework protect me from her, or am I paranoid to feel even more insecure?

No, the *Framework* would not protect someone like you, and yes, you are justified in your feelings of insecurity. Let us suppose, for example, that you were lecturing on William Congreve's *The Way of the World*, one of the materials in your specialty area. Let us further suppose that, in describing the proposal scene between Millamant and Mirabel, you somehow neglected to point out how sexist the whole marriage contract is. *This is systemic discrimination.* If you had actually made eye contact with a student during the pertinent section of the lecture, it could also be grounds for sexual harassment charges, especially if you had just handed back an essay paper and marked that student down.

Surely this is extreme?
Not at all. Zero tolerance means zero tolerance.

Look here. Don't we have adequate laws and constitutional protections to deal with any truly serious acts of harassment and discrimination? Don't you think encoding all this stuff almost guarantees abuses that may prove far greater than any of the problems the Framework *proposes to clear up?*
Double no. And Stephen Lewis says so, too.

Who the hell is Stephen Lewis? In the "Background" section of the Framework, *it states that the government of Ontario's new policy of demanding every university in the province subscribe to harassment and discrimination regulations came about because someone named Stephen Lewis said in June 1992 that it should come about. How did a guy who wasn't even in elected office become so powerful?*
Stephen Lewis saved the Ontario New Democratic Party from extinction, single-handedly restored the United Nations to the powerhouse it is today, brings unprecedented high ratings to CBC Radio's "Morningside," and can cure scrofula with the touch of his hands. Asking what Stephen Lewis has to do with harassment and discrimination policy in Ontario universities is like asking what Torquemada had to do with the Spanish Inquisition. In the new dialectic of zero tolerance, Stephen is the cause and the *Framework* is the effect.

April 1994

Newfoundland's Professor
of the Year

~

An organization screaming for an acronym, The Council for the Advancement and Support of Education, has recently named an English teacher at Memorial University of Newfoundland "Canadian professor of the year." CASE draws its membership from nearly 3,000 universities, colleges, secondary schools, and elementary schools in Canada, the United States, Mexico, and twenty other countries. Since 1981 it has made its business the annual denomination of certain individuals as "professor of the year" or "secondary-school teacher of the year," this honour being attended by a great falderal of press, publicity, and academic preening.

According to the press releases issued by CASE and Memorial University, the process that produced this year's "Canadian professor of the year" involved an exhaustive search and an intensive follow-up scrutiny, including the taking of testimonials from fellow faculty members and students. The net result of the investigation has been to serve up one of my two best friends in Newfoundland as the winner. This is Shane O'Dea, an associate professor in the department of English. You will note that I do not say Dr. Shane O'Dea. He has no doctorate. At this rather late stage in his development (he is well launched into his forties by now), it seems unlikely that he will ever come by one, at least honestly.

The oddity of choosing an undoctored university teacher as "professor of the year" has not been lost on some folk. For example, O'Dea's own departmental head, Professor Averil Gardner, seemed flustered when she was quizzed about the award by a reporter from *The Muse*, Memorial University's student newspaper:

"Concerning the award," the newspaper reported, "Averil Gardner, head of Memorial's English department, said, 'We can't really make a comment because we know little about the award. However we are glad for Mr. O'Dea's sake.'"

Precisely! We are all of us glad for Mr. O'Dea's sake – and none more than I, who once plotted his humiliation and downfall when we were both undergraduates at Memorial. This was in the mid-1960s, and the plot was hatched after a series of provocations culminated in my being blackballed at O'Dea's instigation from a splendid soirée at the home of the Honourable Campbell Macpherson on the ludicrous grounds that I was "a pushy parvenu from the Mainland." The description was not only cruel but unjust. I was in the thrall of all things Newfoundlandish, a condition that would eventually include this disturbing twit who was well over six feet tall and paraded around St. John's in riding boots and breeches like some lost chapter in a novel by Vita Sackville-West.

The unmistakable signs of militant eccentricity were evident in O'Dea at a very early age, aided no doubt by the fact that he was a card-carrying member of the rebel-gentry. For example, he helped organize the first demonstration in Newfoundland against the war in Vietnam. There was a rather small turnout, as far as I can recall, Newfoundlanders being more comfortable protesting against Canada than against the United States.

Nevertheless, it took a certain sang-froid, when the march to the American consul general's residence was over, for O'Dea – still booted and breeched – to say bye-bye to the troops and drop in next door at Government House, where his uncle, the Honourable Fabian O'Dea, was then presiding as lieutenant governor.

Our friendship began only after I had exposed his fraudulent credentials as a radical in a clever little satire submitted to *The Muse*. Shortly after the Macpherson black-ball and the circulation of my satire, we encountered each other at a "social gathering" of the university's dramatic society where he threw his drink in my face. It is not easy to retaliate when you are at least a foot shorter than your opponent and don't talk like Sir Percy Parsnips, but slighted honour will be avenged. While he was busy pontificating, I was able surreptitiously to move a stool behind his back, return to the kitchen for an ice bucket, mount the stool, and pour the half-melted contents over his head. From that moment on, we have been the closest of friends. He is godfather to my daughter, and I to his son, and he has taught me that the obligations of affection and respect are an acceptance of the vagaries of life. Thanks to geography, employment, and family, we have not seen as much of each other over the past two decades as we would have liked; on the other hand, it takes us about twelve seconds to get things back to where they were.

How on earth did CASE discover him? Everyone who knows O'Dea knows that he is among the best teachers in Canada, but no one expects the wider world to discover – let alone appreciate – such things. Still, once he had been singled out, corroboration was enthusiastically furnished. Among the affidavits supporting his selection as "professor of the year" was one that noted, "Mr. O'Dea did not just want to teach – he wanted his students to learn." Another, going into fuller detail, began, "He was always well prepared and introduced students to the leading bodies of critical thought." If this seems a very ordinary qualification for a good teacher, place it against a backdrop of the kind of assembly-line education so many university students know today.

"He [O'Dea] demanded full participation in class from all students," the detailed evaluation continued, "encouraging those who were diffident and retiring to present their opinions. Discussions were wide-ranging and hotly disputed, yet Mr. O'Dea always maintained control of the class. Assignments were well spaced throughout the semester. He expected students to research the topic thoroughly and to present arguments in a precise manner paying close attention to the text. He devoted much energy and thought to the marking of assignments, making time available to all students for full discussion of the paper. His comments were constructive and aimed at helping the student achieve a greater proficiency in writing elegant English and in critical thinking. . . . His sharp sense of humour and wit added an astringency to his classes that I found most welcome. He has that magical power to enthuse students in the love of literature."

Elegant English and all, this is fairly shocking stuff, akin to hearing about a doctor who actually heals a patient without referring him to a specialist, or finding a lawyer who will make a small change to your will for under $200. A teacher who teaches is a contemporary contradiction and should be cherished wherever he or she is found. There is too much undermining good teaching in our universities. Academic snobbery undermines it by overvaluing doctorates, some of which have less value than an honest bachelor's degree. The university tradition of "publish or perish" undermines it by putting a low value on proven teaching skills. Tenure undermines it by conferring indiscriminate sanctity on the good, the mediocre, and sometimes the appalling. Governments undermine it by denying that parsimonious funding has anything whatever to do with the quality of education.

Despite all this, we have Shane O'Dea, a "professor of the year," and there are no doubt others like him around, not nationally recognized, who have stubbornly and bravely stuck to their guns amidst the enveloping gloom. For me, the single most telling tale of my tied-for-best friend in Newfoundland is what he did instead of obtaining the all-important doctorate. Rather than research and write a probing thesis on something useful like the dialectical roles of art and artifice in seventeenth-century social comedy, he pursued a personal agenda of Newfoundland culture. Few know as much as O'Dea about Newfoundland-vernacular kitchen tables or baymen's windows. As a historian of island architecture and artefacts, he has revived an old and rather wonderful concept of the amateur as an enlightened student who pursues a particular field for no other reason than a love of that field. He has travelled extensively throughout his own sainted land, and has made the business of its past – both the observable past and the parts that have become shrouded – his own. Out of this enriching affection he has even managed to persuade the university authorities in Newfoundland to create a course of studies which he teaches himself, thus neatly marrying vocation with amateur passion, and, not incidentally, expressing his gentle, wry Newfoundland patriotism.

I wish with a fervour that would surprise even him that I were a student once again, taking that particular course at Memorial University.

February 1989

The Real Dalai Lama

⌇

O n the day, twelve years ago, that we first climbed the
seemingly endless steps to the Potala Palace, the wind
came swirling down through Lhasa from the broad
plains of the Qinghai Plateau, the highest flatlands in the
world. In theory, we had to climb only five of eight storeys
before reaching the formal entrance hall to the Dalai Lama's
court, but the exterior steps of the first four storeys were so high
and irregular that the ordeal of the ascent conspired with the
dust in the gusty air, thinned of oxygen, to produce a deep physical anxiety. Perhaps the gasping for breath and the visions of
stars in broad daylight were by design. Ego mortification and
the humbling of the body may well be the appropriate compo-
nents of self-perception when presenting oneself to the Dalai
Lama of Tibet, the fourteenth reincarnation of the compassionate *bodhisattva* (or "Buddha-to-be"), Avalokitesvara.

Except, of course, that he wasn't there. He hadn't been anywhere near the Potala Palace for nearly two decades, having
been forced into flight in 1959 when the Chinese Communists

reneged on their promise to allow Tibetan self-rule and instead installed a vicious army of colonial occupation. The group I was travelling with in 1978 was the small foreign press corps resident in Beijing. It was considered at the time something of a historic visit. Other than a few foreign apologists for the Chinese Communists – most notably Han Suyin, the Eurasian novelist and ideological fantast – no outsiders had been permitted to visit the mystical Land of Snows since before the Dalai Lama had retreated just over the border to form his government-in-exile in India.

What we learned on that visit was devastating. During the intervening two decades, more than 1,500 monasteries, temples, and other holy institutions had been destroyed by the Chinese. Hundreds of Buddhist monks, nuns, and priests had been killed, and many more imprisoned. Even today, no one knows how many other loyalists were dispatched into China's vast network of forced-labour camps, but they certainly numbered in the thousands. Religion had been driven underground, where – not surprisingly – it had thrived, but at a terrible cost to ordinary people. Unlucky in both its geography and the politics of its neighbours, Tibet was a country doubly abandoned by the larger world – abandoned, on one hand, to the terrible fate of small nations whose victimization is "not worth a fight," and abandoned on the other hand (at least by many in the West) to a metaphysical limbo that allowed nothing to intrude upon a realm of mysterious and colourful imagination.

The second day of that first trip to Tibet thrust up the dreamland motif. Well, dreamland and burlesque! We gathered slowly on an outside portico of the Potala. As we waited for the others, looking across from the balcony to the old quarter of Lhasa and the golden rooftop of the Jokhang Temple, a French colleague opened up his pack of Gitanes, lit one up, and promptly reeled woozily back. A Chinese official came running with a contraption that looked like a rubber pillow but was inflated with pure oxygen. It was a first-aid kit for foreigners unaccustomed to the altitude. The journalist in question was clearly a fatalist: with the Gitane still burning in one hand, he used the other to hold the nozzle-hose attachment from the pillow; in between gulps of oxygen, he managed to work in quite a few puffs on the cigarette.

While I lingered behind to soak in the extraordinary beauty, the larger group forged on ahead. Realizing that I was in danger of being left behind, I hurried after them into the building proper – and promptly got lost in a maze of unlit rooms; I fancy I might still be there today had I not had the wit to bring along a pocket flashlight. *Dreamland.* Initially, there was the slight sensation of having walked into one of those Enid Blyton pot-boilers for children (*The Temple of Adventure*, possibly), but the impression was quickly replaced by a more accurate literary context: *The Third Eye* by T. Lobsang Rampa, among the most exciting reading I could remember from my boyhood.

The author of this remarkable "autobiography," which sent a *frisson* of excitement down many a spiritually bored North American spine in the mid-1950s, was purportedly a Tibetan lama (or priest), but he wrote in such elegant English, with such a command of drama and fascinating detail, that the whole book seemed a kind of miracle. As it turned out, something less than a miracle was afoot. *The Third Eye* was a fraud, written by the clever son of a Devon plumber who had culled enough from *The Tibetan Book of the Dead* and other sources to put together a vivid narrative. It was, however, one of those books that *should* have been true. As I stumbled rather happily into yet another chamber of the Dalai Lama's formidable residence it seemed to me that T. Lobsang Rampa was my trustiest companion, certainly preferable to the official government guides whose fictions and ignorance were far more repugnant than the Englishman's sprightly and evocative duplicity.

But the reality of Tibet eventually dissipated the charm as

the sense of our missing host – the reincarnated Dalai – grew stronger and stronger. I was not alone in feeling an intruder into his inner sanctum, in recollecting what a terrible wrong had been done to him and his people by the current custodians who held the keys to all the chambers, and in being by turns fascinated and appalled by the lengths to which those custodians would go in order to belittle the Dalai's significance and libel his cause. When I finally caught up with the rest of the group, we had proceeded to crowd into his old bedroom, a humble cell with a small bed, a desk, a low prayer table, book shelves, and an old-fashioned wind-up Victrola. "This room is just as the Dalai Lama left it when he betrayed his people and left the country," the guide announced solemnly. One of us tried unsuccessfully to point out that he had, in fact, left from his summer palace, called Norbulingka, on the outskirts of Lhasa, but the guide was not to be deterred from her script. "See," she continued, "he used a Chinese-made quilt on his bed."

The bedroom had been made up (each day I presumed – or at least before any special, government-approved visit) to suggest hasty departure. The Victrola's turntable held a gramophone record. Some pens (of Chinese manufacture) were spilled haphazardly on the desk. There were bedroom slippers on the ornate carpet, and the quilt in question was studiedly bunched as if thrown off in a hurry. The squashed pillow apparently bore the impression – eighteen years on – of the Dalai's sleeping head on that fateful but nonexistent day he never actually left the Potala for exile in India.

It was two years later, in a wild juxtaposition, that I met the Dalai Lama himself in his bedroom suite at the Royal York Hotel in Toronto, where he was staying on one of his infrequent visits to Canada. He comes here to rally his cause and meet with members of the Canadian-Tibetan community. He was in Canada again a few weeks ago on the same mission and his presence

brought the memories flooding back. For example, the infectious amusement with which he had listened to the account of
his old digs at the Potala: he was disappointed that I could not
tell him which recording had been left on the turntable. "It may
have been significant," he said with a twinkle. "If it was
American, that would have been a sign of decadence. If it was
Chinese, that would have been an indication of China's
'inalienable right to rule Tibet.'"

I pointed out that at his summer palace (about the size of an
ordinary two-storey middle-class Canadian house) I had been
delighted to see he had several recordings of Guy Lombardo and
his Royal Canadians for his portable electric machine. What
would a liking for Guy Lombardo have proved, I asked?

"The worst sort of deviousness," came the quick reply.

The banter at this first interview lasted only a few minutes
and then he questioned me seriously about local conditions and
my interpretation of the latest version of China's notorious
"national minorities policy." Although he remained charming
and interested, I had the distinct impression I had nothing new
to tell him. His information from Tibet is always up to date.
Back in 1980, China had begun a new round of courting the
Dalai Lama, hoping to woo him back to splendid isolation – and
out of harm's way – in a Beijing residence. The quid pro quo was
the promise of periodic visits to a country where the vast majority of the indigenous population considers him both the spiritual and the temporal leader. He declined, and there were
terrible upheavals in Tibet throughout the 1980s. Typically,
however, he has always left the door open for further discussion.

The Dalai Lama's travails in exile have provided the last half
of the twentieth century with one of its few examples of unsul-
lied honour and constancy. He has been wise in his dealings
with the Communists, praising – where appropriate – any modest economic reforms directed towards his people. All peace

overtures extended by Beijing have been acknowledged gratefully and explored to the limits of what he is prepared to
promise. He has never exploited his undoubted capacity to turn
Tibet into complete turmoil and he has travelled the world with
dignity and humility. And with wit.

In Canada a few years ago, he delivered a public homily from
the dais of Convocation Hall at the University of Toronto. The
greater part of the talk was given in Tibetan and translated into
English. I remember the gist of one part of it, which led to a question from a university student sitting in the packed audience.
The Dalai Lama spoke of the need to transmute frustration and
anger into something more positive which would ultimately
ennoble the individual, and shed new, cathartic light on whatever was the source of grievance. He could think of no situation,
he said, that could not be turned to a good account through such
exploration and meditation.

The young questioner turned out to be a devil's advocate. If
there was no situation bad enough to remain unresolved by
appropriate meditation, he asked the Dalai Lama, why had he
then felt it necessary to leave Tibet after the Chinese invaded?
Why had he not simply remained in the Potala and meditated
until the nasty business was resolved?

"Well," said the high and mighty Living Buddha, supreme
ruler of the Order of Yellow Hats, Master of the Lion's Throne,
Lord of the Potala, Great and Precious Conqueror, Ocean of
Wisdom. "Well, no one's perfect."

November 1990

Young and Restless

~

I t is August. We are in Georgian Bay. At the farthest reach of
a cool, sequestered cove, the MV *Gotcha* purrs quietly as it
heads towards the narrow channel separating Band Island
from the mainland and then on out into open water. On the
deck, oiled and bronzed, the pleasingly mature body of a woman
can be made out, shimmering in the summer haze. The woman
is reading a slip of paper, a wry, complex look on her face.
Though its message is brief, even curt, it conjures infuriating
memories – of betrayal, marital larceny, and capital-venture
woes. The woman is perusing her 1988 income-tax acknowl-
edgement from Revenue Canada, forwarded by her accountant.

The growing tendency among a statistically impatient citizenry
to employ accountants to figure out their annual income taxes,
rather than doing it themselves, has meant that many Canadians are no longer familiar with that estimable publication,
the *General Tax Guide*, updated each year by Revenue Canada
as an "aid" to taxpayers. This is a shame because sometime during fiscal 1986-87 there was an editorial revolution at Revenue

Canada. Someone up there in Ottawa had the inspiration of annotating the ledger English with real-life examples, transforming the guide from a Calvinist textbook on pecuniary obligation to a vivid, suspenseful soap opera, full of sociological insights.

Not all at once, of course. Last year's guide (for taxes paid on 1987 income) offered a mercenary, rather petit-bourgeois cast of characters: Michael and Joanne with their joint bank account, David with his $6,000 term deposit, Susan with her CSBs, Mr. and Mrs. Smith with their medical expenses. But this year's guide has got into the modern swing of things. We meet Yuppies: Jon and Zelda, the youngest of whose three kids has an income of $3,500 (from modelling toddler designer jeans for Eaton's?). Mohammed's clipped bonds, Padmini's child-care expenses, and Andrée's allowable claims acknowledge bilingual, multicultural Canada.

And the complications of contemporary relationships are a special feature throughout. Take divorce, Line 128. In former guides, the business of alimony payments was disposed of with distancing briskness. The explication of Line 128 in the 1986 guide, for example, told us:

"If you were divorced or separated, report periodic payments received from your former or estranged spouse under a decree, order, judgement or written agreement. For agreements made after 1983, certain payments that are deemed to be an allowance payable on a periodic basis are income of the recipient. Payments made. . . . before the agreement, decree, order or judgement is signed, but not before the beginning of the previous calendar year, are income of the recipient."

But the 1987 guide not only conceded three possible complications, it also introduced us to the drama of Ron and Jane: "Ron and Jane separated in May 1986, and Jane paid Ron maintenance of $250 a month. They signed their separation agreement in February 1988. The agreement acknowledges the payments that were made to Ron since May 1986. However, Ron only has to report the payments received in 1987 and subsequent years. Payments received from May to December 1986 do not have to be reported as income and are not deductible by Jane." Jane took a bath for $2,000 that first part-year.

But there's worse to come. Much worse. In the 1988 guide, Ron is back again – but married to Ann: "Ron and Ann separated in May 1986, and Ann paid Ron maintenance of $250 a month. . . ." It is not at all clear in the guide whether Ann knew about Jane, but on the boat out in Georgian Bay, Jane's remembered fury at discovering the bigamy has transmitted a sufficiently agitated karma to send a hovering seagull squawking on its way.

Still, it was the 1988 guide that brought the Gallic, saturnine René into her world. In a way, René was a complication, a new subsection ("B") of Line 128: Payments made to you by your estranged spouse, where you had no discretion as to the use of the payment, may have to be included in your income and may be deductible by the payer depending on the date of your order or agreement.

"For example, René received a monthly maintenance allowance plus an additional $200 per month. His agreement stated that he must use the additional $200 to pay the property taxes on his dwelling. In this case, the $200 is considered to be an allowance paid to him for a specific purpose. Even though René has no discretion as to the use of the payment, he may have to include the amount in his income depending on the date of his order or agreement."

A complication? Not in Jane's eyes.

The perfect calm had merged almost imperceptibly into the foretoken of one of those frightening flash storms that seem to come from nowhere on the finest of summer days. The pent-up rage of inchoate Nature suited René's mood as he opened the throttle and let the powerful Evinrude Imperator engine hurl the MV *Gotcha* along the ominously swelling waters of the outer bay.

"Damn her!" he said.

He shouted it out again, over the roar of the Evinrude. "Damn her to hell!"

Jane stuck her handsome head out the cabin door. She had stowed her papers and had been cleaning up the galley when she heard the shout. "Were you calling me, darling?" she asked. Against the lowering horizon, she saw the panoply of the approaching storm and gave an involuntary shudder. "We'd better head for shore."

"That's just what I'm doing," said René. There was irritation in his clipped speech. The oath had not been sworn at Jane – could not have been. Jane was the first good and wholly solvent reality to enter his life since the terrible ordeal of the court settlement nearly two years ago. It was only last year, though, that he had finally comprehended how his ex-wife – he couldn't bring himself to utter her actual name – had managed to tie up his cottage, now his only principal residence, in a forest of red tape.

It would be years before he could sell the cottage and the land. And for what? For a useless $200 a month. It had seemed such a small thing at the time. He'd even thought he'd been clever. How bitter that chimera of cleverness seemed now. Why on earth had he agreed to the additional sum on top of the monthly maintenance? It was special, she said, so that the cottage and island taxes could be paid and the property thus assured for their only child *over whom she had exclusive control*. And then the lawyers managed to get a judicial easement forbidding the sale of all or any part of the land until the child was of bloody age. René hadn't thought to have the extra $200 indexed to increases and the local authorities had now raised the property taxes. "Damn her!"

"Darling," said Jane quietly as she brought him a fresh mug of coffee, "I know you're still angry. But don't let this come between us. It's been such bliss the past few days. I've almost been able to forget Ron."

B - O - O - M.

The thunderclap resounded at the precise moment Jane uttered the name of her husband. Poor Jane. Lucky in business, doomed in love. No other investment counsellor plying the creaky mechanism of Bay Street oiled the levers better than she. No one was more adept at discovering those crucial tidbits of information that made all the difference between humdrum advice and the strategic positioning that brought mega-profits to her favoured clients.

Yet, in love, the clear-eyed assessments that were the hallmark of her success yielded to generosity and blind optimism. The men who littered her private life, for whom she secured safe annuities and had part of her earnings perpetually garnisheed, had proved to be dubious risks, unfixed assets. Ron, the archleech, was the worst of all: the false arbitrageur of her heart. She was paying dearly for that mistake. Each month she had to write out the cheques. *For maintenance!* To maintain him for what?

The first drops of rain came as René's powerful craft returned to the safety of the protected cove behind Band Island. The boat had been her gift to him, in sheer gratitude. She had felt so devastated last April at the news of Ron's perfidy – on top of the monthly payments. With $250 from her and $250 from Ann, Ron was living in luxury. She felt so *used*. And then René came into her life. Cool and exotic, yes, but he, too, was hurting. In their shared hurt they had found solace, and this cruise had been charted in paradise.

The handsomely outfitted launch slowed to a putter as René prepared to ride out the storm in the safe harbour. The tension seemed to lift. The approaching storm was going to be a release. He sensed it. A release – and a sort of inspiration.

"Darling," he said, with that trace of accent she found so disarming. "Let's talk." Jane flushed with pleasure, for he rarely used endearments. At first it had seemed strange that he could be so cold and yet so close, but it only spurred her on to evoke the warmth she knew lay deeply lodged somewhere in his unfathomable heart.

René swallowed the last gulp from his mug and put it down on the latest copy of *Tax Tips,* open at the article on "Capital gains, the new budget, and you."

"You make a damned fine cup of coffee."

He paused, but Jane knew more was to come, because with René a compliment was always prelude to a fugue. She used the serenity of the moment to peruse his tousled hair and chiselled features.

"Darling, I've been thinking about our relationship. I don't think either of us wants to get tied down with legalities after the ordeals we've been through." She shook her head emphatically. "But, you know," he went on, "this boat is coming between us. I sense it, don't you? I mean, if it is really a gift, it should be in my name, shouldn't it? How would you feel?"

Jane was devastated. The gift had been made spontaneously, out of love. But how thoughtless not to do it cleanly, outright. And how decent of René: he had been worrying about her, and her having to pay capital-gains tax on a gift to someone other than a spouse. Her lawyers would fix it up as soon as she got to the city.

"Darling," she said. "You know perfectly well, what's mine is yours."

"You're *ravissante,* babe," said René. "The very best."

B - O - O - M.

From a proposed addition to the 1989 *General Tax Guide,* Line 128, Subsection D:

"René and Jane had a common-law relationship for under one year. During that time, Jane gave René several gifts in cash or kind, including a $189,000 lake cruiser subsequently registered in René's name. In September 1989, René sold the cruiser for cash, at a loss. Jane's gift is taxed as though she had received proceeds at the fair market value of the property at the time of the gift. But, in the light of a recent court decision, René is entitled to claim a capital loss and take it into account in computing his tax. An agreement between René and Jane to reimburse René's estranged spouse with a monthly payment of $200 means that René no longer has to include this sum with his own income."

August 1989

Reciprocity

~

T he debate over a free-trade deal with the United States appears to be reviving that feisty old emotion, righteous indignation. People are getting very, very angry. Some have even stopped talking to each other. Not normally thought of as useful in debates on Canadian policy these days, the anger contrasts curiously with the familiar lobotomized shrug that greets contemporary Canadian issues deemed too big and complicated to worry about.

As with the nation, so it goes at *Saturday Night*, for both the proprietor and the publisher (God forgive them) are ardent free-traders, while the editor knows the whole nasty business is a plot to subvert the destiny of the nation. The other odd socks around here – from the senior editor, associate editors, and contributing editors, to the circulation and advertising managers, cleaning staff, and even the humble, self-effacing comptroller – are all over the map and offer no help whatever in trying to sort out a correct resolution. No help, did I say? We now have a fixed and conveniently acrimonious item on the weekly editorial agenda to carry us through to the twenty-first century.

Although none of this should be exaggerated, there nevertheless does seem to be a refreshing asperity in the air as one goes about the simple tasks of the day. Take for example a perfectly straightforward telephone call to Margaret Atwood to see if the eminently edible lady would care to participate in the great revival of magazine fiction set to take off within these pages as soon as possible:

"When your current work is finished in the spring," I said, "I hope we can count on you."

"What did you say your views on this trade deal were?" Atwood asked sweetly. "I trust they aren't the same as your boss's."

"Clearly the new section won't work unless we have the right balance of offerings from our best writers and the best of our new writers."

"You do realize what it all comes down to, don't you? You saw what [Canadian free-trade negotiator Simon] Reisman said? I am a fascist now. Because I am against this deal, Simon Reisman has said I can now officially be described as a fascist. Not very pretty."

"Well, if we start the new fiction section in May or June, do you think you could oblige . . .?"

"*Oblige!* I won't feel obliged to do anything after our own government has sold us down the river. The reason I won't call it 'free trade' is that there's nothing free for us in it. Why don't we convert the Parliament Buildings into an up-market hotel – the Château Parliament? That way at least somebody will make some money on it."

"So I'll be in touch in June then, shall I?"

"If I'm still here. There won't be much point after this deal goes through, will there?"

Amid the old-world charm of Charles Ritchie's Ottawa apartment, glowing with the patina of bonhomie and experience, the debate takes on a different tone – more even-handed, though no less emphatic. It was a perfect time to strike. The old boy had finished his latest volume of memoirs and the book hustle had just ended:

"I thought, sir, some vignettes or miniature portraits might fit in rather well to the magazine."

"Quite right," said Ritchie, "I couldn't agree more. I am simply going to opt out of the free-trade nonsense altogether. Couldn't make any sense of it anyway."

"Particularly foreign statesmen, sir. With your breadth of experience as an ambassador in so many places. . . ."

"Tea, dear boy, more tea? I take your point, of course, but you see I finally realized that both sides were saying the same thing and that's when I decided I could quit the debate with a clear conscience. The people for free trade tell you that if we don't sign up we will remain hewers of wood and drawers of water forever, while the people against free trade insist that the Americans only want us in the deal as hewers of wood and drawers of water."

"So I can expect to hear from you soon, sir, can I?"

"That's it exactly, but you write it up."

And had I at any time during the past two months been able to get hold of the incomparable Ray Guy somewhere, anywhere, in Newfoundland to tell him that his new meal ticket had moved into the editor's chair at *Saturday Night*, I am quite sure his impeccable sense of irony and historical inevitability would have pushed him towards the free-trade camp somewhat along the following lines:

"Ray! I'm desperate for a piece on Peckford. I'm told he's gone right over the top."

"Yes, me son, I hear you plain. It's all a tremendous vindication for the Crosbie clan."

"No, no. We'll leave Crosbie for the Ottawa columnist. What I want from you is. . . ."

"It was Mr. Ches, you know, who said it first in '48 during the Confederation dust-up. 'Why in the name of Jesus, Mary, and Joseph' – well, Mr. Ches was a Methodist but you get me gist – 'why in the name of Charles Bejeezuz Wesley are we sucking up to those stuck-up miseries in Canada when the whole of the Greater United States lies plump, clucking, and ready for the plucking?'"

". . . the Peckford piece. You'll do it?"

"I le was a man of vision and history was Mr. Ches. Saw the whole picture on free trade forty years ago. A prophet ignored! And never forget he was The Honourable John's daddy. Think about that for vindication."

There is nothing to despair in all this. The unfamiliar ire and enthusiasm may yet be stamped out thanks to the impeccable behaviour of the prime minister, who is pushing the deal but declines to defend it with vigour except at the most primitive level, and the premier of Ontario, who is against it but would prefer quietly to tend his own garden.

Within the dismal confines established by these reticent gentlemen, the real worth of Canadian civility is amply exposed as we ponder our little plunge into economic and social history.

February 1988

The Reverend Doctor Frye

~

The death in January of the great Canadian scholar Northrop Frye brought forth eloquent tributes in the local and national media – for a couple of days. There was also a public memorial service at the University of Toronto's Convocation Hall, which attracted the available literati and Pooh-Bahs from the Ontario government and Toronto academia. In light of Frye's stature as the pre-eminent literary critic in the English-speaking world, a position that it could reasonably be argued had been vacant since the death of Samuel Johnson at the end of the eighteenth century, some of the people attending the memorial service arrived an hour in advance of the anticipated crush to ensure getting seats.

The crush never came. The upper galleries of Convocation Hall remained largely empty. Conspicuous in their scarcity were the students of the very university that Frye had made famous wherever anyone probed the meaning of Western literature. Perhaps the event had not been sufficiently well publicized on campus; perhaps the hour conflicted with too many students' schedules; perhaps the vast majority of those studying English literature at the university supposed there would be little chance of getting a seat. Perhaps, too, not enough students knew enough to appreciate that they had arrived at a memorable juncture in their lives, one hinging the moment when they had lived and studied with Northrop Frye in their midst and the moment when they would not. After he died, Robert Fulford wrote that it was good to live in the Toronto of the Reverend Dr. Frye. Indeed it was, at least for those who actually *knew* they did.

Well, well. Students cannot be criticized without an understanding of the age and neighbourhood of their rearing. Frye himself would have savoured the situation with detached irony. How on earth could a people who so nonchalantly inter their history in order to avoid confrontation and contradictions be expected to savour the passing of a great Canadian who rejoiced in intellectual confrontation and embraced contradiction as a means of penetrating reality? "To participate in anything in human society," he said in 1968, "means entering into a common bond of guilt, of guilt and inevitable compromise. I am not saying that we accept the evils of what we join: I am saying that whatever we join contains evils, and that what we accept is the guilt of belonging to it."

Inside the guilt-ridden stockade of English-Canadian culture, where so many of us are now busy hoarding our store and priming our weapons, the task of coping with the specific bequests of the greatest Canadian thinker of our age is an onerous burden. As a true humanist, he embraced the catholic experience of the world; but, like Yeats's mystic poet, he also knew each fibre of the thatch on his own cottage roof. To make it all doubly uncomfortable, he was so quintessentially Canadian that he could make a crack about being "an undercover agent for the United Church" which was perfectly incomprehensible outside the country and perfectly – hilariously, really – emblematic of our penchant for self-disparaging irony. He was a man burdened by our veneration of accountants and acquainted with

briefs from the Canadian Radio-television and Telecommuni-
cations Commission. Even this was tinged with irony, for in his
work he was the chief actuary of our presiding mythologies, and
in private life he was the high priest of the English-Canadian
cult of purposeful anonymity. Yet for all that, Northrop Frye still
dared to trace the trajectory of our intangible, immortal souls
and it may be another century or so before we see his like again.

For my own part, as far as "bequests" go, I am now enjoined to
correct an inadvertent wrong I committed some years ago in an
excess of zeal spurred on by Frye, who was not so wary of the daily
pressure of newspaper deadlines as he should have been. In
1982, the centenary of the birth of Canada's greatest epic poet,
E. J. Pratt, had passed with hardly any notice. I was then a columnist for The Globe and Mail and had been alerted to the
neglected anniversary by the great Coleridge scholar Kathleen
Coburn. I immediately contacted Frye in his redoubt at the
University of Toronto's Victoria College. He was in phlegmatic
despair. All that had been planned was a small exhibit of
Prattiana at Victoria College where the poet had taught for
more than three decades.

In the United States (with Walt Whitman, for example)
or the United Kingdom (with Virginia Woolf, for another
example), the centennial of the birth of a great literary light
would have been celebrated with a conspicuous reprinting of
key works, new evaluations of his or her life and writing,
television and radio documentaries, a special issue of postage
stamps, and who knows what else. In this way, a nation's literature is revived and made relevant to new generations. Only
in Canada would such a signal event bring such a shrug of
indifference.

Thus inspired by Frye and Coburn, the Globe's columnist, like
Stephen Leacock's horseman, rode madly off in all directions.
I spent a delightful afternoon with Pratt's widow who was then

in her early nineties and living with her daughter Claire in a Rosedale apartment. Viola Pratt may have been the most vigorous nonagenarian in the land, and she was on the warpath. After I had collected a sufficient number of anecdotes to flesh out one column, she let loose a broadside against David Pitt, an academic at Memorial University of Newfoundland, who had had possession of most of the poet's papers for the better part of a decade. "I can't tell you how annoyed I am," said Mrs. Pratt as she drank her tea in vengeful sips. "He's been sitting on this material for years, here's the anniversary of Ned's birth coming, and all he's got are excuses. I trusted him so much. . . ."

Her wrath produced a second column, one that railed away generally at our national forgetfulness and specifically at poor Pitt for not keeping his nose to the grindstone. I was well pleased with this effort until ten days after its publication when I went to Peterborough, Ontario, for the funeral of a venerable academic. Frye had been asked to deliver the homily, and at the reception that followed he motioned to me to take the seat beside him. It was not unpleasant to be asked to sit next to Northrop Frye.

"Those were interesting columns you wrote," he said. "Very useful. Unfortunately there was a mistake in the second one."

I felt the beginnings of a familiar sick lump in my gut. It is a symptom specific to journalism, particularly daily journalism, when confronted with the consequences of hasty writing and easy judgement.

"Pitt's book on Ned has been finished for some years, I'm afraid," said Frye.

My jaw dropped. "Then why didn't he get it to the publishers in time for the anniversary?" I demanded. "Is he a fool?"

"No," said Frye, taking a deep breath. "He's not a fool, he's a gentleman. You see, what you don't know, and I should have told you, was that Ned had an affair. It lasted for a year and Pitt won't publish his biography until Mrs. Pratt is dead."

"Oh my God! I can fix it," I blurted out. My mind raced. "The *Globe* can publish an 'Our mistake' tomorrow."

Frye took in another deep breath and looked at me with genuine sympathy and, I suspect, ironical wonder:

"And how do you propose to word such a correction?"

I saw the dilemma at once. *How would it be worded?* "An article in *The Globe and Mail* incorrectly stated that a biography of E. J. Pratt had not been finished in time for the anniversary of the poet's birth. In fact, the book is written but the author has declined to publish it until . . ." *Until what?* Until the widow's death? Until any untoward revelations will not hurt the living? "Oh my God!" I said again.

"I think," said Frye, "we can't do a thing about it. Someday perhaps you may find an opportunity to correct the record." A relative of the recently departed academic was now approaching the great man to thank him for his homily. "In the meantime," he added quietly, with only a trace of a smile, "we had better deal with the dead at hand."

(Shortly after Mrs. Pratt died a year later, the first volume of David G. Pitt's excellent study of the poet, *E.J.Pratt: The Truant Years, 1882-1927*, was published. This was followed in 1987 by the second volume, *The Master Years, 1927-1964*. These books were widely acclaimed in reviews and commentaries and form the standard work on Pratt's life and writing.)

Northrop Frye presided over the coming of age of English-Canadian literary aspirations. It was not that he was responsible for Morley Callaghan or Hugh MacLennan or Margaret Laurence or Robertson Davies or Mavis Gallant or Mordecai Richler or Alice Munro or Margaret Atwood or Timothy Findley (although he taught Atwood and must have sparred with Callaghan and Davies). It was simply that he loomed so triumphantly over a most extraordinary era in English-Canadian letters, an era that saw our best writers accepted all over the world in spite of the native desire to see ourselves as a dull and plodding folk. He is the cornerstone in a structure of witness, experience, and achievement that cannot be dismantled despite the efficient demolition work of the current grave-diggers of Canada. Whatever happens in the future of the country, the world of Northrop Frye will have to be accounted for and it will be the single most crucial part of whatever it is we come, at last, to rebuild.

April 1991

PART FIVE

Welcome Home to Vietnam

The Last Laugh

I don't remember exactly when I first heard a Newfie joke, although it probably had something to do with how many Newfoundlanders it took to screw in a light bulb. Whatever it was, by the time I first heard it in the mid-1960s I had already spent four rollicking years on the island as a university student and apprentice journalist and had been immersed in real Newfoundland humour, so Newfie jokes didn't strike me as all that funny. I didn't really understand my own sour reaction back then, any more than I understood why the rich, black, self-disparaging wit you could pick up in even the tiniest outport seemed so sad. But the reaction to the Newfie jokes remains vivid. The really stupid ones even left me with some of the queasy feeling I associate with anti-Semitic jokes, no doubt an exaggerated reaction because the spectre of millennial persecution does not haunt Newfoundland – only the loss of nationhood.

All this came winging back at the bleak end of last December when I caught some of the televised obsequies for the late Joseph Smallwood, the first premier of the province of Newfoundland after it joined Canada in 1949, and the adroit propagandist who styled himself "the only living Father of Confederation" at a time – shortly before 1967 – when he wielded almost unquestioned power throughout his fief. That power was so complete that he was able to create a vast pork-barrel cabinet comprising a majority of members in the House of Assembly. This meant that even if every backbencher ratted on him – a most unlikely prospect – he could still control the government.

There is no doubt that Smallwood in his time was the most mesmerizing speaker in Canada. I used to cut lectures just to hear him rant and roar in parliamentary debates because his distinctive style – part Methodist stump preacher, part midway barker – was both colourful and compelling. The delight didn't last long. In no time I came to see him as sinister, someone who had lingered in power so long that he was undoing whatever good he had worked. The effects of his vindictiveness on political or any other kind of enemies, the futility and wastefulness of his Mad Hatter schemes for instant economic salvation, the destructive preening of his insatiable ego: all of these, along with other character flaws, set decent people in Newfoundland against each other and left a bitter residue of distrust and cynicism.

Summed up after his nine decades on earth at his state funeral, however, Joey came off rather well. The prime minister and the current premier of Newfoundland and Labrador spoke glowingly of his achievement, both on behalf of Newfoundlanders and in rounding out Canadian Confederation. He had extended the map of Canada to its "logical" extremity in the east, giving our national motto – "From sea even unto sea" – its full resonance. In return, the charitable instincts of Canadians, in the bureaucratic form of mothers' allowances and old-age-pension cheques, had stretched to embrace "the horny-handed sons of the sea." (I quote Mr. Smallwood.)

For Canadians, it was a reasonable enough bargain. The

feisty little demagogue who had dragged Newfoundland, half of it kicking and screaming, into Canada joined the tedious and fractious world of federal-provincial relations to become chief cheerleader and prize clown. For Newfoundlanders, though, the bargain is still a debatable point. That debate hasn't anything to do with ingratitude at Canadian largess over the years. Nor has it directly to do with the periodic bouts of Canadian contempt for Newfoundlanders and their traditions, of which the Newfie joke is merely a symptom. The business is far more deeply rooted, and we miss the point about Newfoundland at our peril.

The central dilemma in Canada today, the great festering contradiction that has been with us for 125 years, comes down to this: French Canadians aspire to nationhood while English Canadians fear the loss of it. Within our own borders, Newfoundland has the only cautionary example to offer – to everyone.

On the subject of national destiny, for example, Newfoundland has a real tale to tell. Most of the historic forces we claim spurred Canada on to seek independence from colonial ties were at work in the old Dominion of Newfoundland, from heroic service and tragic losses in the First World War to the gradual emergence of goals in trade and foreign affairs that were at variance with British imperial planning. Newfoundland had its own coinage, postage stamps, and national song. As a sovereign country, it enjoyed a salubrious blend of geographical logic, distinctive history, and an emerging cultural consciousness that paralleled what was happening in Canada, New Zealand, and Australia. It was also a small country sitting uncomfortably close to a big and powerful neighbour, and a measurable part of Newfoundland's national feeling was bound up in the perception of things that made it different from that neighbour. In this case, the neighbour was us.

Speaking to the notion held by some in English Canada that

joining a vastly greater neighbouring country is unthinkable, Newfoundlanders can report that the business is no more than cause and effect: just let the political life of your nation sink to the lowest level of venality, just let your economy limp along in a shambles, just drive away the brightest and best of your young people, and just dishearten those who are left with a lack of vision and foreshortened options. The unthinkable deed can be done easily in a mere few years.

To the notion, also held among some in English Canada, that joining a larger neighbour might be the best of all possible solutions, Newfoundlanders can tell you it comes with a heavy price, when – from time to time – you are cheated of your own resources, shackled in your ambitions, despised for your weakness, labelled a loser, and made the butt of cheap jokes.

To the notion that it is impossible for a distinct society (and one lacking the buffer of an officially different language at that) to persist within a larger entity, Newfoundlanders can tell you it's all janny-talk spoken by poor gommels. Quebec has the only cohesive social and imaginative culture in Canada to match Newfoundland's, though Quebeckers now ignore the ways that culture was preserved and extended by the creation of Canada. Newfoundlanders have had few real options in their history, but their reasons for joining in Confederation are more immediately in memory than ours. They have not forgotten that economic reality can supersede national pride, and that it has nothing to do with cultural distinctiveness. Their notions of the worth of union are such a poignant distillation of necessity, calculated self-interest, and gentle ambition that they could form an unwritten constitution far more practical and compelling than the tortured notions we hear on all sides today.

So maybe "the little fellow from Gambo" did, in the end, deserve the fine rhetoric and fancy funeral he got at the Roman Catholic basilica in St. John's – despite pitting Protestant against Catholic to get his way in the Confederation battle of

1948, despite his opportunism and random cruelties, and despite all the corruptions he succumbed to in power. He had a moment when he understood his people's immediate need and self-interest and married them to both his own ambition and a genuine vision of the possible. If it's true that "Great Canada" (I quote Mr. Smallwood again) has been the better for this vision, it is especially important during the current parlous times that we never forget Newfoundland's experience – for we are not immune to the same fate. In this sense *we are all Newfoundlanders*. So never laugh at a Newfie joke unless you want to laugh at yourself.

March 1992

Round Trip from Vietnam

⌇

On Tuesday, December 12, last year, more than 150 policemen and correctional officials from the British crown colony of Hong Kong entered a refugee camp and forcibly removed fifty-one Vietnamese nationals, put them on an airplane, and sent them back to their despised motherland. The operation, according to an unnamed Hong Kong official quoted in Reuter and Associated Press dispatches, went reasonably "smoothly." The police were equipped with helmets, shields, revolvers, and batons. Despite a bit of fuss – before she was quickly and efficiently bundled away, one woman screamed in broken Cantonese, "I don't want to go back to Vietnam!" – the whole business was completed within a few hours.

The authorities were aided by the early hour (3 a.m.), and the fact that the enforcers outnumbered the luckless three to one. Still, nothing was left to chance. In this first of a series of forced repatriations ordered by the British government, those chosen consisted of twenty-six children, sixteen women, and nine men. What ironic echoes are here from the gentlemanly

Empire our grandsires loved and on which the sun set not quite fast enough? Listen closely: *women and children first.*

The shanghai is a done thing. Not really covert, since the parliament at Westminster had been apprised of the intention earlier. The formal announcement of forced repatriation of Vietnamese refugees in Hong Kong was the only government pronouncement made by John Major during his ninety-five days as foreign minister of Great Britain. While it is true that his re-posting was occasioned by the cabinet turmoil that followed the resignation of Margaret Thatcher's chancellor of the exchequer, it seems apt that the public spokesman for one of the most squalid decisions to be announced in the "Mother of parliaments" should beat such a hasty and unlamented retreat.

In Hanoi, where the airplane later arrived under the watchful eyes of the British ambassador to Vietnam and his first secretary, we are told that everything went smoothly as well. But how are we to know for sure? The press was not invited. According to a subsequent report in *The Independent,* a non-aligned London newspaper, "The British said it was an extremely sensitive issue for the Vietnamese [who] . . . wanted no publicity. The Vietnamese said they had been asked by the British to keep reporters away." In this fashion, both the British and the Vietnamese governments conspired to save themselves the nuisance of independent scrutiny should there have been any embarrassing scenes during the unloading of the cargo.

There is a specific price-per-item Britain must pay for these transactions. The Communist regime in Hanoi was not prepared to repatriate its disgruntled citizens without financial consideration and, accordingly, for each child, woman, and man it returned, the British will cough up the curious sum of $620 (U.S., please). Most of this money is apparently to be deployed into "local development projects" to try to create work and housing for the returnees.

The British, to use the old boys' phrase, were prepared to take "a lot of stick" internationally for the forced-repatriation program. Predictably, Amnesty International found it offensive. So also, in more temperate language, did official spokesmen for Canada, the United States, and the United Nations. All things considered, though, outrage has been muted and the British have been clever in their stage management. Perhaps to give the world a short breather in which to assimilate the new reality, the Hong Kong government postponed further repatriation flights for a few weeks. This was sensible. The world and the media have already assimilated greater wrongs in shorter time periods. It took Canada's national newspaper, *The Globe and Mail*, for one, barely twenty-four hours to clear its editorial throat and provide a nicely balanced response. Pointing bravely to the United Nations convention on refugee status (which differentiates between those fleeing genuine political persecution from those merely fleeing poverty), and after briefly conceding that there actually was a "human dimension," Canada's Thunderer went on to conclude:

"Assuming a credible screening process [by the Hong Kong and British authorities] and non-retribution by Vietnam, we have trouble painting Britain or the colony as a villain."

These are hasty assumptions. There is no reason, for example, to credit anything said by officials in Vietnam. Their habit of deceit is as old as the Hanoi Communist regime itself. Say "night" and point to the stars and you'll be told it's daytime. The lies start at the top of the hierarchy and work their way throughout the entire system. The regime lied to the people of the South about their fate under Communism. Twelve years ago, when I interviewed the wily – and now, mercifully, late – premier, Pham Van Dong, he lied about Vietnam's plans to take over Cambodia and Laos. Vietnamese officials lie to international aid agencies, to visiting delegations, to business people, to church leaders. They lie at peace conferences and in the

General Assembly of the United Nations. They are particularly adept at lying about non-retribution. None of this is new information. Just about anyone who has had serious dealings with Hanoi can confirm the basic reality.

Nor should anyone assume that the British are able or willing to set up a credible screening process. The office of the United Nations High Commission for Refugees will not assist in any way with a program of forced repatriation. So we have to trust Great Britain in the business; and its overriding concern – overriding an eroding tradition of fairness and humanity – is, one way or another, to make these refugees go away. More than that: any faith in the process by which some 40,000 Vietnamese boat people, now huddled in camps in Hong Kong, will be screened has to be set against the far larger betrayal Great Britain has in store for Hong Kong itself when the entire colony will be repatriated to another Communist regime not generally noted for its devotion to due process and democratic equitability.

As we tumble into the bizarre last decade of the twentieth century everything seems turned on its head. In Europe, the impossible is happening and the structures of Communist totalitarianism that seemed so impervious to change are miraculously disintegrating. In Asia, the impossible is also happening. A democratic, parliamentary European power is working hand in glove with two notoriously vicious Communist regimes to deliver people into tyranny.

Now, of course, it gets really complicated. Although Great Britain's role in the repatriation affair, both directly and through its colonial administration in Hong Kong, is contemptible, there is a background that has to be acknowledged. More than any other port of entry, Hong Kong has been the most generous in receiving boat people from Vietnam – first, the wave upon wave of mostly ethnic Chinese from the south of Vietnam, and, more recently, the destitute ethnic Vietnamese from the north. The colony has clearly reached its saturation point with refugees. Poor Hong Kong! Like prisoners recruited in Nazi concentration camps to police their own fellows, officials in the crown colony are being made to go through a macabre dress rehearsal of what is in store for themselves in less than a decade. There was a wire photo taken on December 12 of a Hong Kong prison-service officer escorting a young Vietnamese boy out of the Phoenix House Detention Centre to the waiting airplane. The boy's eyes were glazed over in what appeared to be apprehension, but perhaps it was only tiredness, considering the hour. Paternally, the prison officer had an arm around his shoulder. In the background, slightly out of focus, two people clutched each other. Perhaps it was another prison official with a prisoner-refugee. Perhaps it was a refugee couple. Gender, race, and the luck of the draw (whether you were born in Hong Kong or Vietnam) were all impossible to discern. Only the presiding tragedy was clear. It is a picture I fear will come to haunt not only Hong Kong before its own repatriation deadline, 1997, but also all the rest of us thumb-twiddlers.

For who in the world has been prompt with practical help? Not Europe, certainly, although perhaps, with its current historic preoccupations, it can be excused. Not Japan. Japan rarely takes in refugees – it throws money at them to keep them away. Not Australia, not New Zealand, not any of the nations that make up ASEAN. Not the Commonwealth. The Commonwealth can't even come up with a coherent sentence on the subject.

The United States, which did condemn the forced repatriation, nevertheless continues to treat Vietnam as an international pariah, and this is not merely a diplomatic snub – it has practical consequences. There is a growing body of opinion that holds the only effective way to stem the haemorrhage from Vietnam is to assist in the improvement of economic conditions within the country. But this can't be done without a combination of multinational aid and a change in the U.S. government's attitude – an attitude still rooted in its uncomfortable memories of war and defeat. Of course Vietnam has a nasty regime. It may, however, be somewhat less nasty than the Chinese regime President George Bush is courting so assiduously these days. The hypocrisy would be better deployed Hanoi's way at the moment: Vietnam is finally showing signs of coming to terms with economic reforms, urged by the International Monetary Fund, that might improve the general lot of its population and the process should be encouraged.

And what of our own dear home and native land? Canada, as immigration minister Barbara McDougall has pointed out, has led the world in per capita acceptance of refugees over the past few years. That should be something of which to be proud, but the pride is undermined by the fact that our immigration policy is almost impossible to discern and our immigration system is in perfect chaos – backlogged, arbitrary, and all too often reactionary. The lack of a coherent policy is tied directly to our inability as a country to respond with intelligence to a dramatically changing world.

For close to two decades now, we have been toying with the still novel notion that Canada is part of the Pacific basin, too. Our own self-interest, which has always been the litmus test in past immigration policy, points now in the direction of Asia. During the earlier part of this century, when the national need was to populate the prairies, we turned to Eastern Europe to find the bodies. The national need today is to keep expanding our industrial and entrepreneurial base – to make free trade work, to expand into the Pacific market, to meet the challenge of the looming European multinational giant.

It is hard to think of a more qualified immigrant today than a feisty Asian refugee who has experienced first-hand the personal, economic, and social degradation of Communist totalitarianism. If we had had an immigration policy that was coherent and consistent, we would have been able to respond very quickly to this current tragedy in Hong Kong. Instead of watching on the sidelines as those fifty-one boat people were dispatched back into their nightmare, we could have asked Great Britain to send them our way, along with a few thousand more. Not for charity's sake, but for our own. We could also have taken the lead in getting other countries to join us in dealing with the problem directly. As it was, we made our little protest and then washed our hands of the business.

And this was a very great shame. I do not know what anyone else thought upon seeing that wire photo of the bewildered Vietnamese lad as he was being led away from all hope. I myself thought he looked like a fine young Canadian.

March 1990

A Fifty Per Cent Solution

~

U ntil recently, it seemed pretty clear that the monarchy in Canada was a lost cause. Even in that former bastion of royalist sycophancy, the Anglican Church of Canada, the prayers for the sovereign had been quietly interred. In 1989, *Saturday Night* itself carried an essay arguing that the drift away from monarchy was historically and politically inevitable. This year, to settle the matter definitively, the editor in chief of *The Globe and Mail* gave the Queen permission to stay put (because of the affection felt for her by older Canadians), but has ruled out any consideration of her son and heir's coming into his Canadian kingdom.

All this fitted neatly into the presiding propaganda. Few individuals who laid claim to understanding the national psyche – whether they were statesmen, leading authors, high academics, or accountants – had anything positive to say about a "foreign" head of state. Those who did immediately got labelled eccentric or pig-stupid. Since the Queen was mostly absent from the country and her role was almost entirely symbolic, a pervasive sentiment held that the whole creaky packaging of our head of state was a sign of an incomplete country. The other side of the equation was rarely heard any more: that a powerless monarchy is the crowning triumph of a peaceful constitutional arrangement and that, by choosing to retain the services of a royal house whose history has been so inextricably woven into our own, Canadians – however inadvertently – have shown considerable political sophistication.

Then something weird happened. A Gallup poll released late last summer, and published in the republican *Toronto Star*, revealed that fifty per cent of all Canadians did want to retain the Queen as head of state and generally approved of a Canadian monarchy.

Fancy that! *Fifty per cent.* (Those opposed amounted to only thirty-six per cent, while fourteen per cent didn't know what they thought.) After nearly three decades of government embarrassment and confusion over who the head of state actually is; after years of hardly ever playing "God Save the Queen" at official functions; after leaving two generations of schoolchildren largely innocent of the positive underpinnings of a constitutional monarchy; after conscious efforts to transform the office of governor general into either a home-folks presidency (Ed Schreyer) or our very own petty autocracy (the inimitable Jeanne Sauvé): after all this, and despite all this, Good Old Bess is still on her throne across the sea – grumpy on her bad days and smiling gamely on the good ones – and she is more than three times as popular as the majority government we ourselves elected.

Fifty per cent! (And the figure took into account the predictably low statistics from Quebec, where only twenty-three per cent of the population were said to be monarchists and fifty-eight per cent were ready to trot the sovereign off in a constitutional tumbrel.) What is going on here? The Gallup poll made a point of reporting that there was no appreciable difference in response between young people and old and, though it did not break down respondents by ethnic origin, its universe surely incorporated the huge demographic changes wrought by recent immigration – a lot of it from countries with something other than a strong monarchic tradition. How can this be?

The current turmoil in Canada has clarified many things, it seems. For some time, acquiescent English-speaking Canadians had assumed that a "British" monarchy was a significant hindrance to unity. In fact, it now has to be seen as only a minor one and, as hindrances go, can't even begin to compete with the horrors we regularly foist upon ourselves. In any just and mutually acceptable working relationship between Quebec and the rest of the country, the monarchy hardly figures as even a side issue.

Indeed this apparent irrelevance could be the principal means of saving and refurbishing the monarchy as a more useful institution than we have recently allowed. An illogical head of state might make no sense in a logical country. In an illogical country such as Canada, where cantankerous regional and ethnic diversity may yet be our undoing, it may – thanks to the patent neutrality of this particular monarchical system – be as close to astute political wisdom as we are ever going to get. Think about it. Do we really want some wretched honorary president who is going to have to be appointed with the same pork-barrel sensitivity as is a senator from New Brunswick or British Columbia? Or do we want an elected presidency, so that we can further focus our political hatreds and frustrations? Half the country knows the answers to these questions. Half the country prefers the proven professionals already on the job.

I know, I know: the members of our royal family all have those squishy accents. Does it carry any weight to point out that the English have for centuries managed to survive as a coherent nation with monarchs who spoke with thick accents – French accents, Welsh accents, Scottish accents, Dutch accents, German accents – if they even spoke the Queen's English in the first place? We ourselves have made do with governors general stumbling bravely through their incompetence in one, and sometimes both, of our official languages.

The fact that the Canadian sovereign doesn't actually reside among us seems the biggest plus of all. I used to think that a crucial reason the monarchy was dying in Canada was the general neglect it was falling into. How can you maintain popular interest in and loyalty for an institution shrouded in misunderstanding and deprived of attention? In the United States, the cameras practically go into the White House washrooms, so obsessed are the media with covering every waking moment of a president's life.

But this thinking was wrong-headed. It is clear now that the monarchy is going to die of overexposure in Great Britain sooner than it will drift away from underexposure here. Literally. Let poor Prince Andrew go for a discreet skinny dip on a private beach with his three-year-old daughter, unmindful of a telephoto lens, and within days the royal buttocks are served up in millions of newspapers. The recent and grotesquely inflated speculation on the state of the Prince and Princess of Wales's marriage set new journalistic lows even on Britain's royal soap-opera circuit. Given human nature, it is not utterly surprising to learn that the couple might have been going through adjustment problems as their tenth wedding anniversary approached; all other sustained relationships go through such stresses. But few have to endure what Charles and Diana did a few months ago. There could also be a constitutional cost if the burden of the scrutiny wrecks the marriage and scuttles an orderly succession to the throne.

These are not fairyland people in the House of Windsor, however much they dress themselves up or we dress them down. As any Canadian journalist who has covered a royal tour can testify, the Queen goes about her duties in a conscientious and uncontroversial fashion. Controversy and drama come mostly from the fertile minds of reporters and their editors, the minds becoming more fertile in direct proportion to the lack of controversy and drama on the tour. In style, the royal family is relentlessly sensible and middle-class, except of course on those great occasions of state when the ancient mystery and pageantry of monarchy connect our collective past with the present and remind us of the solemn dignity we bestow upon the human condition by maintaining such an institution.

The style is also in wonderfully professional contrast to general pretensions among the high and mighty. I was once invited to attend an annual meeting of officers of the United World Colleges presided over by the Prince of Wales, who was patron of the organization. (Pearson College on Vancouver Island is Canada's contribution to these adventurous high schools for teenagers from all over the world.) One college chairman, Galen Weston, head of the family food conglomerate, whooshed in and out in a flashy helicopter. Another, Armand Hammer, the reptilian zillionaire who made much of his fortune from maintaining good relations with the worst elements of the old Soviet hierarchy, arrived by personal jet. He was then conveyed to a humble Welsh village inn in a cavalcade of two stretch limousines with darkened windows and three lesser vehicles brimful of senior assistants, private security personnel, and assorted flunkies. Before Hammer dared to emerge into the daylight, he was preceded by the security team who set up a bulletproof screen in the sitting room of the inn, behind which he ultimately took a seat. Prince Charles turned up with one aide-de-camp in a Ford Escort.

The modest style, alas, does not prevent the media madness that daily afflicts the role of the monarch in the principal kingdom of the Queen. In missing all this, we are missing nothing. Canada is a noisy, bickering, rather unpleasant nation right now, and having a neutral, aloof head of state who has spent all her life in an act of conspicuous and consistent service to a constitutional ideal seems, as the dust and chicken feathers fly up again, an extraordinary bit of luck. Tattered and undervalued, the monarchy in Canada has somehow made it almost into the twenty-first century. As its former significance recedes, its benefits seem correspondingly precious. Or at least, so say half of all of us, which in the Canada of 1991 amounts to a raging consensus.

November 1991

German Baggage

~

I n Canada, where history often seems inconvenient, the
passage of a couple of years is usually sufficient to obliterate
from the public memory even the worst villains and the
most rancorous events. Not so in Germany. Two generations
have elapsed since the rise of Adolf Hitler, yet the demon of the
twentieth century seems, in some ways, as potent today as he
was in the beer gardens of Munich in the early 1930s. He festers
in the German consciousness – in part, as I discovered a few
years ago when I spent a lot of time travelling around and reporting on the two Germanies, because he festers in our own.

In the West, Hitler is invoked dozens of times each year in
books, in magazine and newspaper articles, in movies, and on
television. He is a motor force within the entertainment and
publishing industries, operating on all levels from the crassest
opportunism (the Hitler "diary" scam of a few years ago) to brilliant scholarship (Modris Eksteins's recently published study
of the foundations of modernism, *Rites of Spring*).

In Eastern Europe, at least until very recently, a similar obsession – differently oriented – could be observed. The old Soviet

empire, always lusting for legitimacy, found its best line of defence in remembrance of the extraordinary sacrifices of its people during the Great Patriotic War. Here, Hitler also helped in blurring the imprint of raw terror that Joseph Stalin himself represented, and in the ensuing triumph of the "lesser evil" can much postwar tragedy be glimpsed.

For many of the Germans I spoke to, the feverish focus of outsiders on the twelve years of Nazi rule seemed endlessly unfair. After all, most of them – East or West – bore no personal responsibility for Hitler's cosmic sins. Yet every time Germans pushed out on the world, their past was brought forward and their noses were rubbed in it. When Boris Becker first emerged a champion at Wimbledon in 1985, the tennis correspondent of *The Times* of London mused whimsically (in a front-page article) on the German enthusiasm for the famous centre court. Curious, he wrote, when you consider how "they" had bombed it during the war.

And now the Germans are reunifying themselves, at breakneck speed. What was virtually impossible to imagine less than a year ago, except in the most theoretical and far-off way, may be a reality before this year is over. Germans and outsiders alike are left breathless in the midst of one of the great historical realignments of the twentieth century, hardly capable of accommodating the dramatic new reality, let alone being able to figure out the implications for the future. And still, to go back to Germany, as I did a few weeks ago, stirs up all the old unwelcome questions, prompts the same convoluted and sometimes self-conscious responses – on one side or the other. The German moment – inexorable as it is logical – has come again, but the baggage of the past still has to be lugged through the turnstile.

In Bonn, the sleepiest of capital cities in the West, certain functionaries are undeniably frisky these days. And who can blame them? The collapse of authority in the Communist regime in

East Germany and the imminent prospect of reunification lie at the heart of a dream most Germans thought unattainable in their lifetimes. Herr D. is a high official with the commission on German unity which, until very recently, was a minor bureau-cratic sop to that dream. In the past, the commission arranged exchange visits between schools in the two Germanies and fos-tered other small-scale friendship projects, thereby allowing the West German government to point to something tangible, however inconsequential, to prove its commitment to even-tual unity.

Now, of course, the official and his office – both slated for upgrading – are riding the reunification crest. Unfortunately, Herr D. has also been chosen as one of the first government spokesmen ("not for direct attribution") to brief a group of visit-ing journalists who have been invited to Bonn to ponder "The German Question." This is an officially organized attempt by the West Germans to be open and forthright about reunification and to waylay any lingering fears that a Fourth Reich is about to rear up in the middle of Europe. As it turns out, none of the visit-ing journalists – from Canada, Finland, Great Britain, Holland, Ireland, Italy, Sweden, and the United States – is unduly con-cerned. Nor does anyone think, despite a certain amount of black humour, that today's Germans are Nazis in sheep's cloth-ing. At least they weren't concerned when they filed into Herr D.'s briefing. By the time they file out, there is a hint of a doubt.

The Dutch journalists have needled the gauleiter about an undue mood of triumphalism they've been detecting in his pro-nouncements. "Look," he says ominously. "This thing [reunifi-cation] is going to happen. And in the end, we are going to remember who our friends have been."

This, of course, serves only to excite the pack, which then pushes him on other points. Herr D. chooses to dig himself in deeper. "If reunification is thwarted by other countries," he

says, "then it might arouse unfortunate national sentiments
of resentment, and we wouldn't want to see that happen, I
don't think."

"No, no, no," say the Dutch journalists, almost in unison and
with mock horror, "we wouldn't want to see that!" They have
bagged their first German official. In the end, during a week-
long tour, we never met another bureaucrat or politician quite
so muscular as this one. The majority were sensible and sensitive, particularly in the foreign ministry and the Bundestag
(federal parliament). All – save Herr D. – seemed weighed down
by the burden of dealing with the thousands of East Germans
who continued to pour daily through the leaky border. But Herr
D. made a notable impact.

Lübeck, on the Baltic Sea, is one of the proud old Hanseatic
cities, independent of any larger German entity right up to the
day Hitler annexed it to the Third Reich in 1937. Now it sits
uncomfortably snug beside the border with the east and waits
with wary patience for its part of the Great Wall of Germany to
come down.

An old friend, Irmgard K., lives here. She is a retired high-
school teacher and principal, and a determined world traveller,
whom I first encountered deep in the interior of China. She is
not one of the mythical "good Germans" (since she would
remind you, in any event, that she's Prussian); she is simply a
good person who has seen terrible things in her lifetime and
overcome them with vigour, common sense, quiet faith, and
twinkling irony.

As passions, we have English literature and German music in
common. Irmgard spent the better part of the 1930s at Trinity
College, Dublin, and makes no bones about the fact that this
gave her "an Irish edge" as she followed events in the father-
land. A dutiful daughter, she spent the war years in Berlin tend-
ing to her parents' welfare and trying to avoid confrontations

with the authorities. Because of her unblemished non-Nazi past, she was among the first Berlin residents allowed by the conquering Allies to teach, and she thus began a hallowed task of nurturing the wounded, and in many cases orphaned, children of a blighted city. Today, she says she never again got to teach students quite so miraculous as those of the immediate postwar years, all of whom had to claw their way out of the nightmare. Each Christmas, in an act of conspicuous remembrance, she brings out the Christmas decorations that some of them made from bits of paper, wood, and metal scavenged from garbage.

"In later years, the students would ask what we did when the Nazis were in power," she told me. "They learned on their own the really terrible things, but what they wanted to understand was the 'normality.' I never believed in avoiding or falsifying reality. So I would tell them the truth. I told them that most people tried to keep their heads low and get through the day."

"Things happen so fast, our memory of great events that took place only a few months ago seems worthless today." Walter Bröker talked quietly in an East Berlin restaurant. He was at the forefront of the movement to bring down the hated Communist regime last autumn and he has been an "activist" for years. I first met him four years ago after a Communion service in Gethsemane (Lutheran) Church. The church stood up to the Communists, having been given a second chance after its craven subservience to the Nazis. A devout Christian, an architect, a devoted husband, and a ridiculously sappy father, he feels – at least when we talked in the early spring – left behind by the pace of events. Still, he remains as brave a man as I know.

Walter is typical of those East Germans who first undermined the seemingly monolithic authority of the German Communist government. In retrospect, he will now admit that he was naive to think his countrymen would accept a gradual, stoical slide into reunion. Impatience and geographical proximity to West German affluence looked after all that. And who can blame the East Germans? For years they were told they had the show-case economy in the East bloc, and now that the Berlin Wall has been transformed into a concrete doily the absurd hollow-ness of the boast seems especially grating.

"We have entered a time when no one wants to think back, just ahead," said Walter. "Just get on with things. Don't stop to analyse." He laughed, but he looked sad and was exhausted – like a victor in a wasting war.

West Berliners certainly forget some things fast. The last time I was in the city, no politician or public pundit failed to trot out the ritualistic, and no doubt heartfelt, line about the indecency of the Berlin Wall. "A government that has to fence in its people is run by nothing more than prison guards," said Greta, a well-known visitors' escort who works freelance for the govern-ment. That was a couple of years ago. After two months of greeting – daily – tens of thousands of East Berlin comrades-in-arms (hundreds of thousands on the weekends), with their dila-pidated, smelly Trabant automobiles, the line has changed. "Finally we had to tell them, 'Enough! You are welcome to come and look at our store windows, but leave your horrid cars at home.'"

The Plötzensee Memorial is not a particularly popular West Berlin tourist spot. Taxi drivers don't like to take you there. It consists of a small and attractively planted garden; a smallish, one-storey, dark-bricked building; and a guardhouse. The entire compound – about half an acre – is surrounded by a contempo-rary brick wall. The building is an execution house, built and first used at the end of the nineteenth century as part of a large prison complex. The means of execution then was the guillo-tine. During the Third Reich, the same building saw the dispatch of special enemies of the Nazis: trade unionists, parliamentarians, Communists, Christians, the July 20, 1944, plotters against Hitler's life. For these, the guillotine was insufficiently horrible and too quick. In its place, five large butcher's hooks were suspended from the single steel beam that runs the breadth of the building, and on these the victims were strung up, often with piano wire. Today, only one hook remains. The floor is earthen. Apart from the hook and the beam, the only other item is the rough concrete sink on a side wall where the executioners washed their hands.

Plötzensee Memorial is important to the West German government because it establishes that there were Germans who opposed Hitler and paid a dreadful price. It has none of the cosmic horror of the concentration-camp memorials maintained to commemorate the Holocaust. At Plötzensee, perhaps only 2,500 or so Germans perished during Hitler's time. But the apparatus of death is so visibly grisly and the sense of the executions so proximate that it shakes you to the bones.

On the morning of my last day in Berlin, I went to Plötzensee. There was only one other visitor. She was an older woman and she was kneeling directly under the hook in prayer, or perhaps simply in deep thought. In front of her, she had placed a small bouquet of freesia on the ground. It was an intolerable collage of sight, smell, and remembrance of things past, and like a coward I fled.

June 1990

Scandal in the Church

~

I n the latest full census, in 1981, Roman Catholicism was confirmed once again as the strongest Christian denomination in Canada – a position it had long held. But the census also reported that Catholics, devout or nominal, accounted for almost half the country's population. Today, nine years later, it's likely that they constitute a clear majority. There is real curiosity here. Following the Reformation, a number of countries switched from Catholic domination to Protestant control. Canada may now be the only Protestant country in the world to have become Roman Catholic.

Census figures, of course, can be as misleading as describing a country by religious affiliation. Many respondents will claim formal connections to a church or faith who can't, in any meaningful sense, be considered denominational adherents. Statistics on regular church attendance, or even nominal attendance (Christmas, Easter, and a wedding or two), confirm the larger reality: by and large, Canadians today have embraced agnosticism or humanism or whatever other fancy word covers a shrug of indifference to religious affairs.

Yet the postwar statistical ascendancy of the Roman Catholic Church in Canada cannot be shrugged off quite so easily. As a national presence, the Church plays a crucial, and sometimes controversial, role in the country. On the positive side, it is the most important nongovernmental institution transcending and often ameliorating the corrosive specifics of the bilingualism debate. Whatever fissures or factions exist within the Church itself, here is a sturdy organization that bridges language and regional differences in a fundamental way. In another sphere altogether, the Church is often the first to reach out to newly arrived immigrants, beginning the crucial process of cultural and social adjustment.

These are areas – and there are others – in which the Roman Catholic Church has played a helpful role in the life of a fractious nation. Elsewhere, the effects of its powerful position are more complicated. During the recession of 1982, the Commission on Social Affairs of the Canadian Conference of Catholic Bishops published "Ethical Reflections on the Economic Crisis." In bringing to bear a critical gaze and censorious rhetoric on the then Liberal administration's economic policies, and on how these policies were affecting ordinary Canadians, the bishops caused major consternation. Precisely because they spoke with a presumed moral authority to a majority constituency, their intervention seemed a bid to wield political influence.

Reciprocally, over the past few decades, governments – which can also read census figures – seem to have bent to the reality of the Catholic ascendancy. (Is it symbolic that no prime minister since Lester B. Pearson has been a non-Catholic?) In Ontario, the Church's educational franchise was extended from separate elementary schools to incorporate a publicly funded separate high-school system which has already proved itself to be vigorous, tenacious, and expansionary. Meanwhile, other provincial governments have for several years engaged quietly in dovetailing their social and remedial programs with already existing Catholic agencies.

None of this is, in itself, sinister, but as a backdrop to recent scandals in Newfoundland and Saskatchewan it does sound an alarm, besides embracing a considerable irony. In the very season of its numerical preponderance in the country, the Roman Catholic Church in Canada has never looked more exposed and corrupt. Yet its involvement is a subject upon which, apart from reporting the specifics of the scandals, the media are still wary of commenting. This is a bad mistake for there is much here to do with the public's rightful business.

That said, it is important first to separate the internal problems of a church in crisis from those dysfunctions that impinge directly on the state. Among "family matters" with which the Church has to wrestle alone, a precipitously declining number of entrants to the priesthood is foremost. Coming immediately behind is the open flouting of Vatican strictures on everything from birth control to theological orthodoxy. The hierarchical and sometimes secretive nature of church governance is also a dilemma for Catholics themselves to struggle with, especially in a country that practises democracy and encourages egalitarianism. Ditto the role of women. Celibacy is the same sort of conundrum, though it is one that the wider world has misunderstood. So often cited glibly as the root cause of the horrors at Mount Cashel Orphanage in St. John's, celibacy may or may not be a contributing factor in the difficulties of recruitment to the priesthood and lay orders. As such, it is a matter for intramural debate and resolution. But it is not the public issue it has been made to seem: the particular aberrational behaviours ascribed as the consequence of celibacy afflict all denominations – and, indeed, other callings – which do not require their practitioners formally to abstain from sexual relations.

Where any of this intrudes upon the life of the body politic is at the precise point where the Church starts pushing out into secular affairs, especially when public money is involved. There is a very good argument to be made for the involvement of any responsible denomination or other religious group in certain areas of public policy and in certain social programs. Generally, the country is the better for the diversity offered by denominationally sponsored schools, refugee programs, old-age homes, youth hostels, halfway houses, hospices, and centres for the handicapped, the disadvantaged, or the homeless. But their sponsorship must not shield such enterprises from audit or policing, must not exempt them from any of the procedures by which a society protects individuals from institutional abuse.

Yet the clear message coming out of the recent and much-publicized scandals is that Roman Catholic institutions are "sacred cows" and not to be held to account. The church connection with the Bosco Homes in Saskatchewan hampered or actually suspended the usual protective monitoring – from media coverage to social-agency scrutiny. In the case of Mount Cashel Orphanage, police investigation was sidetracked and dead-ended. Whether the cover-ups were invited by the Church or automatically applied by a reverent constituency is irrelevant: by accepting them, by translating internal hierarchical indifference or cowardice into the public sector, the Church stored up for itself a fearful reckoning. Its tarnished public face is now diminishing – even degrading – its legitimacy, integrity, and potential dynamism.

For the public interest in the short term, it is an easy enough matter to resolve. Either the Church can clean up its act and run its secular institutions in a manner fit for public scrutiny, or it can't. If it can't, the state has an obligation to intervene and forbid the Church's participation in social-agency work. For the Church itself, there is much more involved than its eroding image and beleaguered social-action policies. The Roman Catholic Church in Canada is also part of a worldwide organization that has carried the weight of human aspiration and human culpability for nearly two millenniums. In many parts of the world – Africa, Eastern Europe, Central and South America – it is not only a crucial agency but often the only standard-bearer of decency, courage, and spiritual renewal. Yet, thanks to a unique history, Catholicism is also encumbered with centuries of forgotten controversies and the dead weight of medieval compromises.

So, in the end, as far as the Church is concerned, everything is connected: the bad with the good, the decaying with the renewing, despair with hope, the profane with the sacred, hierarchical prerogatives with demands for change, the historical legacy with the current dilemma. From the Church in Canada recently, we have been learning more than we ever wanted to know about the dark side of trust. This has to be corrected in a forthright, public manner, no matter how painful the process is. And it will be painful because reforms in the public sector are caught up with all those thorny "family matters" that have to be struggled with urgently and alone.

February 1990

Truth and Consequences

~

S omething basic snapped last year following the failure of the Meech Lake accord. There are those who would say that it snapped a year and a half earlier during the free-trade election, and that in any event it is all Brian Mulroney's fault. Others might argue that the rot set in decades ago: John Diefenbaker was to blame, or Lester Pearson, or – mindful of the venom stored up at the end of his reign – Pierre Trudeau.

A few historians (not generally the ones we care to hear from these days) could point out that the coming together of Canada in the 1860s carried within its process all the ingredients of deconstruction we see today, from the obvious (language rights) to the arcane (Senate prerogatives), and that the nation has always been at risk. Whatever. Something basic has gone out of our collective life, and Canada stands exposed as a nation where the will to survive seems lost.

Certainly the historical and evolving process by which Canada was kept together for nearly a century and a quarter is now thoroughly despised. It was a process requiring a consensus, which might arise from any combination of necessity, vision, expediency, skulduggery, and common sense. We'll have none of it now, thank you very much: we haven't any solutions, but – dammit – we know what we *don't* like any more. In this ultimate triumph of the Canadian penchant for negativism, one thing is abundantly clear: everyone is talking and no one is listening.

We have a prime minister and a leader of the opposition who are both from Quebec and, it could be argued, are well placed to work out either tentative or long-term solutions, but we don't want to listen to either of them even if they had anything to say. Contemporary political logic has become streamlined: we voted for them, therefore we despise them. In Canada today, we don't like anything that reminds us of yesterday, let alone last year or a decade ago.

Quebec itself is definitely not listening to anything from English Canada that does not feed directly into its historic grievances and sense of thwarted nationhood. In this light, most Quebeckers prefer to focus on the few aggrieved communities in English Canada that formally rejected bilingualism, rather than all the other communities that endorsed the concept – communities that a generation ago wouldn't have given French a second thought. Quebec's media had a field day with a ludicrous, mostly geriatric, anti-French revolt in Brockville, Ontario, featuring a pathetic desecration of the Quebec flag, failing to see in the burlesque business – as did many non-francophones – the degree to which mainstream English Canada had forsaken its own old tribalism.

On and on it goes. All of English Canada, in this version, rejected Quebec when the Meech Lake agreement collapsed. But the process, as we allowed it to develop, dictated political unanimity, an absurdity that not even the Lord God Jehovah demanded of the twelve tribes of Israel. This, then, is how three hold-outs – Clyde Wells, Sharon Carstairs, and Elijah Harper – came to represent the stance of all English Canada to Quebec. It was a comprehensive slander, but a popular one.

Quebeckers are in the thrall of their old dreams because right now they know they have a new and unparalleled chance to lunge for sovereignty. Confident in economic survival for the first time in their history, they have reached an idiot's conclusion that it is time to go it alone. God grant them the wisdom of St. Teresa of Avila, who understood what comes to those whose prayers are answered. The French fact has been maintained in North America not just by the constancy and loyalty implicit in Quebec's stirring motto, *Je me souviens*. It has also been sustained, buttressed, and ultimately extended by the uncomfortable and often belligerent alliance with English Canada, which necessitated on Quebec's part a constant inventory and refurbishment of the language arsenal. You don't have to be a cynic to wonder how long it will be before a sovereign government of an independent Quebec, freed from historic vigilance against some 19 million English Canadians, will start making language concessions to the economic reality of 270 million English-speaking North Americans.

In English Canada, also, the deafness is almost complete. Who among us understood that in coming to the bargaining table with the Meech Lake accord, Quebec – for the first time since Confederation – was saying yes to Canada? Who understood the irony?

Who in English Canada is recalling that, up to three decades ago, Canada was, in effect, a unilingual English-speaking nation with minor concessions made to the Catholic peasants huddled on the shores of the St. Lawrence? Who is remembering today that the greatest appeal of applying a relatively modest program of bilingualism to English Canada was not that it was "the decent thing to do" but that it was the best guarantee of Canadian distinctiveness in North America? The stakes we have in each other are so deep that everyone has forgotten them or pays them no regard.

English Canada doesn't give much of a damn about Quebec

at the moment. It is fed up. This is something the intensely myopic Quebec media have been slow to understand, but it is easily as crucial an ingredient in the deconstruction of the nation as Quebec's assertiveness. English Canada is busy putting on regional armour: Prairie reform, Ontario social justice, or Maritime economic union – you name it, there's a lifeboat out there somewhere with a local message that you can swim towards as the SS *Canada* goes under from sea even unto sea.

Is there a way of averting the mess we seem determined to embrace? I don't believe it, although I have read a mother lode of both tough and wimpish advice from a variety of concerned and committed Canadians (and given out dollops of both myself). The deconstruction process looks set to continue apace. Would the Meech Lake accord have changed all this? It might have, but we will never know. Unfortunately, there is a strong though speculative argument to be made that it wouldn't have worked. Still, it would have been a gesture. The nation is in desperate need of gestures from all sides, yet today even gestures have fallen into deficit.

We can, therefore, begin writing the obituary for Canada as we know it. George Grant wrote one in *Lament for a Nation* during the 1960s and it can easily be updated. But why start so recently? During my own parents' time, which begins in 1912 at the outset of King George V's reign, there have been other laments for other ideas of Canadian nationhood. And before that, still other laments for yet different ideas. The only thing that hasn't seemed to alter is the notion of Canada as a *country*. This does not seem to be the same as Canada as a nation. Canada as a country is a place, a state of mind, a forgathering of fortunate souls, an awesome struggle, a birthright, a longed-for destination, an ancestral burying ground, an endless opportunity.

The business of deconstructing the nation may, in the end, destroy the country, but that fate is actually up to all of us. We could start by rethinking our attitude to elected parliamentarians, regional and national, and then fortify them with the strength of our conviction that a beloved country has more than a whimper of support. Elected representatives may be weak vessels, but in a democracy – just in case anyone has forgotten – they are us. If English Canada needs some reciprocal gestures from Quebec, and it does, it is also strong enough to make the first approach in a new round of wooing. If English Canada is weary of wooing, let it – like Quebec – consider the consequences honestly. This has often been a harsh and illogical country, it is true; but Canada has never been an unyielding or unforgiving one. Even to the fools who inhabit it.

March 1991

Up the Creek

~

From *Guide To Happiness In Marriage* by Dr. D. Luck:

> *When two people enter into a marriage, it is like going on a trip on a river in a canoe. There are two destinations on the river. Upstream is Total BLISS AND HAPPINESS, referred to as B&H. Downstream is Total DESPAIR AND UNHAPPINESS, referred to as D&U . . . . I am afraid that even if the canoe is set in the correct direction, the current is against you. There is no motor to help. You must work and work hard to reach B&H. The consequence of not paddling is to drift to D&U. Naturally, if you paddle in the wrong direction you will make it to D&U in a very short time.*

Dr. Luck is a family doctor of Asian-Caribbean background who practises in southern Ontario. The first and only time our paths crossed, many years ago, was because of our mutual interest in China. Recently, though, he sent me his how-to pamphlet (published by JCL Enterprises in Oshawa, Ontario) on gaining and sustaining happiness in long-term relationships. There is not such a wealth of practical guidance on this subject that efforts like Dr. Luck's can be lightly ignored. Much of what is available is far too subtle, requiring as it does a mastery of psychodynamics and exotic sexual gamesmanship. Dr. Luck, on the other hand, is always down-to-earth. "As the means of gaining happiness, marriage has to be considered a high risk investment," he writes. "The amount you can get depends on how much you invest. Of course, like any gamble you can also lose." So the arrival of his pithy guide seemed propitious, especially on a day when everything else was bleak.

On that same day, you see, the papers were overflowing with the news that the Prince and Princess of Wales were going to part:

> LONDON – *The sad end to a royal fairy-tale romance was announced simultaneously yesterday by both Buckingham Palace and British prime minister John Major. The Prince and Princess of Wales are going their separate ways, although they will not seek a divorce. The storm-tossed couple have rarely been out of the headlines the past year. . . .*

And this was also the very day I finished reading Iris Nowell's *Hot Breakfast for Sparrows*, a saddening account of her long and ultimately corrosive affair with the late painter Harold Town, one of the most sensational egoists this country has ever produced:

> *Love in its infinite capacities will hold together even the meanest of unions until the smelling salts of reality are whiffed and the brain clears. My brain cleared when I realized Harold had been taking advantage of me. . . . Harold was a fascinating, dynamic, brilliant man. He was also mean, stingy, selfish, and callous.*

If only Dr. Luck had had a chance to work with Iris and Harold, I feel certain their troubled relationship could have been straightened up. If only he had a chance to work with Charles and Diana, we might have – instead of mutual recrimination and bitterness, or Total D&U – a pair of happy campers paddling together through the swift waters towards the grassy, sunlit uplands of Total B&H.

It's only a matter, after all, of keeping to DR. LUCK'S RULES OF MARRIAGE:

(1) *Keep the promises you made.*
(2) *Learn to enjoy sex together. (Marriages are made or broken up in bed.)*
(3) *Never spend more than you earn. (When money goes out the door, love flies through the window.)*
(4) *Never hit back.*
(5) *There is no boss. (It does not matter who steers the canoe, so long as it is going in the right direction.)*
(6) *Do not fight. (If you fight in a canoe, it will overturn.)*
(7) *Work together. (You must paddle in the same direction or you will get nowhere.)*

In the case of Harold and Iris, Dr. Luck could have told them at once that their affair, which began in 1963 and lasted – off and on – for twenty-four years, was doomed. "TO REACH TOTAL BLISS AND HAPPINESS," he writes in block capitals, underlined for still greater emphasis, "PLEASE DO NOT COMMIT ADULTERY." Never mind that Iris thought Harold brought "more love and joy into my life than I could have possibly imagined"; what with Harold already married and Iris letting herself fall into a subservient position, she should – they both should – have distrusted the pleasure as an illusion. "Let me make one observation on adultery," writes Dr. Luck firmly. "Having sex with a new partner under quite different conditions from having it with your spouse would undoubtedly produce more excitement, more thrills and even more enjoyment – but is it a fair comparison? It takes a lot of maturity to enjoy the same meal at home as much as at a luxurious restaurant."

Iris should have seen the table d'hôte for what it was: an appetizer of chance encounter and furtiveness; a main course of guilt; and a backbiting dessert of rueful bickering. "I am very sorry," says Dr. Luck, "but if you commit adultery, I believe you have knowingly steered your canoe onto a rock, and there is a big hole in it."

The case of Charles and Diana is profoundly different. They are married and for reasons of state they are not going to be allowed a divorce. A couple who cannot disembark from a canoe that will not be allowed to sink can go on paddling contrariwise for only so long, one would think, before sheer exhaustion will lead them to seek guidance and direction. And what does Dr. Luck have to offer?

LOVE YOUR WIFE AS YOU LOVE YOURSELF

First of all you must learn to accept yourself. This is not easy. Many short people would have preferred to be tall. Some men would have preferred to be a different race! . . . Having accepted yourself with all your deficiencies and faults, try to like yourself. If you do not like yourself, how can you expect anyone to like you? If you can accomplish the next step of loving yourself, transferring the same love to your spouse would be a pushover.

Perhaps easier said than done, Dr. Luck! It is not simply that Charles doesn't like himself. He is someone who has gone through a long period of indecision over exactly what other entity he would like to be: a medieval academic, a Bantu bushman, a clerical architect, or a rare species of tulip. The one thing he actually *was* – namely, Heir to the Throne – he has now put in jeopardy, so identifying himself, let alone liking or even loving himself, may be the first difficulty.

Still, if and when Charles gets his identity crisis sorted out, the couple can then address Dr. Luck's sensible nostrum on the dangers of money. "Too much," he writes, "reminds me of the saying, 'It is easier for a camel to pass through the eye of a needle than a too rich man to find happiness in marriage.' . . . To drive home this danger, I would merely ask you to think of the really wealthy people in the world and the results of some of their marriages. . . . I believe their wealth exposes them to more temptations and since they can buy most things with money, they get a little shock to find it does not do the PADDLING."

Giving away all his rents from the Duchy of Cornwall could be a major step, then, but what if it's not enough? What if, even after this, the old canoe is still stuck at Total D&U? Dr. Luck's advice may strike some of you as quaint – even simple-minded – in the light of all we've been told lately about managing relationships to maximize spontaneity, self-actualization, and individual rights to growth. But here it is anyway. For the stuck couple "who will not or cannot get out of the canoe," the steps to take are as follows:

(a) *Swallow your pride;*
(b) *Don't try to find who is at fault;*
(c) *Go to the nearest preacher;*
(d) *Make that [marriage] promise again.*

"What have you got to lose?" the good physician asks at the conclusion of his pamphlet. "You might well ask, 'OK, I will follow these rules but what if my spouse doesn't?' I agree there is no way you can reach B&H in a canoe if your partner is not paddling with you. If for some reason or other you do not get out of it and you follow these rules, take some comfort that when the day of reckoning comes you might reach B&H then."

There you have it then. A comprehensive, almost apocalyptic, solution. Happy paddling.

February 1993

P.S. Dr. Luck contacted me after the publication of this column, blitzing me with other useful pamphlets he had authored. Sadly, I neglected to send along a copy of his *Guide To Happiness In Marriage* to Buckingham Palace, no doubt resulting in the calamity with which we are too familiar.

PART SIX

Who Cares About Canada?

Tales from Beyond

~

Now I hope I have this straight because it is not an easy tale to sort out. It concerns the three great bullfrogs of recent Canadian political punditry: Allan Fotheringham, Jack Webster, and the late Marjorie Nichols:

(1) In the manuscript of her recently published posthumous memoir, *Mark My Words* (Douglas & McIntyre), Ms. Nichols intimated that she, Dr. Foth, and the inimitable Mr. Webster had engaged in some form of editorial collusion one evening.

(2) Dr. Foth, through the medium of his back-page column in *Maclean's*, treated his public to a "pre-review" of the book some time before it was due to be published. In it, he spoke warmly of Ms. Nichols's genius, but mentioned that one incident that was reported in her book never happened.

(3) In some manner Mr. Webster learnt the substance of the about-to-be-published-incident-that-never-happened, whereupon he contacted the book publisher breathing fire and brimstone. But wait. Unlike Dr. Foth, Mr. Webster didn't deny that some sort of incident involving the other two had taken place. What he was at pains to insist was that a fourth person had been

involved. Apparently, the about- to - be- published- incident-that-never-happened- but - actually - did- though- not- as- described was unacceptable to him when reported as a tête-à-tête-à -tête, but perfectly acceptable if reported as, so to speak, a tête-à-quatre.

(4) In the meantime, advance copies of *Mark My Words* had gone out to reviewers, who were pointedly admonished by Douglas & McIntyre to take the slim volume seriously because: "It is a treat: devastatingly honest about Marjorie herself, gracious and opinionated about everyone else, the current state of political journalism in Canada, and the country in general."

(5) Then, in the immediate wake of Mr. Webster's representations to the publishers, a second letter went out to book reviewers from Douglas & McIntyre over the signature of Janice Bearg, the western marketing manager: "Unfortunately, errors crept into . . . advance copies. Would you please send your book back to my attention at Douglas & McIntyre as soon as you receive it. A corrected review copy will be sent out to you as soon as available. . . ."

(6) Finally, *Mark My Words* emerged in October shorn of the offending passage.

Now what does all this say to us? At least three things, it seemed to me, contemplating the whole unseemly flurry. The first concerns "devastating honesty": as Douglas & McIntyre must have learnt the hard way, it's not at all a phrase you want to throw around glibly.

The second lesson concerns "the current state of political journalism in Canada." What is noteworthy here is that three pundits are in dispute not over interpretations but about historical facts. One occasion, three categorically conflicting versions. So if our political reporters can't even agree on what happened, how well is the public, in these troublesome times, being served by their rotund opinions?

The final lesson arises from the little flurry itself – the pre-emptive pre-review, the litigious counterbluster, the smug puffery followed by embarrassed recall. Such agitation! Such a ruffling of feathers! And all from assorted members of the profession that loves to dish it out, let the chips fall where they may. It reminds me of something once said by Richard Ingrams, the founding editor of England's famous satirical magazine, *Private Eye*. The occasion was a libel trial in London's Old Bailey that pitted Ingrams against the wicked press baron Robert Maxwell.

Ingrams is a dark, sardonic fellow and his public persona in those days was full of menace. In the stand, for example, he glowered when Maxwell's oleaginous barrister asked him if he had ever knowingly printed falsehoods in *Private Eye*, and shot back. "Of course I have. Every time I am obliged to publish a legal retraction." But it was later in the trial that he made the relevant point. He was asked whether he could typify the sort of person who tended to sue for slander or libel. "Generally speaking," he replied, "I would say it was other writers or publishers. They're the only ones who actually believe what they read."

November 1992

The Devil We Know

~

Y ou probably don't spend a great deal of time brooding
about Brian Mulroney. Normally I don't either, but
this past summer was different. Partly it was because –
contrary to all vows – I had succumbed to another dose of
constitutional anxiety and it is difficult to think about the
almighty constitution or the governance of this country without
contemplating Mister M.

Partly, though, it came as the result of a piece of political
bumph mailed to my home. Beneath the Ottawa postmark and
above my address, Brian Mulroney's name was printed in large
black type over which had been superimposed a large red "X."
Nostalgia! In China during the Cultural Revolution, to cancel
someone's name in this way was instantly to declare that individual a nonperson. Here the aim was just the opposite, in that
the prime minister was being highlighted as the Archfiend.

And a mysterious thing happened. Without any wild epiph-
any, I quietly realized that the prime minister had ceased to
irritate me. After something akin to a secular exorcism, I was
clear of it.

The timing of the exorcism can't precisely be fixed, but it must have taken place before June 18, which was the date of the postmark. Inside the envelope was an unsurprising fund-raising pitch from the New Democratic Party's deputy leader, Nelson Riis, who was using our Brian as a kind of demon to arouse tribal fear and loathing. The pitch began:

> *Dear Fellow Canadian,*
>   *Are you mad as hell yet?*
>   *Well I am. Here's why: Brian Mulroney's Conservative government policies – the Goods and Services Tax, unfair income tax, corporate freeloading, "free" trade eliminating jobs and closing plants forever, government patronage and corruption, cuts to the CBC, Via Rail, Medicare, pensions and education funding – and that's just the start.*
>   *Pardon my bluntness, but to say Canada is going to hell in a hand basket is an understatement. . . .*

If my response to the hex-marked name on the envelope was a strong inkling of my altered state, the full proof lay in the strange thought that surfaced while I was reading this bleak litany, with its specific references to the nether world: I *wasn't* mad as hell. Worried, maybe – even troubled – but not mad as hell, at any of it. Up to a certain point, before June 18, I had had a lot of problems with Brian Mulroney, but now it was different. Now I found myself feeling that Canada was simply an impossible country to govern at the moment, and I was grateful that someone was prepared to keep trying, even though he stumbled and bumbled. And that's how I still feel.

Take the issue of the Goods and Services Tax. I really was mad as hell when that was brought in. No one likes taxes, and the worst sort of tax is a new tax. But how many other governments in the Western world are honest enough (dumb is a synonym here) to remind everyone, day in and year out, that this damn tax – individually calculated – is going to be there till we reach our graves? In Britain, more often than not, you are simply given one price in which the far nastier Value Added Tax (17.5 per cent versus our seven) is surreptitiously included. In Canada, the government invites a snarl each time we buy a bottle of beer or pay our telephone bill. How can you stay mad as hell at someone who condones such political ingenuousness?

And free trade, for heaven's sake! Over a quarter of a century ago, when Lester Pearson declined to back up his own finance minister in a progam of stringent economic protectionism, anyone who was following national affairs and didn't understand that the Liberals had set us on course towards the closest possible trading relationship with the United States was even less swift than the people who worked out the GST strategy. When the dust and chicken feathers finally settled after the free-trade election in 1988, it seemed to me fairly clear that all Brian Mulroney had done was to make regular what was already a *fait accompli*. Canadians were then, as they are now, unwilling to pay the price it would cost for going it alone, even if we could go it alone any more. And, once again, we damned The Man for his dumb honesty when the fault, if it is a fault, lay within us.

Now, it is possible to bring this kind of sweet reason to all the issues that have got Mr. Riis into his stew and still not feel like snuggling up to our own Irish rover. That's okay too, because you can actually govern Canada while remaining hugely unpopular, and recently Himself appears to have made this breakthrough discovery. It is not at all a new perception, although it had been forgotten. Growing up in Toronto, for example, I'm just old enough to remember the pathological loathing in some circles for William Lyon Mackenzie King. My parents were disposed towards the Liberal Party then, but in the Tory federal riding of Toronto-Eglinton during the 1950s such heresy made them virtually unique. Meanwhile, people of my grandfather's generation talked of Mr. King the way Protestants talked about the pope in the seventeenth century. Yet Mr. King prevailed –

because he was an adroit politician. He could play one part of the country against the other. He could fight in the pit or in the palace. He rarely failed to reward his friends and he *never* forgot Quebec. This is not a national hero we are talking about, merely that endlessly useful item in holding a nation together: a successful politician.

Brian Mulroney is cursed with a personality that restlessly reaches out to seek approval and affection. It has taken him a while to learn that in the world of Canadian politics – our blood sport of choice – love is fickle and not worth the having. It has taken him an even longer time to figure out that the single biggest step he could take to improve his chances for re-election was to stop reaching out and simply shut up. It seemed to me this past summer that whole weeks would go by when we weren't subjected to even one fifteen-second clip of the prime minister on television news. This merciful break in the blather is what also got me thinking about him in a fresh light.

When I used to get mad as hell at Brian, it was because I thought he had no policy beyond expediency, no convictions beyond the latest polls, and no centre to his being beyond the blarney. But I don't think that any more. In economic policy, for example, which is the single most crucial yardstick by which to judge any government, his strategy has been abundantly clear for years: fight inflation, ease trading restrictions, and survive recession without major retreats. It is a fairly conservative recipe, but he's stuck to it, even while making some of the expected concessions to the howls of outrage that always accompany conservative economic policies. It may not be a brilliant record but, comparing just the inflation battle to what's gone on in countries such as the U.S., Britain, or France during the same period, it looks pretty good. Of course I'd still like to bop him on the head for all the foreshortened economic opportunities dealt young Canadians, but frankly in this area I suspect old

Snake-eyes has done less damage in the short term than have Mr. Riis's well-intentioned provincial chums in Ontario over the long haul.

On the question of political conviction, it is fair to say that the prime minister will always have to overcome his manner. And of course, we will always want to bop him over the head for something. My own major gripe is Canada's emerging – and chaotic – refugee policy, which I think is being constructed on a far narrower definition of national necessity than even the stupid opinion polls suggest the public would tolerate. Since this is a field that cries out for courageous and far-sighted leadership, Brian's record of vacillation – one day visionary, the next day craven – is disheartening. Consistency in refugee policy has never been our boy's strongest suit.

On the other hand, the great continuous thread throughout his prime ministership – and the critical test of any Canadian leader – has been his custodianship of the Quebec question. Look at any of our truly successful prime ministers, in wartime or in peace, and you cannot find one for whom the Quebec question was not the paramount issue, because it holds the key to whatever genuine national unity we can maintain. Mulroney can be fairly accused of mistakes and errors of judgement, but armed in his conviction that there is no Canada without Quebec he need take second place to no one in our political history. We have castigated him for the way he "rolled the dice," forgetting that the rules of the contemporary game of Canada were dreamed up by Pierre Trudeau. It is not news that people are fed up with the constitutional wrangling. All I want quietly to suggest is that the commitment Brian Mulroney has consistently brought to the search for a workable national solution has about it, even amid the political arm-twisting and sleaze, a whiff of nobility.

There! I've said it. The "N" word. Does it seem obscene in the context of all the terrible things we have heard and taken as gospel about Muldoon? Maybe. Nevertheless I feel it is true, just as I feel that the manner in which he has borne the slings and arrows of his own particular fortunes – the prying attacks on his family, the constant presumption that he is never up to any good – has a measure of nobility as well.

I'm on a roll now, so hold your noses if you're feeling nauseated. Another reason to admire the old reprobate is that he's not afraid to surround himself with strong cabinet figures. People talk about the constitutional acumen of Joe Clark, or the quiet effectiveness of Don Mazankowski, or the vicelike control over the economy held by Michael Wilson, or the limelight-hogging buffoonery of John Crosbie, but they forget that these outsized and powerful ministers have their licences to operate from a leader who does not feel threatened by whatever national or regional followings they have. It's a very good sign in politics.

The truth is we have scrutinized Brian Mulroney's flaws so often and so minutely that they have become utterly familiar to us and, if the familiarity has brought with it a fair share of contempt, it has also over time strangely neutralized some of the hatred. We are not talking about someone who will ever be beloved in office. Triple-E leaders in Canada (elected, equivocal, and execrated) are, almost by definition, incapable of arousing broad public affection, at least during their actual mandates. (Canonization among the faithful comes later, after they have retired and been put out of harm's way.) Instead, I'm talking about a discredited politician who seems to have come into his own as a leader. Even as the country has allegedly been "going to hell in a handbasket" over the past two years, he has shown grace under fire and courage in office. Who knows, the courage may even prove infectious. Foreseeing the number of letters to the editor about to pour in here – and their gist – I may have caught some of it myself.

September 1992

P.S. Amazingly enough, I did not receive an ambassadorship or even membership in Her Majesty's Canadian Privy Council for this sterling paean to Mr. M. As expected, however, I did get a mother lode of abuse from the faithful, if disgusted, readers of the magazine who subsequently joined the Canadian masses in virtually eradicating Brian's party from the Canadian political landscape. There's just no thanks in this business.

The China Syndrome

~

Wednesday, May 17

Xiao Li called long-distance from Kingston. A great expense for him, so after two minutes of excited talk I told him to hang up and called him right back. Xiao Li is a young economics student who came to Canada over a year ago. A friend of a friend in Shanghai wrote me about him, so we have stayed in touch. Not surprisingly, he was in a state of high euphoria about the democracy demonstrations in Beijing, but his particular excitement today was because he saw one of his best friends on television. The full impact of the global village has hit him, and he's sure China is on the verge of something momentous.

Monday, May 22

Joseph Wong telephoned. Double trouble. He wants me to take part in a large rally at Toronto City Hall next Sunday to support the students in Beijing, whereas I had planned to go to Harbourfront to hear the Orford Quartet. And besides, I don't really believe members of the media should identify themselves with specific causes on public stages. It is hard to explain to Joseph the delicate sensitivities of journalists. He is the physician who, more than anyone, got Chinese Canadians in Toronto to eschew the old, psychologically covert habit of lying low in Chinatown while their rights were abused. This was nearly a decade ago, after CTV aired its notorious "documentary" on how the Chinese were taking over Canadian University faculties. He is a whiz at demonstrations and marches. I mumbled this and that, trying to find an adroit exit. The best I could come up with was a half-hearted "I'll get back to you."

Tuesday, May 23
I have agreed, for better or worse, to take part in the rally.

Wednesday, May 24
The reports from Beijing are ominous. Hardline propaganda is in the ascendant and that's usually a sign of bad things to come. The ad hoc group Joseph Wong has put together will hold a press conference at City Hall to announce the rally. As usual, the name of the group in Chinese is a nice compact sixteen characters, but in English it becomes "The Toronto Committee of Concerned Chinese Canadians Supporting the Movement for Democracy in China." There are to be three "white" faces on the podium: mine, and those of civil-rights campaigner Alan Borovoy and a representative of the Ontario Federation of Students. Politicians of all stripes have sent innocuous statements of support, but have found it prudent not to appear in public.

Joseph Wong had patients up to his eyeballs, as it turned out, so his wife was there instead. Statements were read about the purposes of the committee:

(1) *To urge the People's Republic of China to pursue a democratic society.*

(2) *To recognize the courage and sacrifices of students in bringing about hope for democracy in China.*

(3) *To encourage the Chinese government to endorse freedom of the press.*

(4) *To place international focus on the current crisis, and to maintain vigilant watch over developing events in the People's Republic of China.*

A reporter from CITY-TV picked up on a guarded, but pessimistic, utterance I made during the ensuing discussion. "If you think things are going to turn out so badly, why are you bothering with this rally?" he asked. My Chinese associates at the front, enthusiasts and optimists all, also seemed a trifle irritated at my tone, and I didn't know how to deal with the question efficiently. I muttered something but wanted to say, "Why bother to get out of bed in the morning if you think the day is going to turn out badly?"

Thursday, May 25

Having darkened the press conference yesterday, I still can't shake the gloom. The CBC's "Sunday Morning" is badgering me to do a three-minute thumb-sucker on events in China. I've temporized.

Damn! Six weeks ago I blithely observed to my wife that the whole period of our lives spent in China – from 1977 to the end of 1979 when I was the *Globe and Mail*'s resident correspondent – seemed a faraway dream. It was hard even to summon up specific memories of events that seemed momentous at the time. As hundreds of thousands of students take over Tienanmen Square today, the tiny democracy movement of 1978, which I reported on, seems instantly marginalized.

Then, the demonstrators never amounted to more than 15,000 and they only ever filled a little corner of Tienanmen Square. Deng Xiaoping was the hero of the hour, the man who promised to dismantle Maoism and usher in a new brave age for battered old China. Everyone seems to have forgotten that after this little movement in 1978 served *his* purposes by helping him back to power he had its young leaders packed off to prison. Wei Jingsheng, in the tenth year of his fifteen-year sentence, is still lost in the great void. Ren Wanding, the chairman of the Chinese Human Rights Alliance, on the other hand, was released last year. I wrote about him in the March 1989 Diary.

Another article on Ren Wanding written at the same time by the *Globe's* thirteenth Beijing correspondent, Jan Wong, sent me right up the Great Wall. "China seems to be in the midst of a fundamental change in approach to political dissent," she wrote. "It is, after all, hard to lock people up for their views when establishment economists are calling for an end to such sacred cows as state ownership. Asked whether he has arrested any counter-revolutionaries lately, a police chief laughed." And so on.

Jan Wong depicted Ren as a curious relic from a forgotten era. Me too, I suppose. Maybe that was part of the reason I was angry. Vanity? Anyway, the last paragraph left me ranting:

"Ignored at home, Mr. Ren is hoping to get his message out in the foreign press. Last month, in the *International Herald Tribune*, he urged other countries to withhold aid and investment until China's [human] rights record improves. And how did the government react to this provocation? It wrote a letter to the editor."

My wife, as usual, was wise. "She hasn't had a friend arrested yet. Give her time to learn."

Late Thursday night

I said I'd do the "Sunday Morning" piece. When I was a reporter in China I was taught a cardinal rule: whatever you say, give yourself a back door through which to leave. Hedge every assertion, undermine every ostensible fact. That seemed a silly rule tonight and so, in a very stark and sombre mood, I turned to the word processor. "The Chinese people, once again, have to play out their terrible drama alone, while the rest of us hold our breath." Strong sentence, but back it up. "Historically, in the cycle of repression and revolt that the Chinese Communist Party has presided over since 1949, this stage in a populist movement from the masses is the most dangerous of all. It has invariably been at the time of the last-ditch stand that a new generation of martyrs is served up for the higher purposes of the unyielding state. It is a dreadful moment, a moment when aspiration and reality collide head on."

I'm worried that the whole screed is going to end up sounding like a dire sermon on some old-time revivalist "Prophecy Hour," so I've promised myself to rethink it before the recording tomorrow at the CBC's old radio building on Jarvis Street.

Friday, May 26

I recorded the piece, mostly unchanged. In fact, I had to do it twice. The first time I must have sounded like a funeral-home director because, though timed for three minutes, it took over four. In the end, I was not pleased. I thought I talked in riddles and wondered if there was a psychological malaise called "the Cassandra syndrome."

Sunday, May 28

The great rally went off without a hitch. Close to 5,000 people jammed into Nathan Phillips Square. Alan Borovoy was very effective with his warning to the Chinese government not to touch "one hair" on the Beijing students' heads. I started off with a few words in Mandarin which earned me howls of approval. Xiao Li was at the rally. The euphoria of a week ago has evaporated, and now he is very worried about being seen by (Chinese) consular officials. But he wanted to do something, so he and some friends took the bus to Toronto. He is going to stay in town for a few days to solve a bureaucratic visa problem, so we agreed to meet later. It's horrible to see the familiar fear return to the face of a young Chinese idealist, especially one that so recently radiated hope and great expectations.

Friday, June 2

A weaponless regiment of the People's Liberation Army tried to amble into Tienanmen Square and was repulsed, not just by the students in the square but also by ordinary residents of the capital. One news report I caught on radio was optimistic, suggesting that the government will now be forced into dialogue because of the impotence of the army and the determination of the people. *Aaargh!* When did we see this little scenario before? In April 1979, two days before an extensive wave of arrests ended the Xidan Democracy Movement, there was a half-hearted effort by the Public Security Bureau to cordon off the wall-poster wall at the corner of Xidan and Chang An avenues. The police never seemed so inept or ineffective, and they retreated amidst some ridicule and a few dust-ups with young rowdies and *provocateurs*. In retrospect, foreign journalists realized it was a setup for a bigger – and awesomely well-organized – operation. Marx says that when history repeats itself, once it is tragedy but twice is a farce. Marx is wrong. Tragedy cannot be transmuted.

Saturday, June 3

The stupidest thing to do in Toronto on the weekend is to look for a house. With prices in downward spiral, there are tempting offers all over, but no one can sell his own humble abode, so what's the point in hunting? In the midst of inspecting an "open house" in Cabbagetown during the afternoon, I heard that the real army has moved into Tienanmen Square. Seventeen people have been killed, maybe more.

Back home, I finally discovered – a year and a half after the fact – why it was I subscribed to CNN's twenty-four-hour news service on cable television. It is horrible, mesmerizing stuff, updated every half hour. The kill estimates go up periodically as more details are pieced together – a regular update, like the rally for party seats on election night.

Joseph Wong called again. The committee is organizing a massive demonstration and protest march for tomorrow. People are to gather in Chinatown and then march up Beverley and St. George streets to the Chinese consulate general. The Chinese consulate is precisely sixty-four steps from my own front door. For several weeks, the RCMP have been providing the building with twenty-four-hour protection. Coming home from the house hunt, though, I noticed six police vehicles crowding the nearby corner of St. George Street, along with a van full of crowd-control fences.

Sunday, June 4

Early radio reports have put the death toll at over 2,000. It *can't* be true. At the early Communion service at our church, the priest declined to read the concluding Gloria from the Book of Common Prayer. "I don't feel like saying it," he said, "after the events in China." I never felt so far from God in all my life. I took Communion like an automaton.

How do you organize a bourgeois Sunday? Easy. Daughter Number One to a birthday party. Daughter Number Two to a friend's house. Daughter Number Three – the baby – stays with Wife (one and only) but ends up in the march, being pushed in her carriage from Chinatown to the Chinese consulate. Father stays home to await negotiated return of Daughter Number One and then joins the throngs.

On the last stage of the march, two blocks from our home, some of the "brothers" at a fraternity house on upper St. George Street were on their balcony guzzling cans of beer. This upset some of the (non-Chinese) marchers who shouted up at them: "They're killing students in Beijing. Why aren't you down here marching too?"

Each segment of the long march, which has brought together an estimated 15,000 people, demonstrated for ten or fifteen minutes in front of the consulate. We ended sitting on our front lawn and, as each succeeding segment concluded, it dispersed right past us. We knew many people in this crowd and an impromptu demonstration tea party soon began. Not surprisingly, the RCMP started to notice us, and I had a brief chat with an amiable, curious officer, who wanted to know what sort of a "meeting" I was holding. "It's a tea party. That's all." From Chairman Mao's little red book of quotations: "A revolution is not a tea party. It is not nearly so nice or so gentle. . . ."

Xiao Li came to town again for the demonstration and elected to stay overnight with us to see if he can't get his visa problems straightened up definitively. I informed him that visa problems can never be solved definitively – it is a contradiction in terms.

Monday, June 5

I turned forty-five today and tried to keep it a dark secret. That's a lie. I let someone at the magazine know and got a box of cream-centred cookies to help keep my weight down. Oh well, middle-class vanity about ageing is somewhat peripheral at the moment. I discovered, to my chagrin, that after nearly two years at a monthly magazine my instincts remain lodged in daily journalism, at least when the blood is up and the craving for an immediate outlet is strong. When the *Financial Post* called to see if I would do an essay on China, I said yes. And then sat down to write about . . . Hong Kong. Although the images from China are uniformly appalling, my mind seemed stuck at an oblique angle: I could not get Hong Kong and its fate detached from the larger tragedy. Maybe it's because we can do so little about China, but might – in a crunch – help to rescue the people of Hong Kong from the fate the British government has in store for them when the crown colony is handed over to the killers in Beijing in 1997.

There is no respite from the expanding horror, though. At the Chinese consulate, a Buddhist nun has established herself in front of the main entrance. Apparently she will stay there for a week. She sits cross-legged on the ground and beats out a mournful death tattoo on her drum, banging it about every five seconds for hours on end. You can hear it from our bedroom window, and it lacerates the soul. Hundreds of people have begun massing outside the premises, leaving flowers on the police fences. Traffic has been diverted and, for the first time since we bought our house eight years ago, kids can play on the street. At the consulate, there is no sign of internal activity or of the Chinese staff. No one comes, no one leaves. The crowds focus on the nun. They listen to the drum and, I suppose, think about the dead. It's worse than a wake, for there seems no catharsis for the grief.

When I got home, I discovered that Xiao Li was not attending to his visa problems. Instead, he had stayed glued all day to CNN. The service has been available in some tourist hotels in Beijing: a new thing since my day. We forced Xiao Li to come with us for dinner at the home of our friend Robin. Inevitably, we all ended in front of the television set. The dynamite footage was of a lone man standing before a column of tanks. "My God," said Robin. I looked over at him to share in the astonishment, but saw, instead, Xiao Li. He was doubled over, sobbing.

Friday, June 9

The "Cassandra syndrome" returned with a vengeance. It is a sickness to have such a complete vision of what is coming. Everything that is going to happen has happened before, in one form or another. Trumped-up charges, arrests, torture, public confessions, purges, show trials, summary execution: all these things are only a few days away. It is impossible to account for the small solace that comes in writing such things down, except to note that it occurs. So I wrote another screed, words of impotent warning and frustrated rage spilling out all over the place. A messy piece, but I sent it off anyway to the editor of the *Globe*, unsolicited and with apologies. The piece finished with a plea for people to remember the Chinese in their abiding humanity, and not in the agony of such cruel repression. To remember them after their tragedy becomes familiar – or too difficult to cover – and leaves the front pages.

Tuesday, June 13

In Vancouver, to address the 1989 Western Magazine Awards dinner.

I could barely manage a few jokes and threw away what I had intended to say. Instead I talked about Wei Jingsheng, still in prison from the 1978 democracy movement. He was a magazine editor and writer too, and sometimes, when referring to "the billion Chinese," it makes a lot of sense just to concentrate on one individual. Before the awards dinner, I made the mistake of talking to K. in Hong Kong, who informed me that the authorities in Beijing had picked up Ren Wanding. So there's the sequel to my March Diary – he's back in the dark void. Ren was asked a few months ago whether he dreaded ever being sent back to prison. No, he said, "I am no longer afraid. I've already died once in prison. Once you have been there, you are never really afraid of anything again." I cannot get the first lines of a hymn out of my skull: "Turn back, O man, forswear thy foolish ways. Old now is earth and none may count her days." Who would want to count them? They are filled with too much criminal stupidity and grief.

Wednesday, June 14

The flight back from Vancouver was ghastly. It was my bad luck to sit next to a penny-ante anthropologist who noticed that I was reading the *New York Times* coverage of events in China. The police and army are arresting hundreds of people all over the country. "The Chinese aren't ready for democracy," my neighbour observed, perfectly unbidden by me. "They're nice people, but they stick together too much."

Saturday, June 17

Show trials of "hooligans" have begun.

Wednesday, June 21

The executions have started.

Friday, June 23

Joe Clark has summoned businessmen, academics, and no doubt a few senior bureaucrats to a seminar in Ottawa on what to do about China. Surprise, surprise, surprise: the representative of the Wheat Board said we must protect our wheat sales to China. The academics urged Joe not to sever hard-won links. The businessmen talked about the two-way Sino-Canadian trade total last year: $3.6-billion. In a newspaper report, Marcel Dufour, president of Lavalin International, was quoted as saying: "You cannot expect the Chinese to have a democracy within five years. It might never happen. The Chinese have their own way to settle matters . . . and what they did, they've been doing for the last thousand years."

On "The Journal" last week, I predicted it would be business as usual within six months of the slaughter in and around Tienanmen Square. What ignorance! It took less than three weeks.

October 1989

P.S. All things come to pass – triply. In the spring of 1994, the New Democrat premier of Ontario, Bob Rae, travelled to China on the eve of the fifth anniversary of the Tienanmen Square massacre. He was accompanied by leading Ontario businessmen and, echoing Prime Minister Jean Chrétien and – more notoriously – U.S. President Bill Clinton, he "delinked" trade and human rights. It will be interesting to hear what these jokers will say when the next catastrophe occurs. For example, will they have urged young democracy activists to "lighten up" because their campaign is hurting trade? Then the linkage will come full circle: trade with no human rights whatsoever.

Musical Chairs

~

The constant shining light among Canada's chamber-music ensembles over the past twenty-five years has been the Orford Quartet, an organization embodying so many national themes of the 1960s and 1970s – from the crucial importance of the Canada Council to a particular definition of what constitutes a Canadian perspective in the performing arts – that people might be forgiven for thinking it had been invented to provide the background music for Pierre Trudeau's Liberal vision of the country. A few weeks ago, the Orford announced that it would disband next July, following a final concert. For those who care, the sense of calamity and impending loss was considerable. At the same time, it has to be acknowledged that this extraordinary ensemble has had an eerie and almost symbiotic relationship with the national political agenda.

A string quartet is one of the smaller denominations in music-making and yet, if you transpose the standard anatomy of a quartet, its four constituent parts can be seen to parallel the country's regional divisions: first violin as Ontario (dominant and often unconsciously arrogant), second violin as the Atlantic provinces (apparently necessary), viola as the West (forever misunderstood), and the cello as Guess Who (complex, passionate, often sulky, and independence-minded). Only someone who has got politics and culture hopelessly muddled together in his mind would want to push this metaphor any further, but there does exist some concrete and less fanciful evidence that after the Orford Quartet was founded in 1965 at the legendary Jeunesses Musicales camp at Mount Orford, Quebec, some such intertwining of artistic and national agendas occurred.

At the time the four founding members (Andrew Dawes, first violin; Kenneth Perkins, second violin; Terence Helmer, viola; and Marcel St-Cyr, cello) were brought together, for example, there was no full-time, professional string quartet in the country, and remedying the lack appears to have been a top priority for leading cultural and musical establishment figures from Peter Dwyer, head of the Canada Council, to Arnold Walter, dean of music at the University of Toronto. This is, admittedly, retrospective analysis, based on the speed and enthusiasm with which the Orford was assisted financially and given a home at the U of T. But it is backed up by contemporary observers and participants such as Gilles Lefebvre, the director of Jeunesses Musicales, who sent the quartet on a perishing cross-country launch tour, and officials of the external-affairs department, who quickly started using the quartet to represent Canada abroad culturally. In the heady days of centennial-induced nationalism, the ensemble became a standard-bearer. Dawes's violin case always carried a Canadian flag decal, as if to buttress the point.

Less than ten years later, before the Orford had even built up its repertoire to include the entire cycle of Beethoven's string quartets, a young and somewhat breathless music critic of the nationalist school was able to write in *Saturday Night* that the "simplicity and directness" of the Orford's distinctive style had produced an "unostentatious and wholly effective emotion" which was, in a word, "Canadian."

The Orford Quartet has played the world over since then, and garnered far more than enough laudatory, high-profile foreign reviews to persuade the most self-consciously suspicious Canadian that it is properly numbered among the half-dozen best quartets in the world. Its quarter-century anniversary this year was therefore considered something more than ordinarily worthy of celebration, and those celebrations were going along very nicely until just before the Meech Lake crisis exploded. Then the first violinist, Andrew Dawes, turned broody – and not for the first time – announcing that at long last he was going to go solo. The Orford's continuing existence immediately came under threat, and within a couple of months the remaining three members gave up the struggle to find a new first violinist. The quartet's timing, as usual, was apt – this time horribly so, even if the metaphor gets a trifle warped in light of the fact that Dawes is supposed to represent the Ontario element.

Then again, the original Quebec element (founding cellist Marcel St-Cyr) had dropped out years before, so there may yet be hope for both the quartet and the country. St-Cyr quit the Orford in 1980 to pursue an obsession for old instruments, and to escape the grind of relentless rehearsal and remorseless touring that has been the quartet's life since its inception. Now it is not uncommon for a quartet to change its parts. Only one of its founding members still plays with the famous Juilliard Quartet. The Kneisel Quartet (the first great American ensemble) had nine changes in thirty-two years, and the Budapest Quartet had seven in thirty years. Actually, the Orford – up until the last half-decade, at least – was famous for its ability to hold together.

Always, the fear is that change will injure the dynamics of relationships, interpretation, and performance. The repertoire for string quartet is extensive, intensely intellectual, and often very exacting of both performers and listeners. "Do you think I worry about your lousy fiddle when the spirit speaks to me?" demanded Beethoven of the foremost string player of his day, Ignaz Schuppanzigh, who had complained about the immense difficulties of one of the composer's quarters. A wholehearted acceptance of the technical and emotional costs, and the excellence to which the Orford has always committed itself, have paid huge dividends in performances and recordings. But they have also exacted a toll, of which Dawes's soul-searching and eventual decision provide only a glimpse.

This is because a string quartet is the oddest relationship in the music world. "Being in a quartet is almost like being in a marriage," Michael Tree of the Guarneri Quartet once said, "and in some respects it's harder than a marriage." To spend so much time together in such close proximity would bring stress to any relationship, and when things go sour in a quartet they can go very sour. As well, the dynamics of hierarchy are a periodic source of tension – ultimately irresolvable. There are wicked stories about any number of famous international quartets (the Juilliard Quartet in particular) where the acrimony of the personal relationships increased in direct proportion to the economic imperatives of staying together, until the members rehearsed with their backs to each other, and used an outside party to communicate. These accounts are probably apocryphal, but they occur with such regularity that they can be regarded as cautionary tales.

The Orford has its own variants. All the members, past and present, are tight-lipped about departures, but there have been a sufficient number in recent years – the most spectacular prior to Dawes's announcement being that of the cellist Denis Brott in 1988 – that they tend to highlight the dramatic tension of the intimacy. For Orford aficionados like me, the most intriguing change in the quartet's chemistry was the appearance, in 1987, of a new violist and its first woman – the young, technically vibrant, and beautiful Sophie Renshaw. Describing Renshaw's stage presence as romantic and dreamy is not gratuitous. Shortly after she was chosen, word emerged from the very bosom of the quartet – to the affectionate if mischievous delight of its fans – that Mrs. Dawes and Mrs. Perkins would henceforth be taking turns chaperoning the quartet on its arduous tours. It was not a question of lack of trust, one of the astute spouses was reported to have said, just "common sense." This all fitted nicely into the presiding artistic style of the Orford which does, after all, feature directness and clarity of purpose. (It also helped distract public attention and concern from the departure of the founding violist, Terence Helmer.)

In the end the marriage metaphor is sustained because a leave-taking is a kind of divorce, whatever the reasons. Brott's replacement, for example, the less flamboyant but probably more sensitive Desmond Hoebig, was considerably agitated by Dawes's farewell announcement: he himself had just turned down a handsome position with an important orchestra to renew his commitment to the quartet. The Orford being the Orford, you could tell from the prevailing atmosphere of militant calm and excruciating politeness that everyone was hugely upset.

Andrew Dawes is the Orford member I have come to know best over the years. He is a beautiful interpreter, a formidable technician, and a wonderfully generous personality. Indeed, he seems admirable on so many fronts that I find it hard to judge his decision to depart, throwing the Orford into the tailspin that led to its sad announcement. Actually, Dawes pulled this stunt once before, the first time he became convinced he had sacrificed a solo career. This was in 1970, coinciding – naturally enough – with the imposition of the War Measures Act. The Orford, in effect, disbanded, although now it is referred to as a "sabbatical."

Like the country with which the quartet has so identified itself, it may thus be premature to give up on the Orford. Let us pretend to humour its members, especially Dawes, during what we might winkingly acknowledge to be their "final" year together. Let each of them go his or her own way because, heaven knows, another "sabbatical" has been earned. But let us also badger them to re-evaluate their midlife crisis when a year or two has passed. The music-loving audiences of Canada owe the Orford a lot, but it is not a one-way relationship. The best string quartet this country has ever produced also owes us. And we can wait.

October 1990

P.S. So much for sound advice. The Orford Quartet never did regroup after 1990, but it has left behind many wondrous recordings. None are finer than the complete Beethoven quartets which now sound more luminous with each passing year.

The Orphan King

~

The summons to attend upon "His Majesty King Michael of Romania" at the behest of the Canadian Institute of International Affairs (CIIA) came out of the blue, but was not entirely unexpected. Not that I had been waiting breathlessly to meet King Michael, or anything like that, but when the invitation did come in mid-March, in advance of His Exiled Majesty's cross-Canada tour, it seemed, well . . . about time.

Michael has been bobbing around the surface of twentieth-century European history for seven decades, like a cork from an obscure bottle of vintage wine. Twice enthroned and twice dethroned before he was out of his twenties, he has actually survived long enough to see an electrifying change in his family's prospects, thanks to the collapse of the Communist regimes in Eastern Europe. These seismic political shifts have taken place so quickly it is hard for any of us to assimilate all the major consequences, let alone fit in footnotes like the implications for the current titleholder of a remote branch of the Hohenzollern clan.

Yet here he was planning to be among us, on his first visit to Canada, a three-city tour (Toronto, Kitchener, and Vancouver) sponsored by regional branches of the CIIA, and paid for by Canadian Airlines, which had coughed up enough to send him, his queen (Anne), and his eldest daughter (Margarita) winging across the Precambrian Shield in style. Michael's mission was to tell us about the future of Romania and Eastern Europe in the post-Communist era – a somewhat meatier topic, I have to admit, than squared with my picturesque imaginings. Because, one way or another, I've been thinking of him for a long time as a romantic, if shopworn, anachronism.

The notion of Romania implanted in my childhood mind, starting with an attraction to its most famous province, Transylvania, and its sinister old count, Dracula, was of a dark and deliciously Gothic mountain fastness in Eastern Europe. I moved on to *The Prisoner of Zenda* and the luckless young king of Ruritania who was spirited away by evil plotters and traitorous agents. Having played the role of Count Rupert in a schoolboy production of *Zenda*, I became a connoisseur of the plots and star-crossed adventures appropriate to the better sort of Gothic court circles.

Michael of Romania fitted perfectly into these mists. Born in 1921, he came to the throne five years later when his bizarre father, Carol, renounced his right of succession before his own father's death (and also ditched Michael's mother) in favour of exile and the arms of his dangerously alluring mistress, Magda Lupescu (hereafter referred to by her correct title, "the notorious Madam Lupescu"). The story of Little King Michael was a novel and popular news item; a delightful headline in *The New York Times* of August 3, 1927, gives the flavour:

MICHAEL LEAVES HIS TOYS; PRESIDES OVER REGENTS
While They Discuss Romanian Affairs the Boy King
Considers Using 'Scooter' in Throne Room

This sweet scene didn't last long. Three years later, Carol claimed he had renounced his mistress and demanded his throne after all. Michael and his abandoned mother were ushered out the back door, King Carol II was duly crowned, and two months later the notorious Madam Lupescu dropped by for a visit and declined to leave. Now I ask you: is this Romania or Ruritania?

Carol turned out to be an authoritarian, although a mild one in comparison to the ferocious dictators the era was spawning. Caught out by the fascist ground swell in his own country, he was forced to abdicate in 1940 by a local stooge of Hitler's named Ion Antonescu, who went on to usurp to himself the powers of head of state. The monarchy was popular, though, so Generalissimo Antonescu felt obliged to let Carol's son assume the actual crown.

Poor Michael. At eighteen, he found himself back on the throne, but with no power and no real role. His only clear asset was an adroit and courageous adviser in the person of his redoubtable mother (Princess Helen of Greece). Together they watched Romania's fortunes collapse as Europe was transformed into a charnel house. The pair achieved one final and memorable Ruritanian stroke: in 1944 Michael pulled off a successful palace coup against Antonescu and got Romania to change sides from the Axis powers to the Allies. His reward for this act of daring was to suffer two humiliating years as a figurehead for the vile postwar Communist regime before being forced to abdicate in 1947.

After that, it was exile and political oblivion: the life of a remittance man in Switzerland; bittersweet relations with ruling or other dispossessed royalty; melancholy gatherings with outcast compatriots; the sad, steady march of the years. As for Romania/Ruritania, it remained lost in the mists, but this time there was an Iron Curtain in between.

The curtain lifted first, for me, in 1978, when I witnessed

the presiding Communist monster of Bucharest, Nicolae Ceauşescu, dancing a little jig with a group of Chinese "Young Pioneers" in Beijing's Tienanmen Square. I was so close, I could almost smell the blood on his breath when he smiled. Eleven years later President and Madam Ceauşescu's summary trial and their execution in a hail of counter-revolutionary bullets transfixed an international television audience. Not pretty. And poor old Romania is still stuck in a purgatory run by half-baked Communists and fully formed opportunists. Ruritania vanished forever, however, when the photographs of Romanian AIDS babies first started to appear in the West, and I realized there was still an enslaved nation longing for respite and redemption.

And here is Michael, bobbing up yet again, a candidate for a third stint on his throne. This time, though, he comes with a few wisps of a real record – a curious sidebar turned up by postwar scholarship. To set the scene: for centuries, it seems, Romania was one of the most deeply anti-Semitic of European countries. Throughout the nineteenth and early twentieth centuries, Romanian governments of all political stripes had institution-alized systematic discrimination against Jews, discrimination periodically supported by the Church – and by the court. Not so much in Carol's reign, though. Michael's enigmatic father finally came a cropper in 1940 not simply because Hitler didn't want him, but also because he took unto himself, and would not give up, the notorious Madam Lupescu. Madam Lupescu was a Jew.

Here is where history comes a little unstuck. Although Romanian Jewry suffered grievously during the Second World War, with nearly half of its 800,000 members perishing in pogroms and camps, it's still true that over half actually survived. This happened in almost no other country where Nazi Germany held sway. According to Theodor Lavi, who published a study of Romanian Jewry during the Holocaust for the Israel Universities Press, the main reason was the practised alertness of Romanian Jews. There were no illusions that "things are bound to get better," and this state of preparedness for the worst saved many lives. So also did a deep ambivalence at the heart of the anti-Semitic Romanian soul. According to Lavi, entrenched anti-Semitism bred a kind of antibody, and even Romanian fascists balked at the Final Solution. All the political parties, he writes, had "approved of economic discrimination [in the past] and of a restriction of the political rights of Jews, but they could not accept mass-murders or total extermination. It would appear important to stress the timing of [the mid-war] protests [against the extermination of the Jews]. They were all voiced within Romanian political circles before Stalingrad, and the prospective defeat of German arms. They must therefore be attributed to specific motives which were deeper than mere opportunism."

Michael's own role in this business was passive-honourable. His mother, who was his closest adviser throughout the war years, is even now being mentioned in Israel as a Righteous Gentile for small but – considering the times and the precarious position of the monarchy – courageous acts on behalf of specific Jews. Her son followed her lead closely. Add to this the pair's palace coup on behalf of the Allies and there is, at least, a bit of something to reckon with. If a return to the monarchy in Bucharest is really in the cards, then Michael may yet break out of the footnote his life became. Or not.

This century has less than nine years remaining to it, and the fate of the ex-king of Romania, though it resonates through so many turbulent decades and is genuinely curious, may be the least of what we are going to be served up. For the life of me, I can't figure out whether to embrace Michael's recent emergence from the mists, or acknowledge the unfocused dread that he will once again become a creature of terrible events over which he will have no control.

But I accepted the CIIA's invitation anyway.

May 1992

Before the Camera

~

I n the outpouring of grief and admiration that followed
Barbara Frum's untimely death at the end of March, what
became clear was that, in some curious manner, television,
and Mrs. Frum's role on TV, had concealed the rounded, complex human being who now emerged from the tributes and
laments. On television, the cool, trenchant intelligence was
unmistakable – but not the courage of her private eighteen-year
battle with leukaemia. The wit and attack were on view –
but not the patient, methodical way she went about nurturing
and embellishing the lives around her. Above all, and because
her professional function was to ask questions, her insatiable
curiosity was displayed night after night – but rarely the causes
to which she kindled, the private values by which she lived, her
loyalties, her own opinions. In this she was rather like Irene
Forsyte in John Galsworthy's *Forsyte Saga*, who was an important catalyst in the novels but whose character had to be
inferred from her effect on the other figures. On television, the
real Mrs. Frum, too, could only be inferred.

This being said, the notion that Barbara Frum was without passionate views – and actions to back them up – is a bit of a joke to anyone associated with *Saturday Night*. The simple truth is that, at the worst moment in the magazine's 105-year history, Barbara Frum came charging to our rescue. The story unfolds in 1974. Although she never wrote for my predecessor, Robert Fulford, she was by this time a close friend of his and fully aware of the economic perils through which the magazine was staggering, month after month. That October, the magazine gasped its apparent last breath and folded. Obituaries were published.

A few days after the suspension of publication was announced, or perhaps it was a few weeks, she was at a social event crowded with members of the Toronto arts and letters community. As she made the rounds, she discovered that *Saturday Night* was at the centre of many conversations, but it wasn't grief that was being expressed. It was *glee*. The magazine's time had clearly passed, she heard. Fulford had got what he deserved. *Saturday Night* was a bore. It was élitist. It was irrelevant. It was . . . well, it was whatever the cocktail-party pundits wanted to say to prove their belief that the universe was unfolding as it should. Mrs. Frum could not understand how the very people who should have been fighting to save *Saturday Night* could be cackling at its demise. She left the party in a rage and kept nattering at her husband, Dr. Murray Frum, until he retreated exhausted to bed. In the morning, he awakened to find his wife calm and armed for battle. She had, she said, found a solution for *Saturday Night*.

"What's your solution?" asked Dr. Frum.

"I'm going to give them you," said Mrs. Frum.

And so she did. Dr. Frum, a creative and energetic organizer as well as a successful developer, became chairman of a new board of directors, working with Fulford and a new publisher to get the magazine going again. It was his idea to canvass *Saturday Night*'s loyal subscribers to see if they would commit themselves to the magazine's future. They did, and *Saturday Night* rose phoenix-like from its ashes. Dr. Frum stayed the course and guided the "higher" affairs of *Saturday Night* astutely for half a decade.

Barbara Frum stayed the course as well. She was a crucial ally for Fulford throughout the nineteen years of his remarkable editorship and, though I never knew what she felt about his controversial leave-taking five years ago and my subsequent arrival, in different and rather wonderful ways she continued to support the magazine. Not the least of those contributions were two of her talented children: Linda Frum, whose deliciously inflammatory article on Canadian universities still holds the record for bringing in the most letters to the editor we have ever received; and David Frum, whose every published word when he wrote regularly for us from 1987 to 1989 seemed to end up as either a battle cry for the Right or a gauntlet flung down for the Left. David Frum's articles became such a lightning rod for outrage in some quarters that his mother once said to him wickedly: "Your father and I aren't being asked out a lot any more, David. But *we don't blame you*."

This magazine has another reason to be well aware of Barbara Frum's capacity for opinions. Though it has not been much dwelt on, she began her career as a print journalist and one of her first assignments was a series of columns for *Saturday Night*. This was in 1967, the columns were on the subject of television, and boy! did she have views. Here is a sampling.

- The fact is TV-viewers don't like change . . . you have only to check the programme listings to prove it. The situation comedies, the quizzes, the panel shows – programmes all designed for the so-called mass audience – only have to hook firmly onto an audience to keep it. As in marriage, it's the first year that's critical; if a show can scrape through that one season, it's likely to survive six more before the seven-year-itch for change threatens it. . . . On television, it would seem, familiarity breeds no contempt.

- A viewer attuned to gestures can cut through the sham and contrivance of many TV images. Take "Sunday" for example . . . there's Ian Tyson, relaxed, accustomed to entertaining crowds, a slick performer, he leans back and away from you, smugly crosses his arms across his chest and almost defies you not to like him. But Peter Reilly, a journalist, not really show biz, is obviously embarrassed in that bear pit and tells you so by his gestures. His head is held slightly hangdog as he periodically makes quick flicks of his nose with his right index finger, hopefully unobtrusive but not at all so. Larry Zolf, not so embarrassed but not really at home either, his pet gesture reinforces his reputation for hearty vulgarity, a thumb-forefinger pinch of the nostrils, like the last part of a nose-blowing, but with no handkerchief in sight.

  And lastly on "Sunday" . . . there's Jack Webster "up to his old tricks in B.C.," a belligerent and common fellow who revels in his man-of-the-people origins and indicates them with a long, backhand wipe of the nose that starts at the wrist and ends savouringly at the fingertips.

- Women, generically, may be TV Public Affairs' newest "problem" subject. . . . now that the medium has pretty well plumbed poverty and picked over Viet Nam. Witness the recent trio of half-hours on "Take 30," CBC Public Affairs afternoon uplift-with-coffee-break for ladies. Undoubtedly conceived as three penetrating and helpful looks at the post-forty woman (the menopausal mess once again), it comes out as an unintentionally brutal vision of women annihilated in every sphere of life by the closing down of their reproductive systems. The message of the series: Hey there, you with the bulging waistline and atrophying ovaries, you'd better learn how to sublimate, because you're in real trouble now you've hit forty.

• The . . . gimmick of this television season is the spending of large amounts of money on single properties to be broadcast as "specials!" Over 300 are scheduled – Gielgud in "To Chekhov With Love," CBC's "Swan Lake," Gogol's "Diary of a Madman," The Royal Shakespeare Company's "Macbeth". . . . Lest the naively optimistic start believing that television is at last upgrading its taste, I caution that the special itself is just an idea, this year's idea. And like all new television ideas it, too, will pall and shortly be replaced.

• Recently I was told by a television public relations man that there are really only two kinds of critics, those who like what "the people" like, and are therefore presumably worth listening to, and those who don't. And he coyly implied I fell into the latter category.

  Perversely, I take that as a compliment. If the TV ratings prove that "the people" like "The Beverly Hillbillies," "The Smothers Brothers," "Ed Sullivan," and "Bonanza," then okay, I don't like what the people like.

There were only nine columns in all, and inevitably they are dated by their references to particular programs and personalities. But they have more than mere curiosity value: here was the real Mrs. Frum using her journalist's eye and her fastidious sensibility to critique the medium she soon set out to conquer. Television being what it is, she never had public occasion to be so forthright on the subject again.

June 1992

The Summit's Crowning Glory

~

The International Journalists' Summit, being held this year in Toronto from June 19 to 22, offers Canadians a unique opportunity to see close up the working style and social habits of the most powerful figures in the West. Often criticized as so much ritualistic posturing, these annual gabfests – organized by the United States, Canada, France, West Germany, Italy, Great Britain, and Japan – nevertheless bring together the key players who shape and direct public reaction to the economic policies of their seven patron governments. The Toronto summit marks the first occasion the meetings have been held in a major North American metropolis, and the city is understandably bracing itself for the kind of political posturing and undignified scrummages that have now become such a familiar feature of the events.

It was not supposed to be this way. When the summit was conceived by the French in 1975, it had been optimistically thought that something of substance could be achieved if the top 300 journalists forgathered quietly in Paris, the first site. Right from the beginning, though, heads of government felt abandoned and insisted upon coming, although they agreed to bring only skeletal support staff and further pledged to remain mute and sequestered in the inconsequential village of Rambouillet, a good sixty kilometres from all the action in the French capital. With these concessions the media delegates felt they could hold their meeting unmolested.

Thirteen years ago, the journalists did not even want to call their gathering a summit. Instead, they saw relaxed, off-the-record informality as the key to useful conversations on the divisive issues of the day. The unattributable quotation and the unidentified source were concerns of the American and British delegations, for example, while the establishment of an internationally acceptable norm on fabricated expense accounts was the fixation among the code-conscious French. For their part, the Italians were angry about the rise of exclusive one-on-one interviews with terrorists.

Sadly, the illusion of a low-key working retreat was shattered in short order. Cut off entirely from the fourth estate, the government leaders plotted amongst themselves to force a press conference or, at the very least, a brief media opportunity. Boldly eluding their own security precautions, the politicians mustered in a village mayor's office and demanded coverage of a mysterious and hastily conceived document called "the final communiqué." Since news is news, no matter how brazenly contrived, the journalists resignedly left their pleasant deliberations at the cafés and bistros along boulevard du Montparnasse, and journeyed to the rural squalor of Rambouillet. Thus was born the journalistic necessity of actually having to work at some point during the summit, and the attendant ambition to keep it to a minimum.

Within two years, the format with which we are now all too familiar began emerging. By this time, journalists from Canada, who had inexplicably been excluded at Rambouillet, were allowed full membership; inevitably, Canadian government leaders also insisted upon coming. Together, the seven leaders surreptitiously increased government representation to include key figures in the various foreign affairs and economic ministries, along with their chief aides, executive assistants, academic advisers, stenographic staff, and security personnel – which meant that the journalists had little choice but to increase their own numbers to deal with the quantum leap in background briefings, calculated leaks, and measured assessments of the final communiqué. Any hope of a return to the initial intimacy of Paris/Rambouillet was lost forever. Today, organizers for the Toronto summit estimate that anywhere from 4,000 to 7,000 media worthies will come to the city, trailed by a proportionate number of government officials.

Apart from the ballooning size of the twin delegations, the other key development during these years was the emergence from obscurity to pivotal importance of the so-called "sherpas." Named after those intrepid Nepalese guides who lead climbers to the tops of mountains, and – significantly – down again, the summit sherpas have been recruited from the highest ranks of the various bureaucracies. Their chief task is to mediate between the journalists and the government leaders. On one hand, they supply the politicians with a plausible script complete with controlled drama, apparently substantive issues, and a portentous-sounding but harmless consensus to be reached. On the other hand they guarantee the journalists that their own pursuits will not be interrupted by surprises and that they will be spared any need to think for themselves. To protect their own unique role, the sherpas have taken to reinforcing feelings of confusion and inferiority among government leaders, while neutralizing identical feelings among the journalists who must cover what they do not understand. In the encompassing incomprehension are the reputations of successful summits made.

For the past three or four years, the archsherpa – or "first among equals" – has been a Canadian: the redoubtable Dr. Sylvia Ostry, our former chief statistician. While the summit is actually being held, Dr. Ostry never speaks "on the record" (and is known to the public only as "a senior government official"). Still, she manages successfully to service both media and government leaders, and such is her reputation that her arrival for a briefing at the Canadian press centre during the 1985 Bonn summit was preceded by cries of "Sylvia's coming! Sylvia's coming!" from joyous journalists concerned about a lack of "heft" in their copy. Ostry is esteemed for her no-nonsense demeanour, her lucid analysis of the inexplicable, and her noble – if Sisyphean – efforts to keep the current Canadian government leader from trying to butter his political parsnips at inappropriate moments.

Those in Canada who have never before closely followed a summit may not be aware of this background, but it is crucial for understanding what goes on: what they read in newspapers or see on television is as carefully orchestrated as a solemn *Te Deum*. Everything has been worked out weeks beforehand by the sherpas. For the benefit of the uninitiated, this outline of the ordained "Order of Service," suitable for clipping, is offered. (1) *Introit and Processional*. The stately preliminaries commence ten to fourteen days before the first session of the summit. They are obtrusive only in the host country because of the duty incumbent on the local media to provide maximum coverage. Senior journalists with previous summit experience are required to write endless op-ed speculations on and analyses of some of the major, and all of the minor, issues. The tone expected here is cool authority. Junior sherpas make themselves available as sources. As the summit gets closer, judiciousness is jettisoned and a different sort of journalist is brought forward whose job it is to whip up stories from details "leaked" by more senior sherpas, focusing on potential contention and divisiveness. (2) *Arrival of the Senior Clergy*. Every summit begins with a formal media opportunity, and for this significant event are assembled the scripted villains, accuser-victims, and peacemakers – roles that are interchangeable from year to year. A villain is that country whose economy has been most successful during the preceding year; accuser-victims are those with chronic deficits based on general mismanagement and specific ineptitude; the peacemaker is always chosen from among the least influential whose opinions are irrelevant and therefore of maximum apparent disinterest (Canada always vies with Italy for this post).

(3) *Litany*. Each successive summit features "unprecedented security precautions" to protect journalists and government delegations. Thus, a special summit vocabulary emerges for a couple of days. Security officials, for example, will demand of a journalist, "Have you been magged yet?" in a reference to magnetic metal detectors. "Macro" and "micro" are also key elements in security clearance: a journalist or government figure who cannot talk meaninglessly for fifteen minutes on macroeconomics is *ipso facto* suspect. A host city is inevitably "tense" prior to the beginning of a summit, and "relieved" when it is over. Details, such as police helicopter surveillance above, and underwater (or sewer-drain) inspection sweeps below, are mandatory, although a bomb scare is optional.

(4) *Consecration*. One crucial tradition of Rambouillet has been maintained. It is still thought expedient to hide government leaders from public view (except for brief glimpses when they sip coffee or Bovril, or go to the washroom) until it comes time for the sacred rite of the final communiqué. The leaders once hinted they should have full media exposure throughout the two working days of the summit, but it was unilaterally decided that this would interfere with the journalists' agenda,

strained as it already is with such crucial coverage as the shopping habits and clothing styles of the government leaders' spouses, or the cost of local accommodation. (At the Venice summit, a renegade correspondent reported in his newspaper that accommodation for journalists was $420 per night. A cost-conscious Canadian Press editor wired his reporter in shock demanding both confirmation and explanation of this charge. The answer came back: "Report accurate. Price includes breakfast.")

(5) *Recessional.* The elevation of "the final communiqué" marks both the high point and the conclusion of the government summit. The document itself – only slightly less relevant than a contemporary papal bull – represents a shopping list of items government summiteers disagree upon least. Generally, it can be assumed that "the final communiqué" of the Toronto summit, like all the others, will be for mothers, against the senseless slaughter of innocent people, and "concerned" about all the things the summit was unable to resolve. The media, in a time-honoured ritual, are required to pronounce the communiqué worthless even as they sanctify it with 800 to 2,000 words. That concludes their extracurricular obligations.

This is, of course, a very simplified guide to the Journalists' Summit, which is an extremely complex process. There is not space here, for example, to explain fully the intricate negotiations involved in allocating journalists' hotel bedrooms. The vicious dispute which erupted last year in Venice after an ancient hack from *The Toronto Star* was assigned a spacious room overlooking a romantic piazza beside a canal, while the Toronto *Globe and Mail's* prize-winning European correspondent found himself with windows opening on a well no bigger than a laundry chute, has not yet been resolved.

Despite the engrossed fatuousness of these affairs, let it be said that the international summit does, in the end, provide a useful opportunity for oppressed journalists to flee their spiteful editors and drown tears of frustration in a different country's beer each year. This is not an epic accomplishment, but it is better than war.

June 1988

Who Cares?

~

Happy 125th birthday, Canada! Apparently, things have never been worse: the economy's in a shambles, the constitution remains a mess, the language dispute is as bitter as usual, regional divisions are getting wider, public services are at historic levels of shoddiness, racism and sexism are perceived to be rampant, the Reichmanns have come a cropper, our lawmakers are spiritually exhausted, the citizenry is already disgusted and bored, and the CBC is moving up all the bad news from ten o'clock to nine p.m. to make completely sure we don't sneak off to bed with even a scintilla of hope.

On top of all this, we have been told so often and from so many quarters that Canada is an illogical nonsense of a nation that today's conjunction of maximum peril and seemingly intractable difficulties conspires to make many Canadians doubt there ever was a coherent country worth a patriotic cheer, let alone dying for or struggling to maintain. So then, what on earth are we going to do about our "glorious" 125th?

Personally, I think we should all pretend it's the 127th or the 123rd, and head for the hills as normally as possible. These numerically portentous anniversaries are the pits unless you know how to handle them properly. My ancient cousin, Miss Louise Hill of Fredericton, New Brunswick, for example, managed to sneak past her ninetieth birthday not so long ago by announcing she would brook no celebration until her centenary in 2001, when she would be pleased and proud to receive a message of congratulations from her sovereign.

Cousin Louise is a model figure for me, as is my excellent friend Ralph Heintzman of Ottawa, who – like me – is attending upon his half-century within a couple of years. Forget 125! The ominous figure of fifty is out there winking and grimacing on the horizon and I long to creep stealthily past its irritating force field of summation and evaluation. Knowing Heintzman, however, he will turn the event into a triumphant celebration of ripeness attained. He's like that. He could pluck a juicy moral from a crab tree in the dead of winter.

My friend Heintzman and my cousin Louise have never heard about each other except through me, but they are both historians and writers, and fans of Canada, and when I want to feel good about the country I live in I think of them and other people I love who are like them. People I know.

Samuel Taylor Coleridge saw the network of ordinary personal affections as the strongest single link in human civility and decent endeavour. Such affections, he wrote in *Lectures on Revealed Religion*, expand "like the circles of a lake – the love of our friends, parents, and neighbours leads us to the love of country, to the love of all mankind." That is the only sensible definition of Canada I have ever come across, even if it was written about seventy years before Confederation.

I was put in the way of this passage a long time ago by my friend Heintzman, who was best man on my wedding day and gave me two handsome volumes of Coleridge's essays as a present. In my library, I also have two volumes of Cousin Louise's lifetime work, *The Old Burying Ground*, a careful catalogue with commentary of Loyalist graves in the oldest cemetery in Fredericton. She's hard at work today completing the third and final volume, and if it seems an amazing thing that a person born in 1901 should be harassing a volunteer computer inputter and bargaining with recession-weary publishers in 1992, that is simply part of the measure of Cousin Louise.

Her life's credo is brisk and pointed: fear God, honour the Queen, love the land. Her father was a hero during the First World War, winning the Military Cross and emerging a briga-dier general. She was a dutiful daughter and, after her mother died, she tended to him until his death nearly half a century ago. For many years she was the librarian at the New Brunswick pro-vincial legislature, where she watched the passing parade of provincial politicians with a certain wry detachment. It was Cousin Louise who told me a few years ago that Richard Hat-field's Conservatives were in real trouble. This was long before the pundits – or even poor Hatfield himself – figured it out. In the subsequent election, when the premier went down to igno-minious defeat and not a single Tory got elected, Cousin Louise expressed astonishment that "Mr. Hatfield did as well as he did."

My friend Heintzman, unlike Cousin Louise, does not have an ironical nature. If you could imagine a Queen's Scout as an Ottawa civil servant, and throw in some steely passion, you've got my man. In his most essential professional guise, he is an English-Canadian historian of French Canada. His love for Quebec and for French Canadians, for the French reality in Canada, runs so deep that I've never been able to plumb it. He understands, and embodies, what Sir John A. Macdonald meant when he said: "Treat them [French Canadians] as a nation and they will act as a free people generally do – generously."

Ralph Heintzman is also the principal draftsman of the par-liamentary *Report of the Special Joint Committee on a Renewed Canada*, chaired by Senator Gérald Beaudoin and Dorothy

Dobbie, MP. The report, when it was finally released a few months ago, was hailed by the prime minister as one of the most important documents in Canadian history. The prime minister and I are of the same view on this matter.

I understand very well that the reports of vast political inquiries such as this are always put through the political mill. I also know my friend Heintzman's style and mind. I could spot his paragraphs a mile off. Paragraphs like these:

"The challenges facing our country are so enormous, and our emotions so stretched, that it is sometimes hard to imagine that we should be able to meet both our external and internal needs at the same time.

"We are not given to this view. It does not do anything approaching justice to the very great Canadian achievements of the last decades. . . . Nor does it do justice to the authentic and underlying convictions of Canadians, what they believe in their heart of hearts. . . .

"Canadians sometimes seem to think that the Canadian experiment is a much more fragile or artificial one than it really is. But that view does not take account of the roots of contemporary Canadian life, which are far deeper and older than many Canadians today are inclined to think. It does not do justice to the very long journey that Canadians have taken together toward the ideals of Canadian life – a journey that, in the eyes of the world, is a noble one, and of great worth."

Heintzman's still hacking away in the same difficult terrain, only now he's advising Joe Clark on the wretched Senate. I can't think what he'll do there, but whatever it is I know this: he always stands on guard, and Canada is lucky he does.

Three years ago, I walked around the old Loyalist burial grounds in the heart of Fredericton with Cousin Louise. She was on a bit of a rant about the inadequate upkeep of the graveyard when she spied a large weed that had grown up in front of the final resting place of one of her favourite Loyalists. I can't remember the name, except that he was a soldier, so she had a special affection for him. As she recited all his pertinent dates and relatives and business dealings, transporting me back to the eighteenth and early nineteenth centuries as if it were only yesterday, she aimed her walking stick at the weed and then tried quite dramatically to smite it a mighty whack.

"Missed!" she said in disgust. "I wish it had been the gardeners I'd hit."

I asked her curiously whether she thought people in Canada today really cared any longer about the Loyalists and their flight from the American Revolution to live under the British Crown in the Canadian colonies.

"Care?" she said a little angrily, and then she paused a long time. It crossed my mind that the wrath of God was about to descend upon me, but she was only trying to think of the right answer. My cousin Louise has always enjoyed a pointed conversation. She pushed her stick into the heart of the weed and ground it into the earth.

"I care."

In the caring, affections are nurtured. In the nurturing, a nation is sustained. God bless this good and patient land of all our families and all our friends.

July 1992

One Last Rant

⌣

"The freedom to be cruel is one of journalism's uncontested privileges," wrote Janet Malcolm, the controversial American reporter and author, in her celebrated 1993 *New Yorker* article on the late poet Sylvia Plath. Uh . . . not quite. Let me contest it, for example. The notion that somehow cruelty is a journalistic privilege – a *right* really, almost an obligation – seems to me to be a symptom of the prevailing dysfunction which has afflicted my profession for the past thirty years. And while we're at it, what about the "uncontested privilege" or right to be lazy? Or to be vituperative? And then there's the right to fake objectivity and the right to distort facts and quotes – or to ignore them altogether. Such things are part of a journalist's publicly perceived identikit now and are buttressed by example in all media on an hourly, daily, weekly, bimonthly, monthly, quarterly, and annual basis.

I'm going to eschew the wonderful world of television reporting here and stick to print, which I know best. For my purposes, print is sufficient to depict the malaise, especially since so much

television reporting is first lifted from newspapers and magazines: in my world, the halt still lead the blind. Much as my colleagues lament the fact, there *are* real reasons why journalism is
held in such low esteem these days, and if some of the reason
is the public's dislike for difficult stories or "bad news," that is
now the lesser part of the conundrum. Ordinary people are onto
our game, and they have discovered that beyond the laws of libel
and slander, we tend to make up our own rules of employment
and then issue them as if they had been written in stone. Rules
and privileges like Ms. Malcolm's.

Some time ago in the dim, dark past of the history of journalism – about the time Richard Nixon and his U.S. presidency
were on the ropes over the Watergate scandal – the avocation of
reporting, a hitherto modest craft that was the last safe redoubt
of the generalist, took on cultic overtones, complete with
priestly practitioners. However honourable were the intentions
of the two mighty journalists at *The Washington Post* who broke
and sustained the Watergate story, they have nevertheless
spawned several generations of second- and third-rate Carl
Bernsteins and Bob Woodwards. We've been paying the price
ever since in the demolition of respect for public institutions, in
the declining quality of our political leaders, and in the stultify-
ing cynicism of a public that now needs to be mainlined with
any old trashy exposé in increasingly frequent and deadly doses.
If old-fashioned journalism can fairly be accused of too often
ignoring political cupidity and ethical malefactions, new-style
journalism is far more guilty of manufacturing scandal and
human failure out of innuendo, out of suspicion, and – often
enough – out of thin air.

Do you remember, for example, when the Canadian general
Lewis MacKenzie was the subject a couple of years ago of nasty
news service stories which suggested that the hero of the United
Nation's peacekeeping command in former Yugoslavia was in
reality a war criminal? I recall it vividly because I was so shocked

I went to the trouble to track down the sources, all of whom turned out to be anonymous members of a certain faction inside the terrible Bosnian conflagration. For weeks, these stories hinting at atrocities involving General Mackenzie made it into most Canadian newspapers. And then, as mysteriously as they started, they died away. So far as I was able to discern, not one newspaper or news agency tried to do a proper investigation or follow-up and point out the spurious, slanderous origin of the stories. In the end, it was left to the poor general himself to explain that no, actually, he hadn't been party to the raping of widows or the killing of prisoners-of-war.

How did it come to be that the Reichman brothers, because of an almighty business catastrophe associated with worldwide recession, were transformed from financial wizards and social benefactors to third-rate development goons whose family may have had – or, then again, may not have had – dubious business interests during the Second World War? How did ordinary and perfectly decent political figures like Joe Clark, John Turner, Audrey McLaughlin, David Peterson, or Kim Campbell become so demonized that even their facial features took on sinister casts? *How? Why? What?* I find myself asking these questions about my profession all the time and lately I find myself increasingly going back to root causes.

Perhaps a little unfairly, I trace much of it back to journalism schools, which don't just feed into the post-Watergate cynicism and distrust of anything or anyone worthy of an "investigative" report or "in-depth" profile, they positively foster institutional rancour and disbelieving zealotry with a righteousness no longer to be found in even a fundamentalist divinity school. I can sniff journalism grads a hundred miles away, and increasingly at *Saturday Night* I tried to avoid them, unless they could prove to me that they had repented of nearly everything they were taught. The task, as an editor, of deprogramming journalism students is unpleasant because it is not simply specific practices you have to get at, but a presiding ethos and self-identification. Tell a young buck journalist today to give the subject of his story the benefit of doubt and you'll be called "Mrs. Bobbit." Tell a doe and you end up a sexist pig. Remember Ms. Malcolm: "The freedom to be cruel is one of journalism's uncontested privileges."

Mea culpa, mea culpa. I have been on the boards of journalism schools. I fought to save the graduate school of journalism at the University of Western Ontario, but it was with a heavy heart. What I would really like to do is eliminate the whole lot, take the budding journalists by their collars and pants, and force march them into literature courses, philosophy courses, psychology courses, political science courses, law courses, theology courses, even basket-weaving courses – anything that would keep them away from Journalism 100.

Good journalists have to start with two basic, innate traits: curiosity and a desire to communicate. These traits can be taken in many directions, but the best direction is broad general knowledge and a few areas of specialization. Distinctive writing skills come, first, from wide reading and emulation, and later from relentless practice and rigorous editing. Curiosity, on the other hand, is a far more precarious commodity because it is so easily diverted down cul-de-sacs or stifled altogether in the useless badinage of "correct journalistic practice." In this way, journalism courses cut off inquiry by emphasizing technique; they cut off normal human compassion and fairness by assumptions of implied guilt that arise thanks to the arbitrary methodology involved in getting "to the bottom of the story"; and, worst of all, they cut off any real sense of responsibility by invoking a higher calling.

Take the issue of objectivity, for example. Every journalist is supposed to strive towards the cardinal virtue of "objectivity," yet this must be one of the vainest, most intangible, and ultimately unobtainable goals a humble craft ever set itself. There is no such thing as a strictly objective story. It isn't possible. Everything – from the structure of an article to the choice of facts – is filtered through a particular outlook and a prejudiced mind. All stories are weighted in some direction. All stories, in newspapers or magazines, leave out pertinent facts, either by design or inadvertently. This is true equally of a modest news agency report and an "in depth" political feature. Not even the most detailed *Saturday Night* or *New Yorker* profile can provide a comprehensive view of a subject's life where, even with the best of intentions, distortions are varied and manifold. There are tangible reasons why most eminent journalists and editors are so reluctant to be profiled, or, if they do agree, why they become such neurotic control freaks, setting out "guidelines" and "parameters" and "off-the-record" understandings. They know better than anyone how they can be served up. If you want to discover the proof of all this, just listen to the moral outrage of journalists whenever letters of complaint are sent to the editor. A friend of mine once supervised the letters to the editor section of *The Globe and Mail* and regularly regaled me with little horror stories of my colleagues going ballistic whenever criticism came through the mailbox. Usually, the letter-writers were accused of not seeing a particular article in context, of manipulating the writers' words, of being unfair, of being wrong, of being stupid. Sometimes the reporters would lobby higher authorities in the newsroom to keep the letters out of the paper. On one notable occasion at *Saturday Night*, a writer even threatened legal action over a letter to the editor. I double-dared him.

Intelligent readers know all this, of course. They know they have to read widely to get a decent grip on any subject, including the life of a public figure. The most you can hope for, the only thing you should be able to count on, is relative honesty, and the very best (i.e., the most honest) journalists always let their readers know their specific prejudices and the general nature of the intellectual equipment through which they distill their stories. All claims to any higher ordering in the reporting of the affairs of men and women are bunk. There are no exceptions.

The self-delusion of so many journalists as they skate across the surface of life is almost beyond comprehension, and this has grown proportionately to their expanding self-esteem. Few stories ever probe deeply, usually because of laziness, but sometimes because such probing will complicate a story line already decided upon. Unless, of course, there's a hint of hanky-panky, but even here all we usually get is the hint. No publication in Canada over the past seven years devoted more of its energy and its proportionate editorial space to investigative reporting than *Saturday Night*. It is an arduous, expensive, and exhausting business, rife with the possibilities of litigation and prone – even under the best of circumstances – to factual elision and character defamation. Without exception, every article we published in this genre was subjected to intense checking, legal advice, and a constant blitz of questioning from all the editors at the magazine about its fairness. And still, from time to time, we erred, and when we did it seemed to me a grievous, self-inflicted wound which we would go to considerable efforts to correct, even at the expense of humiliating a reporter or an editor or a checker.

Perhaps I should admit here that my views are coloured by experience. When I was posted in China for *The Globe and Mail* in the late 1970s, I lived among the best journalists the world had to offer. So comprehensive was the authoritarian pall which still shrouded the population, that at this time no outsider – least of all a distrusted, resident correspondent – had any meaningful contact with the citizens of the People's Republic. Yet when the so-called Peking Spring unfolded and young Chinese people found the courage to tell the truth about life under Chairman Mao, there were precisely four foreign correspondents (out of over fifty!) who didn't feel threatened by this uncontrolled expression from real Chinese people. I found myself surrounded by colleagues who didn't want to know anything different from what they thought they already knew, who were frightened of such encounters, and who would later expend considerable effort undermining the work of the four who were – however tentatively – trying to decipher one of the most important stories of the day. Frankly, it's the same tale back home, and the proof can be found with the pack journalism of the press gallery in Ottawa. Of course there are notable exceptions, but if ever you want a totally dispiriting experience, go off to a good news agent when things are politically hot in the nation's capital and buy a dozen newspapers published from sea even unto sea. To compare and contrast this superficial, knee-jerk, junk coverage is to abandon all hope.

And this, too. The power of the media is such these days that journalistic vanity is left largely unchecked. It is not a pleasant experience to encounter the smug certitudes of the accredited messengers and soothsayers of our society. About the only corrective around is the "Remedial Media" column of *Frank* magazine, that nasty little compendium of journalistic follies. Often inaccurate, "Remedial Media" nevertheless regularly administers painful enemas to bloated egos and strutting ambitions, but what a dreadful statement on our times and this profession when we have to cite the hackery of *Frank* as the best available antidote.

And *Frank* rarely gets at the root cause, perhaps because it has a satirical stake in maintaining the status quo. There's a joker from a prominent graduate school of journalism who pontificates from time to time in both broadcasting and print as a self-styled media analyst. Any time he has talked about something I have had practical experience of, I have been staggered by how far off the mark he is, but on a self-confidence scale of one to ten he's at the top. I once telephoned him after he pronounced a verdict on the future of general interest magazines (gloomy) and

Saturday Night in particular (dead). He didn't turn out to be an evil fellow, quite the contrary in fact, but so set was he in his theories that my feeble efforts to inject a few basic facts into his consciousness had all the effect of waves washing up against the Rock of Gibraltar. *The Ryerson Journalism Review*, published annually in Toronto, is one of the most respected journals of its kind, right up there with the *Columbia Journalism Review*. On one level it is brilliant: a compendium of all the teaching tricks dished out to journalism students – tough and probing, strictly objective, no favour or fear allowed – and yet its articles and analyses are usually so wrong or so biased that the information provided is of little value. In a recent issue, for example, a student writer under the direction of teachers and editors castigated *The Toronto Star* for abandoning the newspaper's historic support for "the little man." This thesis was the engine propelling the whole article. Now there are many criticisms which can be levelled at *The Toronto Star*, Canada's largest daily, but the one thing it could never be accused of – and which even the enemies of the *Star* would never accuse it of – is abandoning "the little man." The newspaper may be a trifle unhinged when it finds itself inside the realm of political correctness, its economic nationalism may be stuck in a time warp, and so on, but it does retain a distinctive viewpoint and it now has far more of value to "the little man" than even the grunty *Sun* tabloids, which seem to have abandoned their once rigorously populist posture.

In my experience at *Saturday Night* there was only one exception which made me question my growing unease with the methodology and results of journalism schools, and yet this particular exception became so complicated I'm still – three years after the events – not sure what to make of all the lessons to be learned. A young, fresh graduate of the journalism school at Ryerson, Sean O'Malley, turned up at our offices. Unlike most journalism grads, I was predisposed to like him because his dad was Martin O'Malley, a fine journalist of the old school and a former colleague of mine at *The Globe and Mail.* (Yes, Virginia, editors play favourites and have been known to look sympathetically upon the progeny of their friends, although the connection usually only serves to get a foot in the door). After a bit of a general chat, we got onto the subject of Bryan Johnson, my successor at *The Globe* in two posts (theatre criticism and the Beijing bureau), and for the young O'Malley a childhood hero and role model. Johnson, who by this time had left *The Globe,* was well remembered for his "insightful" reports on The Philippines. He wrote a wonderful book on Cory Aquino's "People's Revolution" and, among the chattering classes, was particularly esteemed for a famously sensitive article on the child prostitutes of Manila.

The story Sean O'Malley started telling me was almost beyond comprehension. Bryan, said Sean, had returned to live in Manila and had gone "native" in a particularly sensational way: he was now a part-owner of a girlie bar in the seamy Ermita district of the Philippine capital. If true, this was a tale right up there with the life of Kurtz in Joseph Conrad's *Heart of Darkness,* but I didn't – couldn't – believe it. On the other hand, O'Malley was lusting to explore the Far East for exotic job possibilities, and at the time I had access to free transportation for him and a small expense account. So off he went on what I fully expected to be a story more rumour-ridden than factual, but hell, what can you do about the young.

In the end, the story turned out to be only too true, and Sean took a terrific stab at the article which, on its first draft, was too heavily overlaid with metaphors from *Heart of Darkness.* He worked with a good editor at the magazine, Bruce Headlam, and every one else also pitched in. In the end, Sean pulled off what I still cite as a masterpiece of journalistic honesty, although he had to abandon some – not all – of the rules he had studied at journalism school. What made the story so compelling, what propelled it towards magazine awards and even a movie contract, was the simple device of honesty. Sean didn't try to disguise his own voice in objectivity. In fact, rereading the article today, I am still awed by the way he managed to deploy his naivety to draw readers into his tale.

He was even scrupulously fair to Johnson, somewhat buying into a specious spiritualism in which this proprietor of a tawdry girlie club tried to depict himself as a saviour bringing material and protective solace to young girls. No regular journalist could have got this extraordinary story, which ended up telling us so much about the hypocrisy towards the Third World which afflicts the affluent West, which encumbers male and female relationships, and – last but not least – which poisons journalism itself. Although this was an exceptional case, I will never get out of my mind the feelings of admiration – hell, envy – I felt for Johnson when he was castigating society and governments for allowing the trade of child prostitutes to flourish and the feelings of nausea at how it all ended up.

It was also a difficult story for me to preside over because of my own previous association with Johnson and because the success of the story left me with a troubled young journalist (O'Malley) who needed a few months to recover from the experience. But it was all too horribly emblematic of things that frightened me in my profession, and this turmoil was not alleviated by the reaction from mutual colleagues of Johnson's and mine. A number of journalists raked me over the coals, from quite different perspectives, but the underlying message – beyond being told that the story was too "in" or that Johnson was not a worthy figure to be profiled – was that I had fouled my own professional nest. In every case, these professionals were not graduates of journalism schools, so I try to keep a little perspective on my venom.

But enough negativism. The antidote to all this comes in two guises: great editing and humility among the scribes. By humility, I mean a recognition of the limits of journalism and an honest presentation of self. This does not mean letting crooked politicians off the hook, but it does mean that a political reporter might know a bit about the profession of politics before he or she stands in almighty judgement. That's one end of the problem. At the other end, it also means that a journalist should strive to do something more than rewrite a press release, and that he or she is prepared to dig deeply for factual information and context. My predecessor as editor at *Saturday Night*, Robert Fulford, has always been such a journalist, one whose premises have always been open for scrutiny. So, in a very different and distinctive way, is his fellow columnist at *The Globe and Mail*, Rick Salutin. You never mistake their prejudices, even if you disagree with what they are saying. Indeed, one often enthusiastically disagrees with them. The point is that they engage you responsibly by extending new information and viewpoints and by respecting a reader's own ability to reason and make sense of things.

One of my other heroes in this business is Peter Worthington, the founding editor of *The Toronto Sun* and now a widely published columnist. Since I once called him an asshole after a public sparring match, I suppose I better explain my own premises. I first encountered Worthington at the old Toronto *Telegram*, where I started my career in journalism as a summer-time copy boy in 1960. A decade later, when I worked full time at the *Telegram* during the last year and a half of its existence, Worthington had returned from Russia, and his anti-communism marked him off to many in our profession as a right-winger almost as deranged as Lubor J. Zink, another columnist at the *Telegram*. As copy boys, we used to stuff Zink's mail box with any left-wing literature we could get hold of. We loved the sight of him angrily hurling the bumph into a trash can. None of us knew anything of Zink's background, his courage when he lived under a communist regime in Eastern Europe, his unyielding zeal to make sure the world never forgot Stalin's atrocities. When, decades later, the Soviet empire came tumbling down, there were very few of us who stood up and said, "Lubor J. Zink was right." Zink is now an old man and remains massively unhonoured in the country where he told the truth.

Peter Worthington, on the other hand, has never worried too much about vindication, and because he was posted in Moscow he knew early on that Lubor J. Zink was not a nut or even a silly-sounding name. One of the least vain journalists I have ever encountered, his populist sense of fairness is innate. He drives some people crazy and makes dangerous alliances with almost anyone or any cause that he feels isn't getting a decent shake in the media. Although his ideology is on the Right, this has never distracted him from identifying with an underdog. He fights with passion and conviction. When you read Worthington, all his prejudices are on view and no reader can be in any doubt about his premises. The glee with which he exposes hypocrisy can be positively frightening. Yet shining through all this is a clear humanity and decency that seems to drive a lot of journalism professors manic with bitterness and anger. If a young tyro asked me who would be a good model for an honest, action journalist, I'd point immediately to Worthington, especially if the kid was from journalism school. The initial look of shock would be worth the price of the advice alone.

You couldn't find a journalist more different from Worthington than Anne Collins, a distinguished author (her book on the CIA's drug experiments in the 1950s, *The Sleep Room*, won the Governor General's Award for non-fiction) and a senior editor at *Saturday Night*. I suppose her ideological slant is soft-Left, but I've never been very much aware of it. What I did see was a selfless editor who seemed to live for other writers, willing them to take chances, to smarten up their prose, and – above all – to be fair. In Canadian journalism today, there are very few editors of Anne Collins' calibre.

There are reasons for this. For one thing, she is a cracking good writer herself with an authentic voice, the most salient feature of which is transparent honesty. She is also a real fighter, but one with a helpless compulsion towards fairness. The strength of her own writerly voice is clearly a source of personal confidence, but curiously it is also allied to a genuine humility – or selflessness – when she puts on her editor's cap. To edit well requires keeping a writer's voice intact and, at the same time, pushing for more and better in a collaborative relationship that does not leave the writer either abandoned or encumbered by an editor's personal agenda. All this Anne Collins does wonderfully well at *Saturday Night*, and the writers she worked with went into print sounding far more salient and judicious than they had intended to be when their first drafts arrived on our premises.

Most journalists are not pushed like this. Most aren't pushed much beyond their own definition of perfection. The consequences of this editorial vacuum, which is evident in so many of our publications, have had much to do with the escalating deterioration of public information and debate in Canada. Very few editors at newspapers ever send back stories for second and third rewrites, unless they are trying to be vindictive. Often the writers are more knowledgeable about editing than the editors, and because the editors-in-chief don't put a high premium on forceful editing, nothing is ever done to correct the problem.

In all the agony which the recession has brought to the Canadian media, all the cutting back of resources and the letting off of staff, all the rethinking of the "market audience" and the redesigning of "product," I have seen no evidence of any real attention paid to the basic flaws of poor reporting and dismal editing. In terms of the media's challenge, nothing actually has changed. What are the real stories that mean something to people today? How honestly can they be reported? How well can they be crafted? How strikingly can they be presented?

Nothing else really matters. Nothing else ever did.